T0323260

MOROCCO.

SCENE OF THE FÊTE OF THE BIRTH OF MAHOMET AT TANGIERS.

MOROCCO:

ITS PEOPLE AND PLACES.

BY

EDMONDO DE AMICIS.

TRANSLATED BY C. ROLLIN-TILTON.

With Original Illustrations.

———◆———

DARF PUBLISHERS LIMITED

LONDON

1985

First Published 1882
New Impression 1985

ISBN 1 85077 055 7

Reprinted in Great Britain by A. Wheaton & Co. Ltd, Exeter

CONTENTS.

LIST OF ILLUSTRATIONS.

———◆◇◆——

Landing at Tangiers.

MOROCCO.

CHAPTER I.

TANGIERS.

THERE are no two countries in the world more entirely different from each other than the two which are separated by the Straits of Gibraltar; and this diversity is peculiarly apparent to the traveller who approaches Tangiers from Gibraltar, where he has left the hurried, noisy, splendid life of a European city. At only three hours' journey from thence the very name of our continent seems unknown; the word " Christian " signifies enemy; our civilisation is ignored, or feared, or derided; all things, from the very foundations of social life to its most insignificant particulars, are changed, and every indication of the

B

neighbourhood of Europe has disappeared. You are in an
unknown country, having no bonds of interest in it, and everything to learn. From its shore the European coast can still be
seen, but the heart feels itself at an immeasurable distance, as if
that narrow tract of sea were an ocean, and those blue mountains
an illusion. Within three hours a wonderful transformation has
taken place around you.

The emotion, however, which one naturally feels on first
setting foot on that immense and mysterious continent, which
has moved the imagination since one's childhood, is disturbed by
the manner of disembarkation. Just as we began to see distinctly from the vessel the first white houses of Tangiers, a
Spanish lady behind us cried out, in a voice of alarm, "What
can all those people want?" I looked, and beheld behind the
boats that were coming to take off the passengers a crowd of
half-naked ragged Arabs, standing up to their hips in the water,
and pointing out the ship with eager gestures, like a band of
brigands rejoicing over their approaching prey. Not knowing
who they were, or what they wanted, I descended with an
anxious mind into the boat with the other passengers. When
we had come to within twenty paces of the shore all this brick-
coloured crew swarmed into our boat and laid hands upon us,
vociferating in Spanish and Arabic, and making us understand
that the water being too low for us to land from the boats, we
were to be transported upon their shoulders; which information
dissipated our fears of robbery, and imposed in their stead the
dread of vermin. The ladies were borne off in triumph upon
stools, and I made my entrance into Africa upon the back of an
old mulatto, with my chin resting upon his bare skull, and the
tips of my toes in the water.

The mulatto, upon reaching the shore, unloaded me into the
hands of an Arab porter, who, passing through one of the city
gates, led me at a run through a deserted alley to an inn not far
off, whence I almost immediately issued again with a guide, and
proceeded to the more frequented streets.

I was struck at once, and more forcibly than I can express, with the aspect of the population. They all wear a kind of long white cloak of wool or linen, with a large pointed hood standing upright on the head, so that the city has the aspect of a vast convent of Dominican friars. Of all this cloaked company some are moving slowly, gravely, and silently about, as if they wished to pass unobserved; others are seated or crouched against the walls, in front of the shops, in corners of the houses, motionless, and with fixed gaze, like the petrified populations of their legends. The walk, the attitude, the look, all are new and strange to me, revealing an order of sentiment and habit quite different from our own, another manner of considering time and life. These people do not seem to be occupied in any way, nor are they thinking of the place they are in, or of what is going on about them. All the faces wear a deep and dreamy expression, as if they were dominated by some fixed idea, or thinking of far-distant times and places, or dreaming with their eyes open. I had hardly entered the crowd when I was aware of a peculiar odour, one quite unknown to me among Europeans; it was not agreeable, and yet I began to inhale it with a vivid curiosity, as if it might explain some things to me. As I went on, the crowd, which at a distance had seemed uniform, presented many varieties. There passed before me faces white, black, yellow, and bronze; heads ornamented with long tresses of hair, and bare skulls as shining as metallic balls; men as dry as mummies; horrible old men; women with the face and entire person wrapped in formless rags; children with long braids pendant from the crown of the otherwise bare head; faces of sultans, savages, necromancers, anchorites, bandits; people oppressed by an immense sadness or a mortal weariness; none smiling, but moving one behind the other with slow and silent steps, like a procession of spectres in a cemetery.

I passed through other streets, and saw that the city corresponded in every way to the population. It is a labyrinth of

B 2

Types of the Natives of Tangiers.

crooked lanes, or rather corridors, bordered by little square houses of dazzling whiteness, without windows, and with little doors through which one person can pass with difficulty ; houses which seem made to hide in rather than live in, with a mixed aspect of convent and prison. In many of the streets there is nothing to be seen save the white walls and the blue sky; here and there some small Moorish arch, some arabesque window, some strip of red at the base of a wall, some figure of a hand painted in black beside a door, to keep off evil influences. Almost all the streets are encumbered with rotten vegetables, feathers, rags, bones, and in some places dead dogs and cats, infecting the air. For long distances you meet no one but a group of Arab boys in pointed hoods, playing together, or chanting in nasal tones some verses from the Koran; or a crouching beggar, a Moor riding on a mule, an overloaded ass with bleeding back, driven by a half-naked Arab; some tailless mangy dog, or cat of fabulous meagreness. Transient odours of garlic, fish, or burning aloes, salute you as you pass; and so you make the circuit of the city, finding everywhere the same dazzling whiteness, the same air of mystery, sadness, and *ennui*.

Coming out upon the only square that Tangiers can boast, which is cut by one long street that begins at the shore and crosses the whole town, you see a rectangular place, surrounded by shops that would be mean in the poorest of our villages. On one side there is a fountain constantly surrounded by blacks and Arabs drawing water in jars and gourds; on the other side sit all day long on the ground eight or ten muffled women selling bread. Around this square are the very modest houses of the different Legations, which rise like palaces from the midst of the confused multitude of Moorish huts. Here in this spot is concentrated all the life of Tangiers—the life of a large village. The one tobacconist is here, the one apothecary, the one *café*—a dirty room with a billiard-table — and the one solitary corner where a printed notice may be sometimes seen. Here gather the half-naked street-boys, the rich and idle Moorish gentlemen, Jews talking about their business, Arab porters awaiting the arrival of the steamer, *attachés* of the Legations expecting the dinner-hour, travellers just arrived, interpreters, and impostors of various kinds. The courier arriving from Fez or Morocco with orders from the Sultan is to be met here; and the servant coming from the post, with his hands full of journals from London and Paris; the beauty of the harem and the wife of the Minister; the Bedouin's camel and the lady's lapdog; the turban and the chimney-pot hat; and the sound of a piano from the windows of a consulate mingles with the lamentable chant from the door of a mosque. It is the point where the last wave of European civilisation is lost in the great dead sea of African barbarism.

From the square we went up the main street, and passing by two old gates, came out at twilight beyond the walls of the town, and found ourselves in an open space on the side of a hill called Soc-de-Barra, or exterior market, because a market is held there every Sunday and Thursday. Of all the places that I saw in Morocco this is perhaps the one that impressed me most deeply with the character of the country. It is a tract of bare ground, rough and irregular,

Street of the Soc-de-Barra, Tangiers.

with the tumbledown tomb of a saint, composed of four white walls, in the midst. Upon the top there is a cemetery, with a few aloes and Indian figs growing here and there; below are the turreted walls of the town. Near the gate, on the ground, sat a group of Arab women, with heaps of green-stuff before them; a

GENERAL VIEW OF TANGIERS.

long file of camels crouched about the saint's tomb; farther on were some black tents, and a circle of Arabs seated around an old man erect in their midst, who was telling a story; horses and cows here and there; and above, among the stones and mounds of the cemetery, other Arabs, motionless as statues, their faces turned towards the city, their whole person in shadow, and the points of their hoods standing out against the golden twilight sky. A sad and silent peacefulness seemed to brood over the scene, such as cannot be described in words, but ought rather to be distilled into the ear drop by drop, like a solemn secret.

The guide awoke me from my reverie and re-conducted me to my inn, where my discomfiture at finding myself among strangers was much mitigated when I discovered that they were all Europeans and Christians, dressed like myself. There were about twenty persons at table, men and women, of different nationalities, presenting a fine picture of that crossing of races and interlacing of interests which go on in that country. Here was a Frenchman born in Algiers married to an Englishwoman from Gibraltar; there, a Spaniard of Gibraltar married to the sister of the Portuguese Consul; here again, an old Englishman with a daughter born in Tangiers and a niece native of Algiers; families wandering from one continent to the other, or sprinkled along the coast, speaking five languages, and living partly like Arabs, partly like Europeans. All through dinner a lively conversation went on, now in French, now in Spanish, studded with Arabic words, upon subjects quite strange to the ordinary talk of Europeans: such as the price of a camel; the salary of a pasha; whether the Sultan were white or mulatto; if it were true that there had been brought to Fez twenty heads from the revolted province of Garet; when those religious fanatics who eat a live sheep were likely to come to Tangiers; and other things of the same kind that aroused within my soul the greatest curiosity. Then the talk ran upon European politics, with that odd disconnectedness that is always perceptible in the discussions of people of different nations—those big, empty phrases which they use in talking of the politics of distant countries, imagining absurd alliances and impossible wars. And then came the inevitable subject of Gibraltar—the great Gibraltar, the centre of attraction for all the Europeans along the coast, where their sons are sent to study, where they go to buy clothes, to order a piece of furniture, to hear an opera, to breathe a mouthful of the air of Europe. Finally came up the subject of the departure of the Italian embassy for Fez, and I had the pleasure of hearing that the event was of far greater importance than I had supposed; that it was discussed at Gibraltar, at Algesiras, Cadiz, and Malaga, and that the caravan would be a mile long; that there were several Italian painters with the embassy, and that perhaps there might even be a

An Arab Asleep.

representative of the press—at which intelligence I rose modestly from the table, and walked away with majestic steps.

I wandered about Tangiers at a late hour that night. There was not a single light in street or window, nor did the faintest radiance stream through any loophole; the city seemed uninhabited, the white houses lay under the starlight like tombs, and the tops of the minarets and palm-trees stood out clear against the cloudless sky. The gates of the city were closed, and everything was mute and lifeless. Two or three times my feet entangled themselves in something like a bundle of rags, which proved to be a sleeping Arab. I trod with disgust upon bones that cracked under my feet, and knew them for the carcase

of a dog or cat; a hooded figure glided like a spectre close to
the wall; another gleamed white for one instant at the bottom
of an alley; and at a turning I heard a sudden rush and scamper,
as if I had unwittingly disturbed some consultation. My own
footstep when I moved, my own breathing when I stood still,
were the only sounds that broke the stillness. It seemed as if
all the life in Tangiers were concentrated in myself, and that if
I were to give a sudden cry, it would resound from one end of
the city to the other like the blast of a trumpet. Meantime
the moon rose, and shone upon the white walls with the splendour
of an electric light. In a dark alley I met a man with a lantern,
who stood aside to let me pass, murmuring some words that I
did not understand. Suddenly a loud laugh made my blood run
cold for an instant, and two young men in European dress went
by in conversation; probably two *attachés* to the Legations. In
a corner of the great square, behind the looped-up curtain of a
dark little shop, a dim light betrayed a heap of whitish rags,
from which issued the faint tinkle of a guitar, and a thin, tremulous, lamentable voice that seemed brought by the wind from a
great distance. I went back to my inn, feeling like a man who
finds himself transported into some other planet.

The next morning I went to present myself to our *chargé
d'affaires,* Commendatore Stefano Scovasso. He could not
accuse me of not being punctual. On the 8th of April, at
Turin, I had received the invitation, with the announcement
that the caravan would leave Tangiers on the 19th. On
the morning of the 18th I was at the Legation. I did not
know Signor Scovasso personally, but I knew something about
him which inspired me with a great desire to make his acquaintance. From one of his friends whom I had seen before
leaving Turin, I had heard that he was a man capable of riding
from Tangiers to Timbuctoo without any other companions than
a pair of pistols. Another friend had blamed his inveterate
habit of risking his life to save the lives of others. When I
arrived at the Legation I found him standing at the gate in

the midst of a crowd of Arabs, all motionless, in attitudes of profound respect, seemingly awaiting his orders. Presenting myself, and being at once made a guest at head-quarters, learned that our departure was deferred till the 1st of May, because there was an English embassy at Fez, and our horses, camels, mules, and a cavalry escort for the journey were all to be sent from there. A transport-ship of our military marine, the *Dora*, then anchored at Gibraltar, had already carried to Larrace, on the Atlantic coast, the presents which King Victor Emmanuel had sent to the Emperor of Morocco. The principal scope of our journey for the *chargé d'affaires* was to present credentials to the young Sultan, Muley el Hassen, who had ascended the throne in September, 1873. No Italian embassy had ever been at Fez, and the banner of United Italy had never before been carried into the interior of Morocco. Consequently, the embassy was to be received with extraordinary solemnities.

My first occupation when I found myself alone was to take observations of the house where I was to be a guest; and truly it was well worthy of notice. Not that the building itself was at all remarkable. White and bare without, it had a garden in front, and an interior court, with four columns supporting a covered gallery that ran all round the first floor. It was like a gentleman's house at Cadiz or Seville. But the people and their manner of life in this house were all new to me. Housekeeper and cook were Piedmontese; there was a Moorish woman-servant of Tangiers, and a Negress from the Soudan with bare feet; there were Arab waiters and grooms dressed in white shirts; consular guards in fez, red caftan, and poignard; and all these people in perpetual motion all day long. At certain hours there was a coming and going of black porters, interpreters, soldiers of the pasha, and Moors in the service of the Legation. The court was full of boxes, camp-beds, carpets, lanterns. Hammers and saws were in full cry, and the strange names of Fatima, Racma, Selam, Mohammed, Abd-er-Rhaman flew from

mouth to mouth. And what a hash of languages! A Moor
would bring a message in Arabic to another Moor, who trans-
mitted it in Spanish to the housekeeper, who repeated it in Piedmontese to the cook, and so on. There was a constant succession

A Moorish Soldier.

of translations, comments, mistakes, doubts, mingled with
Italian, Spanish, and Arabic exclamations. In the street, a
procession of horses and mules; before the door, a permanent
group of curious lookers-on, or poor wretches, Arabs and Jews,

patient aspirants for the protection of the Legation. From time
to time came a minister or a consul, before whom all the turbans
and fezes bowed themselves. Every moment some mysterious
messenger, some unknown and strange costume, some remarkable face, appeared. It seemed like a theatrical representation,
with the scene laid in the East.

My next thought was to take possession of some book of my
host's that should teach me something of the country I was in,
before beginning to study costume. This country, shut in by
the Mediterranean, Algeria, the desert of Sahara, and the ocean,
crossed by the great chain of the Atlas, bathed by wide rivers,
opening into immense plains, with every variety of climate,
endowed with inestimable riches in all the three kingdoms of
nature, destined by its position to be the great commercial high
road between Europe and Central Africa, is now occupied by
about 8,000,000 of inhabitants—Berbers, Moors, Arabs, Jews,
Negroes, and Europeans—sprinkled over a more vast extent of
country than that of France. The Berbers, who form the basis
of the indigenous population—a savage, turbulent, and indomitable race—live on the inaccessible mountains of the Atlas, in
almost complete independence of the imperial authority. The
Arabs, the conquering race, occupy the plains—a nomadic and
pastoral people, not entirely degenerated from their ancient
haughty character. The Moors, corrupted and crossed by Arab
blood, are in great part descended from the Moors of Spain,
and, inhabiting the cities, hold in their hands the wealth, trade,
and commerce of the country. The blacks, about 500,000,
originally from the Soudan, are generally servants, labourers,
and soldiers. The Jews, almost equal in number to the blacks,
descend, for the most part, from those who were exiled from
Europe in the Middle Ages, and are oppressed, hated, degraded,
and persecuted here more than in any other country in the
world. They exercise various arts and trades, and in a thousand
ways display the ingenuity, pliability, and tenacity of their race,
finding in the possession of money torn from their oppressors a

recompense for all their woes. The Europeans, whom Mussulman intolerance has, little by little, driven from the interior of the empire towards the coast, number less than 2,000 in all Morocco, the greater part inhabiting Tangiers, and living under the protection of the consular flags. This heterogeneous, dispersed, and irreconcilable population is oppressed rather than protected by a military government that, like a monstrous leech, sucks out all the vital juices from the State. The tribes and boroughs, or suburbs, obey their sheikhs; the cities and provinces the cadi; the greater provinces the pasha; and the pasha obeys the Sultan — grand schereef, high priest, supreme judge, executor of the laws emanating

A Moor of Tangiers.

from himself, free to change at his caprice money, taxes, weights and measures; master of the possessions and the lives of his subjects. Under the weight of this government, and within the inflexible circle of the Mussulman religion, unmoved by European influences, and full of a savage fanaticism, everything that in other countries moves and progresses here remains motionless or falls into ruin.

Commerce is choked by monopolies, by prohibitions upon exports and imports, and by the capricious mutability of the laws. Manufactures, restricted by the bonds laid upon commerce, have remained as they were at the time of the expulsion of the Moors from Spain, with the same primitive tools and methods. Agriculture, loaded heavily with taxes, hampered in exportation of produce, and only exercised from sheer necessity, has fallen so low as no longer to merit the name. Science, suffocated by the Koran, and contaminated by superstition, is reduced to a few elements in the higher schools, such as were taught in the Middle Ages. There are no printing-presses, no books, no journals, no geographical maps; the language itself, a corruption of the Arabic, and represented only by an

A Jewish Money-changer in Tangiers.

imperfect and variable written character, is becoming yearly more debased; in the general decadence the national character is corrupted; all the ancient Mussulman civilisation is disappearing. Morocco, the last western bulwark of Islamism, once the seat of a monarchy that ruled from the Ebro to the Soudan, and from the

Niger to the Balearic Isles, glorious with flourishing universities, with immense libraries, with men famous for their learning, with formidable fleets and armies, is now nothing but a small and almost unknown state, full of wretchedness and ruin, resisting with its last remaining strength the advance of European civilisation, seated upon its foundations still, but confronted by the reciprocal jealousies of civilised states.

As for Tangiers, the ancient Tingis, which gave its name to Tingistanian Mauritania, it passed successively from the hands of the Romans into those of the Vandals, Greeks, Visigoths, Arabs, Portuguese, and English, and is now a city of about 15,000 inhabitants, considered by its sister cities as having been " prostituted to the Christians," although there are no traces of the churches and monasteries founded by the Portuguese, and the Christian religion boasts there but one small chapel, hidden away among the Legations.

I made in the streets of Tangiers a few notes, in preparation for my journey, and they are given here, because, having been written down under the impression of the moment, they are perhaps more effective than a more elaborate description.

I am ashamed when I pass a handsome Moor in gala dress. I compare my ugly hat with his large muslin turban, my short jacket with his ample white or rose-coloured caftan—the meanness, in short, of my black and grey garments with the whiteness, the amplitude, the graceful dignified simplicity of his—and it seems to me that I look like a black-beetle beside a butterfly. I stand sometimes at my window absorbed in contemplation of a portion of a pair of crimson drawers and a gold-coloured slipper, appearing from behind a column in the square below, and find so much pleasure in it that I cannot cease from gazing. More than anything else I admire and envy the *caic*, that long piece of snow-white wool or silk with transparent stripes which is twisted round the turban, falls down between the shoulders, is passed round the waist, and thrown up over one shoulder, whence it descends to the feet, softly veiling the rich colours of the dress beneath, and at every breath of wind swelling, quivering, floating, seeming to glow in the sun's rays, and giving to the whole person a vaporous and visionary aspect.

No one who has not seen it can imagine to what a point the Arab carries the art of lying down. In corners where we should be embarrassed to place a bag of rags or a bundle of straw, he disposes of himself as upon a bed of down. He adapts himself to the protuberances, fills up the cavities, spreads himself upon the wall like a bas-relief, and flattens himself out upon the ground until he looks like a sheet spread out to dry. He will assume the form of a ball, a cube, or a monster without arms, legs, or head; so that the streets and squares look like battle-fields strewn with corpses and mutilated trunks of men.

The greater part have nothing on but a simple white mantle; but what a variety there is among them! Some wear it open, some closed, some drawn on one side, some folded over the shoulder, some tightly wrapped, some loosely floating, but always with an air; varied by picturesque folds, falling in easy but severe lines, as if they were posing for an artist. Every one of them might pass for a Roman senator. This very morning our artist discovered a marvellous Marcus Brutus in the midst of a group of Bedouins. But if one is not accustomed to wear it, the face is not sufficient to ennoble the folds of the mantle. Some of us bought them for the journey, and tried them on, and we looked like so many convalescents wrapped in bathing-sheets.

I have not yet seen among the Arabs a hunchback, or a lame man, or a rickety man, but many without a nose and without an eye, one or both, and the greater part of these with the empty orbit—a sight which made me shiver when I thought that possibly the globe had been torn out in virtue of the *lex talionis,* which is in vigour in the empire. But there is no ridiculous ugliness among these strange and terrible figures. The flowing ample vesture conceals all small defects, as the common gravity and the dark, bronzed skin conceal the difference of age. In consequence of which one encounters at every step men of an

c

indefinable age, of whom one cannot guess whether they are old or young ; and if you judge them old, a lightning smile reveals their youth ; and if you think them young, the hood falls back and betrays the grey locks of age.

The Jews of this country have the same features as those of our own, but their taller stature, darker complexion, and, above all, their picturesque attire, make them appear quite different. They wear a dress in form very like a dressing-gown, of various colours, generally dark, bound round the waist with a red girdle ; a black cap, wide trousers that come a little below the skirts of the coat, and yellow slippers. It is curious to see what a number of dandies there are among them dressed in fine stuffs, with embroidered shirts, silken sashes, and rings and chains of gold ; but they are handsome, dignified-looking men, always excepting those who have adopted the black frock-coat and chimney-pot hat. There are some pretty faces among the boys, but the sort of dressing-gown in which they are wrapped is not generally becoming at their age. It seems to me that there is no exaggeration in the reports of the beauty of the Jewesses of Morocco, which has a character of its own unknown in other countries. It is an opulent and splendid beauty, with large black eyes, broad low forehead, full red lips, and statuesque form—a theatrical beauty, that looks well from a distance, and produces applause rather than sighs in the beholder. The Hebrew women of Tangiers do not wear in public their rich national costume ; they are dressed almost like Europeans, but in such glaring colours— blue, carmine, sulphur yellow, and grass-green—that they look like women wrapped in the flags of all nations. On the Saturdays, when they are in all their glory, the Jewish quarter presents a marked contrast to the austere solitude of the other streets.

The little Arab boys amuse me. Even those small ones who can scarcely walk are robed in the white mantle, and with their high-pointed hoods they look like perambulating extinguishers. The greater part of them have their heads shaven as bare as your hand, except a braided lock about a foot long pendent from the crown, which looks as if it were left on purpose to hang them up

Jewesses.

by on nails, like puppets. Some few have the lock behind one ear or over the temple, with a bit of hair cut in a square or triangular form, the distinctive mark of the last born in the family. In general they have pretty, pale little faces, erect

c 2

slender bodies, and an expression of precocious intelligence. In the more frequented parts of the city they take no notice of Europeans; in the other parts they content themselves with looking intently at them with an air which says, "I do not like you." Here and there is one who would like to be impertinent; it glitters in his eye and quivers on his lip; but rarely does he allow it to escape, not so much out of respect for the Nazarene as out of fear of his father, who stands in awe of the Legations. In any case the sight of a small coin will quiet them. But it will not do to pull their braided tails. I indulged myself once in giving a little pluck at a small image about a foot high, and he turned upon me in a fury, spluttering out some words which my guide told me meant, "May God roast your grandfather, accursed Christian!"

I have at last seen two saints—that is to say, idiots or lunatics, because throughout all North Africa that man from whom God, in sign of predilection, has withdrawn his reason to keep it a prisoner in heaven, is venerated as a saint. The first one was in the main street, in front of a shop. I saw him from a distance and stayed my steps, for I knew that all things are allowed to saints, and had no desire to be struck on the back of the neck with a stick, like M. Sourdeau, the French consul, or to have the saint spit in my face, as happened to Mr. Drummond Hay. But the interpreter who was with me assured me that there was no danger now, for the saints of Tangiers had learned a lesson since the Legations had made some examples, and in any case the Arabs themselves would serve me as a shield, since they did not wish the saint to get into trouble. So I went on and passed before the scarecrow, observing him attentively. He was an old man, all face, very fat, with very long white hair, a beard descending on his breast, a paper crown upon his head, a ragged red mantle on his shoulders, and in his hand a small lance with gilded point. He sat on the ground with crossed legs, his back against a wall, looking at the passers-by with a discontented expression. I stopped before him: he looked at me. "Now," thought I, "he will throw his lance." But the lance remained quiet, and I was astonished at the tranquil and intelligent look in his eyes, and a cunning smile that seemed to gleam within them. They said, "Ah! you think I am going to make a fool of myself by attacking you, do you?" He was certainly one of those impostors who, having all their reason, feign madness in order to enjoy saintly privileges. I threw him some money, which he picked up with an air of affected indifference, and going on my way presently met another. This was a real saint.

He was a mulatto, almost entirely naked, and less than human in visage, covered with filth from head to foot, and so thin that he seemed a walking skeleton. He was moving slowly along, carrying with difficulty a great white banner, which the street-boys ran to kiss, and accompanied by another poor wretch who begged from shop to shop, and two noisy rascals with drum and trumpet. As I passed near him he showed me the white of his eye, and stopped. I thought he seemed to be preparing something in his mouth, and stepped nimbly aside. "You were right," said the interpreter; "because if he had spat on you, the only consolation you would have got from the Arabs would have been, 'Do not wipe it off, fortunate Christian! Thou art blessed that the saint has spat in thy face! Do not put away the sign of God's benevolence!'"

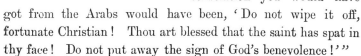

A Saint.

This evening I have for the first time really heard Arab music. In the perpetual repetition of the same notes, always of a melancholy cast, there is something that gradually touches the soul. It is a kind of monotonous lamentation that finally takes possession of the thoughts, like the murmur of a fountain, the cricket's chirp, and the beat of hammers upon anvils, such as one hears in the evening when passing near a village. I feel compelled to meditate upon it, and find out the signification of those eternal words for ever sounding in my ears. It is a barbaric music, full of simplicity and sweetness, that carries me back to primitive conditions, revives my infantile memories of the Bible, recalls to mind forgotten dreams, fills me with curiosity about countries and peoples unknown, transports me to great distances amid groves of strange trees, with a group of aged priests bending about a golden idol; or in boundless plains, in solemn solitudes, behind weary caravans of travellers that question with their eyes the burning horizon, and with drooping heads commend themselves to God. Nothing about me so fills me with a yearning desire to see my own country and my people as these few notes of a weak voice and tuneless guitar.

The oddest things in the world are the Moorish shops. They are one and all a sort of alcove about a yard high, with an opening to the street, where the buyer stands as at a window, leaning against the wall. The shopman is within, seated cross-legged, with a portion of his merchandise before him, and the rest on little shelves behind. The effect of these bearded old Moors, motionless as images in their dark holes, is very strange. It seems themselves, and not their goods, that are on exhibition, like the "living phenomena" of country fairs. Are they alive, or made of wood? and where is the handle to set them in motion? The air of solitude, weariness, and sadness that hangs about them is indescribable. Every shop seems a tomb, where the occupant, already separated from the living world, silently awaits his death.

I have seen two children led in triumph after the solemn

ceremony of circumcision. One was about six, and the other five years old. They were both seated upon a white mule, and were dressed in red, green, and yellow garments, embroidered with gold, and covered with ribbons and flowers, from which their little pallid faces looked forth, still wearing an expression of terror and amazement. Before the mule, which was gaily caparisoned and hung with garlands, went three drummers, a piper, and a cornet-player, making all the noise they could; to the right and left walked friends and parents, one of whom held the little ones firm in the saddle, while others gave them sweet-

Moorish Shopkeeper.

meats and caresses, and others, again, fired off guns and leaped and shouted. If I had not already known what it meant, I should have thought that the two poor babies were victims being carried to the sacrifice; and yet the spectacle was not without a certain picturesqueness.

This evening I have been present at a singular metamorphosis of Racma, the minister's black slave. Her companion came to call me, and conducted me on tip-toe to a door, which she suddenly threw open, exclaiming, "Behold Racma!" I could scarcely believe my eyes, for there stood the negress, whom I

FESTIVAL OF THE CIRCUMCISION.

had been accustomed to see only in her common working dress,
arrayed like the Queen of Timbuctoo, or a princess from some
unknown African realm, brought thither on the miraculous
carpet of Bisnagar. As I saw her only for a moment, I
cannot say exactly how she was dressed. There was a
gleam of snowy white, a glow of purple and crimson, and a
shine of gold, under
a large transparent
veil, which, together
with her ebony black-
ness of visage, com-
posed a whole of bar-
baric magnificence and
the richest harmony of
colour. As I drew
near, to observe more
closely, all the pomp
and splendour vanished
under the gloomy Mo-
hammedan sheet-like
mantle, and the queen,
transformed into a
spectre, glided away,
leaving behind her a
nauseous odour of black
savage which destroyed
all my illusions.

Negro Servant.

Hearing a great outcry in the square, I looked out of my
window and saw passing by a negro, naked to the waist and
seated upon an ass, accompanied by some Arabs armed with
sticks, and followed by a troop of yelling boys. At first I
thought it some frolic, and took my opera-glass to look; but
I turned away with a shudder. The white drawers of the negro
were all stained with blood that dropped from his back, and the
Arabs were soldiers who were beating him with sticks. He had

stolen a hen. "Lucky fellow," said my informant; "it appears they will let him off without cutting off his right hand."

I have been seven days at Tangiers, and have not yet seen an Arab woman's face. I seem to be in some monstrous masquerade, where all the women represent ghosts, wrapped in sepulchral sheets or shrouds. They walk with long, slow steps, a little

Punishing a Thief.

bent forwards, covering their faces with the end of a sort of linen mantle, under which they have nothing but a long chemise with wide sleeves, bound round the waist by a cord, like a friar's frock. Nothing of them is visible but the eyes, the hand that covers the face, the fingers tinted with henna, and the bare feet, the toes also tinted, in large yellow slippers. The greater part of them display only one eye, which is dark, and a small bit of yellowish-white forehead. Meeting a European in a narrow street, some of them cover the whole face with a rapid, awkward movement, and shrink close to the wall; others venture a timid glance of curiosity; and now and then one will launch a provoking look, and drop her eyes smiling. But in general they wear a sad, weary, and oppressed aspect. The little girls, who are not of an age to be veiled, are pretty, with black eyes, full faces, pale complexions, red lips, and small hands and feet. But at twenty they are faded, at thirty old, and at fifty decrepit.

I know now who are those fair-haired men, with ill-omened visages, who pass me sometimes in the streets, and look at me with such threatening eyes. They are those Rifans, Berbers by race, who have no law beyond their guns, and recognise no authority. Audacious pirates, sanguinary bandits, eternal rebels, who inhabit the mountains of the coast of Tetuan, on the Algerian

Berbers of the Rif.

frontier, whom neither the cannon of European ships nor the armies of the Sultan have ever been able to dislodge; the population, in short, of that famous Rif, where no foreigner

WEDDING PROCESSION IN TANGIERS.

may dare to set his foot, unless under the protection of the saints and the sheikhs; about whom all sorts of terrible legends are rife; and the neighbouring peoples speak vaguely of their country, as of one far distant and unknown. They are often seen in Tangiers. They are tall and robust men, dressed in dark mantles, bordered with various colours. Some have their faces ornamented with yellow arabesques. All are armed with very long guns, whose red cases they twist about their heads like turbans; and they go in companies, speaking low, and looking about them from under their brows, like bravoes in search of a victim. In comparison with them, the wildest Arab seems a life-long friend.

We were at dinner in the evening, when some gunshots were heard from the square. Everybody ran to see, and from the distance a strange spectacle was visible. The street leading to the Soc-de-Barra was lighted up by a number of torches carried above the heads of a crowd that surrounded a large box or trunk, borne on the back of a horse. This enigmatical procession went slowly onwards, accompanied by melancholy music, and a sort of nasal chant, piercing yells, the barking of dogs, and the discharge of muskets. I speculated for a moment as to whether the box contained a corpse, or a man condemned to death, or a monster, or some animal destined for the sacrifice, and then turned away with a sense of repugnance, when my friends, coming in, gave me the explanation of the enigma. It was a wedding procession, and the bride was in the box, being carried to her husband's house.

A throng of Arabs, men and women, have just gone by, preceded by six old men carrying large banners of various colours, and all together singing in high shrill voices a sort of prayer, with woeful faces and supplicating tones. In answer to my question, I am told that they are entreating Allah to send the grace of rain. I followed them to the principal mosque, and not being then aware that Christians are prohibited from entering a mosque, was about to do so, when an old Arab suddenly flew at

me, and saying in breathless accents something equivalent to
"What would you do, unhappy wretch?" pushed me back
against the wall, with the action of one who removes a child
from the edge of a precipice.   I was obliged to content myself

Praying for Rain.

with looking at the outside only of the sacred edifice, not
much grieved, since I had seen the splendid and gigantic
mosques of Constantinople, to be excluded from those of Tangiers, which, with the exception of the minarets, are without
any architectural merit.   Whilst I stood there, a woman behind
the fountain in the court made a gesture at me.   I might record

that she blew me a kiss, but truth compels me to state that she
shook her fist at me.

I have been up to the Casba, or castle, posted upon a hill
that dominates Tangiers. It is a cluster of small buildings,
encircled by old walls, where the authorities, with some soldiers,
and prisoners are housed. We found no one but two drowsy
sentinels seated before the gate, at the end of a deserted square,
and some beggars stretched on the ground, scorched by the sun,
and devoured by flies. From hence the eye embraces the whole
of Tangiers, which extends from the foot of the hill of the
Casba, and runs up the flanks of another hill. The sight is
almost dazzled by so much snowy whiteness, relieved only here
and there by the green of a fig-tree imprisoned between wall and
wall. One can see the terraces of all the houses, the minarets
of the mosques, the flags of the Legations, the battlements of
the walls, the solitary beach, the deserted bay, the mountains
of the coast—a vast, silent, and splendid spectacle, which would
relieve the sting of the heaviest home-sickness. Whilst I stood
in contemplation, a voice, coming from above, struck upon my
ear, acute and tremulous, and with a strange intonation. It was
not until after some minutes' search that I discovered, upon the
minaret of the mosque of the Casba, a small black spot, the
muezzin, who was calling the faithful to prayer, and throwing
out to the four winds of heaven the names of Allah and
Mahomet. Then the melancholy silence reigned once more.

It is a calamity to have to change money in this country.
I gave a French franc to a tobacconist, who was to give me back
ten sous in change. The ferocious Moor opened a box and began
to throw out handfuls of black, shapeless coins, until there was
a heap big enough for an ordinary porter, counted it all quickly
over, and waited for me to put it in my pocket. " Excuse me,"
said I, trying to get back my franc, " I am not strong enough
to buy anything in your shop." However, we arranged matters
by my taking more cigars, and carrying off a pocketful of that
horrible money. It appears that it is called *flu*, and is made of

copper, worth one *centime* a-piece now, and sinking every day in
value. Morocco is inundated with it, and one need not inquire
further when one knows that the Government pays with this
money, but receives nothing but gold and silver. But every
evil has its good side,
they say, and these *flu,*
bane of commerce as
they are, have the in-
estimable virtue of pre-
serving the people of
Morocco from the evil
eye, thanks to the so-
called rings of Solomon,
a six-pointed star en-
graven on one side—an
image of the real ring
buried in the tomb of the
great king, who, with it,
commanded the good and
evil genii.

The Castle.

There is but one
public promenade, and
that is the beach, which
extends from the city to
Cape Malabat, a beach
covered with shells and
refuse thrown up by the
sea, and having numerous
large pieces of water,
difficult to guard against at high tide. Here are the Champs
Elyseés and the Cascine of Tangiers. The hour for walking
is the evening, towards sunset. At that time there are
generally about fifty Europeans, in groups and couples, scattered at a hundred paces' distance from each other, so that
from the walls of the city individuals are easily recognised. 1

can see from my stand-point an English lady on horseback, accompanied by a guide; beyond, two Moors from the country; then come the Spanish Consul and his wife, and after them a saint; then a French nurse-maid with two children; then a number of Arab women wading through a pool, and uncovering their knees—the better to cover their faces; and further on, at intervals, a tall hat, a white hood, a *chignon*, and some one who

The Beach, Cape Malabat.

must be the Secretary of the Portuguese Legation, wearing the light trousers that came yesterday from Gibraltar—for in this small European colony the smallest events are public property. If it were not disrespectful, I should say that they look like a company of condemned criminals out for a regulation walk, or hostages held by the pirates of a savage island, on the look-out for the vessel that is to bring their ransom.

It is infinitely easier to find your way in London than among this handful of houses that could all be put in one corner of Hyde Park. All these lanes, and alleys, and little squares, where one has scarcely room to pass, are so exactly like each

D

other, that nothing short of the minutest observation can enable
you to distinguish one from the other. At present, I lose myself
the very instant that I leave the main street and the principal
square. In one of these silent corridors, in full daylight, two
Arabs could bind and gag me, and cause me to vanish for ever
from the face of the earth, without any one, save themselves,
being the wiser. And yet a Christian can wander alone through
this labyrinth, among these barbarians, with greater security
than in our cities. A few European flags erected over a terrace,
like the menacing index finger of a hidden hand, are sufficient
to obtain that which a legion of armed men cannot obtain among
us. What a difference between London and Tangiers! But
each city has its own advantages. There, there are great palaces
and underground railways; here, you can go into a crowd with
your over-coat unbuttoned.

There is not in all Tangiers either cart or carriage; you hear
no clang of bell, nor cry of intinerant vendor, nor sound of busy
occupation; you see no hasty movement of persons or of things;
even Europeans, not knowing what to do with themselves, stay
for hours motionless in the square : everything reposes and
invites to repose. I myself, who have been here only a few
days, begin to feel the influence of this soft and somnolent
existence. Getting as far as the Soc-de-Barra, I am irresistibly
impelled homewards; I read ten pages, and the book falls from
my hand; if once I let my head fall back upon the easy chair,
it is all over with me, and the very thought of care or occupation
is sufficient to fatigue me. This sky, for ever blue, and this
snow-white city form an image of unalterable peace, which, even
with its monotony, becomes, little by little, the supreme end of
life to all who inhabit this country.

Among the numerous figures that buzzed about the doors of
the Legation, there was a young Moor who had from the first
attracted my eye : one of the handsomest men whom I saw in
Morocco ; tall and slender, with dark, melancholy eyes, and the
sweetest of smiles ; the face of an enamoured Sultan, whom

Danas, the malign genius of the "Arabian Nights," might have placed beside the Princess Badoura, instead of Prince Camaralzaman, sure that she would have made no objection to the change. He was called Mahomet, was eighteen years of age, and the son of a well-to-do Moor of Tangiers, a big and honest Mussulman protected by the Italian Legation, who, having been for some time menaced with death by the hand of an enemy, came every day with a frightened visage to claim the protection of the Minister. This Mahomet spoke a little Spanish, after the Moorish fashion, with all the verbs in the infinitive, and had there made acquaintance with my companions. He had been married only a few days. His father had given him a child of fifteen for a wife, who was as beautiful as he. But matrimony had not changed his habits; he remained, as we say, a Moor *of the future*—that is to say, he drank wine under the rose, smoked cigars, was tired of Tangiers, frequented the society of Europeans, and looked forward to a voyage to Spain. In these days, however, what drew him towards us was the desire of obtaining, through our intervention, permission to join the caravan, to go and see Fez, the great metropolis, his Rome, the dream of his childhood; and with this end he expended salutations, smiles, and grasps of the hand with a prodigality and grace that would have seduced the entire imperial harem. Like most young Moors of his condition, he killed time in lounging from street to street, and from corner to corner, talking about the Minister's new horses, or the departure of a friend for Gibraltar, or the arrival of a ship, or any topic that came uppermost; or else he stood like a statue, silent and motionless, in a corner of the market-place, with his thoughts no one knows where. With this handsome idler are bound up my recollections of the first Moorish house in which I put my foot, and the first Arab dinner at which I risked my palate. His father one day invited me to dinner, thus fulfilling an old wish of mine. Late one evening, guided by an interpreter, and accompanied by four servants of the Legation, I found myself at an arabesque

D 2

door, which opened as if by enchantment at our approach; and crossing a white and empty chamber, we entered the court of the house. The first impression produced was that of a great confusion of people, a strange light, and a marvellous pomp of colour. We were received by the master of the house and his sons and relations, all crowned with large white turbans; behind them were some hooded servants; beyond, in the dark corners, and peeping through doorways, the curious faces of women and children; and despite the number of persons, a profound silence. I thought myself in a room until, raising my eyes, I saw the stars, and found that we were in a central court, upon either side of which opened two long and lofty chambers without windows, each having a great arched doorway closed only by a curtain. The external walls were white as snow, the arches of the doors dentellated, the pavements in mosaic; here and there a window, and a niche for slippers. The house had been decorated for our coming : carpets covered the pavement; great chandeliers stood on either side of the doors, with red, yellow, and green candles; on the tables were flowers and mirrors. The effect was very strange. There was something of the air of church decorations, and something of the ball-room and the theatre : artificial, but very pretty and graceful, and the distribution of light and arrangement of colours was very effective.

Some moments were spent in salutations and vigorous grasps of the hand, and we were then invited to visit the bridal chamber. It was a long, narrow, and lofty room, opening on the court. At the end, on either side, stood the two beds, decorated with a rich, dark red stuff, with coverlets of lace; thick carpets covered the pavement, and hangings of red and yellow concealed the walls. Between the two beds was suspended the wife's wardrobe : bodices, petticoats, drawers, gowns of unknown form, in all the colours of the rainbow, in wool, silk, and velvet, bordered and starred with gold and silver; the trousseau of a royal doll; a sight to turn the head of a ballet-dancer, and make a columbine die with envy. From thence we passed into the dining-room. Here also were carpets and hangings, flowers, tall chandeliers standing on the floor, cushions and pillows of all colours spread against the walls, and two gorgeous beds, for this was the nuptial chamber of the parents. The table stood all prepared near one of the beds, contrary to the Arab custom, which is to put the dishes on the floor, and eat with the fingers; and upon it glittered an array of bottles, charged, to remind us, in the midst of a Moorish banquet, that

Tea at the House of Mahomet.

Christians existed. Before taking our places at table, we seated ourselves cross-legged on the carpets, around the master's secretary, who prepared tea before us, and made us take, according to custom, three cups a-piece, excessively sweetened, and flavoured with mint; and between each cup we caressed the shaven head and braided tail of a pretty four-year-old boy, Mahomet's youngest brother, who furtively counted the fingers on our hands, in order to make sure that we had the same number as a Mussulman, and no more. After tea we took our seats at table, and the master, being entreated, seated himself also; and then the Arab dishes, objects of our intense curiosity, began to circulate. I tasted the first with simple faith. Great heaven! My first

impulse was to attack the cook. All the contractions that can
be produced upon the face of a man who is suddenly assailed
by an acute colic, or who hears the news of his banker's failure,
were, I think, visible on mine. I understood in one moment
how it was that a people who ate in that way should believe
in another God, and take other views of human life than ours.
I cannot express what I felt otherwise than by likening myself
to some unhappy wretch who is forced to satisfy his appetite
upon the pomatum pots of his barber. There were flavours of
soaps, pomades, wax, dyes, cosmetics—everything that is least
proper to be put in a human mouth. At each dish we exchanged
glances of wonder and dismay. No doubt the original material
was good enough—chickens, mutton, game, fish ; large dishes
of a very fine appearance, but all swimming in most abominable
sauces, and so flavoured and perfumed that it would have seemed
more natural to attack them with a comb rather than with a
fork. However, we were in duty bound to swallow something,
and the only eatable thing seemed to be mutton on a spit. Not
even the famous *cùscùssù*, the national Moorish dish, which bore
a perfidious resemblance to our Milanese *risotto*, could we get
down without a pang. There was one among us who managed
to taste of all : a consolatory fact which shows that there
are still great men in Italy. At every mouthful our host
humbly interrogated us by a look ; and we, opening our eyes
very wide, answered in chorus, " Excellent ! exquisite ! " and
hastened to swallow a glass of wine to revive our drooping
courage. At a certain moment there burst out in the court-
yard a gust of strange music that made us all spring to our
feet. There were three musicians come, according to Moorish
custom, to enliven the banquet : three large-eyed Arabs, dressed
in white and red, one with a theorbo, another with a mandolin,
and the third with a small drum. All three were seated on the
ground in the court-yard, near a niche where their slippers were
deposited. Little by little, our libations, the odour of the
flowers, and that of aloes burning in carved perfume-burners

of Fez, and that strange Arab music, which, by dint of repetition, takes possession of the fancy with its mysterious lament, all overcame us with a sort of taciturn and fantastic dreaminess, under the influence of which we felt our heads crowned with turbans, and visions of sultanas floated before our eyes.

The dinner over, all rose and spread themselves about the room, the court, or the vestibule, looking into every corner with childlike curiosity. At every dark angle stood an Arab wrapped in his white mantle like a statue. The door of the bridal chamber had been closed by a curtain, and through the interstices a great movement of veiled heads could be seen. Lights appeared and disappeared at the upper windows, and low voices and the rustle of garments were heard on all sides. About and above us fermented an invisible life, bearing witness that though within the walls we were without the household; that beauty, love, the family soul, had taken refuge in the penetralia; that we were the spectacle, while the house remained a mystery. At a certain moment the Minister's housekeeper came out of a small door, where she had been visiting the bride, and, passing by us, murmured, " Ah, if you could see her ! What a rosebud ! What a creature of paradise ! " And the sad lamenting music went on, and the perfumed aloe smoke arose, and our fancies grew more and more active, more so than ever when we issued forth from that air filled with light and perfume, and plunged into a dark and solitary alley, lighted only by one lantern, and surrounded by profoundest silence.

One evening we received the not unexpected intelligence that the next day the *Aissawa* would enter the city. The *Aissawa* are one of the principal religious confraternities of Morocco, founded, like the others, under the inspiration of God, by a saint called Sidi-Mohammed-ben-Aissa, born at Mekïnez two centuries ago. His life is a long and confused legend of miracles and fabulous events, variously related. The *Aissawa* propose to themselves to obtain the special protection of heaven, praying continually, exercising certain practices peculiar to

themselves, and keeping alive in their hearts a certain religious fever, a divine fury, which breaks out in extravagant
and ferocious manifestations. They have a great mosque at Fez,
which is the central house of the order, and from thence they
spread themselves every year over the provinces of the empire,
gathering together as they go those members of the brotherhood
who are in the towns and villages. Their rites, similar to
those of the howling and whirling Dervishes of the East, consist in a species of frantic dances, interspersed with leaps, yells,
and contortions, in the practice of which they grow ever more
furious and ferocious, until, losing the light of reason, they
crush wood and iron with their teeth, burn their flesh with
glowing coals, wound themselves with knives, swallow mud and
stones, brain animals and devour them alive and dripping with
blood, and finally fall to the ground insensible. The *Aissawa*
whom I saw at Tangiers did not go to quite such extremities,
and probably they seldom do, but they did quite enough to leave
an indelible impression on my memory.

The Belgian Minister invited us to see the spectacle from
the terrace of his house, which looked over the principal street of
Tangiers, where the *Aissawa* generally passed on their way to
their mosque. They were to pass at ten o'clock in the morning,
coming in at the Soc-de-Barra. At nine the street was already
full of people, and the tops of the houses crowded with Arab and
Jewish women in all the colours of the rainbow, giving to the
white terraces the look of great baskets of flowers. At the given
hour all eyes were turned towards the gate at the end of the
street, and in a few minutes the leaders of the procession appeared. The street was so thronged with people that for some
time nothing could be seen but a waving mass of hooded heads,
amid which shone out a few shaven skulls. Above them
floated here and there a banner; and now and then a cry as of
many voices broke forth. The crowd moved forwards slowly.
Little by little a certain order and regularity in the movement
of all these heads became visible. The first formed a circle;

others beyond a double file; others again beyond another circle;
then the first in their turn broke into a double line, the second

Entry of the Aissawa into Tangiers.

formed in a circle, and so on. But I am not very sure of what
I say, because in the eager curiosity which possessed me to

observe single figures it is possible that the precise laws of
the general movement escaped me. My first impression as
they arrived below our terrace was one of pity and horror combined. There were two lines of men, facing each other, wrapped
in mantles and long white shirts, holding each other by the
hands, arms, or shoulders, and, with a rocking swaying motion,
stepping in cadence, throwing their heads backwards and forwards, and keeping up a low eager murmur, broken by groans
and sighs, and sobs of rage and terror. Only "The Possessed,"
by Reubens, "The Dead Alive," by Goya, and "The Dead Man
Magnetised" of Edgar Poe, could give an idea of those figures.
There were faces livid and convulsed, with eyes starting from
the sockets, and foaming mouths; faces of the fever-stricken
and the epileptic; some illuminated by an unearthly smile, some
showing only the whites of their eyes, others contracted as by
atrocious spasms, or pallid and rigid, like corpses. From time
to time, making a strange gesture with their outstretched arms,
they all burst out together in a shrill and painful cry, as of
men in mortal agony; then the dance forwards began again,
with its accompaniment of groans and sobs, while hoods and
mantles, wide sleeves and long disordered hair, streamed on the
wind, and whirled about them with snake-like undulations.
Some rushed from one side to the other, staggering like drunken
men, or beating themselves against walls and doors; others, as
if rapt in ecstasy, moved along, stiff and rigid, with head
thrown back, eyes half closed, and arms swinging; and some,
quite exhausted, unable any longer to yell, or to keep on their
feet, were held up under the arms by their companions, and
dragged along with the crowd. The dance became every
moment more frantic, and the noise more deafening, while a
nauseous smell came up from all those bodies like the odour of a
menagerie of wild beasts. Here and there a convulsed visage
turned upwards towards our terrace, and a pair of staring eyes
were fixed on mine, constraining me to turn away my face.
The spectacle affected me in different ways. Now it seemed

a great masquerade, and tempted me to laugh; then it was a procession of madmen, of creatures in the delirium of fever, of drunken wretches, or those condemned to death and striving to deaden their own terror, and my heart swelled with compassion; and again, the savage grandeur of the picture pleased my artistic sense. But gradually my mind accepted the inner meaning of the rite, and I comprehended what all of us have more or less experienced—the spasms of the human soul under the dread pressure of the Infinite; and unconsciously my thoughts explained the mystery. Yes; I feel Thee, mysterious and tremendous Power; I struggle in the grasp of the invisible hand; the sense of Thee oppresses me, I cannot contain it; my heart is dismayed, my reason is lost, my garment of clay is rent. And still they went by, a pallid and dishevelled mass, raising voices of pain and supplication, and seeming in their last agony. One old man, an image of distracted Lear, broke from the ranks, and tried to dash his head against a wall, his companions holding him back. A youth fell head foremost to the ground, and remained there insensible. Another, with streaming hair and face hidden in his hands, went by with long steps, his body bent almost to the earth, like one accursed of God. Bedouins were among them, Berbers, blacks, mummies, giants, satyrs, cannibal faces, faces of saints, of birds of prey, of Indian idols, furies, fauns, devils. There were between three and four hundred, and in half-an-hour they had all gone by. The last were two women (for they also belong to the order), looking as if they had been buried alive, and had escaped from their tomb, two animated skeletons dressed in white, with hair streaming over their faces, straining eyes, and mouths white with foam, exhausted, but still moving along with the unconscious action of machines; and between them marched a gigantic old man, like an aged sorcerer. Dressed in a long white shirt, and stretching out two bony arms, he placed his hands now on one head, now on the other, with a gesture of protection, and helped them to rise when they fell. Behind these three spectres came a throng of armed Arabs, women, beggars, and children ; and all the mass of barbarism and horrid human misery broke into the square, and was dispersed in a few minutes about the city.

Another fine spectacle that we had at Tangiers was that of

The Horsemen at the Fête of Mahomet.

the festival of the birth of Mahomet; and it made the greater impression upon me that I saw it unexpectedly. Returning from a walk on the sea-shore, I heard some shots in the direction of the Soc-de-Barra. I turned my steps in that direction, and at first found it difficult to recognise the place. The Soc-de-Barra was transfigured. From the walls of the city up to the summit of the hill swarmed a crowd of white-robed Arabs, all in the highest state of animation. There might have been about three thousand persons, but so scattered and grouped that they

FÊTE OF THE BIRTH OF MAHOMET.

appeared innumerable. It was a most singular optical illusion. On all the heights around, as upon so many balconies, were groups seated in Oriental fashion, motionless, and turned towards the lower part of the Soc, where the crowd—divided into two portions—left a large space free for the evolutions of a company of cavalry, who, ranged in a line, galloped about, discharging their long guns in the air. On the other side an immense circle of Arab men and women were looking on at the games of ball-players, fencers, serpent-charmers, dancers, singers and musicians, and soldiers. Upon the top of the hill, under a conical tent open in front, could be discerned the enormous white turban of the Vice-Governor of Tangiers, who presided at the festival, seated on the ground in the midst of a circle of Moors. From above could be seen in the crowd the soldiers of the Legations, dressed in their showy red caftans, a few tall hats, and European parasols, and one or two artists, sketch-book in hand, while Tangiers and the sea formed a background to the whole. The discharge of musketry, the yells of the cavalry, the tinkle of the water-sellers' bells, the joyful cries of the women, the noise of pipes, horns, and drums, made up a fitting accompaniment to the strange and savage spectacle, bathed in the burning noon-day light.

My curiosity impelled me to look everywhere at once, but a sudden scream of admiration from a group of women made me turn to the horsemen. There were twelve of them, all of tall stature, with pointed red caps, white mantles, and blue, orange, and red caftans, and among them was a youth, dressed with feminine elegance, the son of the Governor of Rif. They drew up in a line against the wall of the city, with faces towards the open country. The son of the Governor, in the middle, raised his hand, and all started in full career. At first there was a slight hesitation and confusion, but in a moment the twelve horsemen formed but one solid serried line, and skimmed over the ground like a twelve-headed and many-coloured monster devouring the way.

Nailed to their saddles, with heads erect, and white mantles streaming in the wind of their career, they lifted their guns above their heads, and, pressing them against their shoulders, discharged them all together, with a yell of triumph, and then vanished in a cloud of smoke and dust. A few moments after they came back slowly and in disorder—the horses covered with foam and blood, their riders bearing themselves proudly—and then they began again. At every new discharge, the Arab women, like ladies at a tourney, saluted them with a peculiar cry, that is a rapid re-petition of the monosyllable *Jù* (or in English *yù*) like a sort of joyous trill.

We went to look at the ball-players. About fifteen Arab boys and men—some of the latter with white beards—some with sabres, some with guns slung across their shoulders, were tossing a leathern ball about as big as an orange. One would take it, let it fall, and send it

The Ball-Players.

into the air with a blow of his foot; all the others rushed to catch it before it fell. The one who caught it repeated the action of the first; and so the group of players, always following the ball, were in constant movement from one point to another. The curious part of it was that there was not a word, nor a cry, nor a smile among them. Old men and boys, all were equally serious and intent upon the game, as upon some necessary labour, and only their panting breath and the sound of their feet could be heard.

At a few paces farther on, within another circle of spectators, some negroes were dancing to the sound of a pipe and a small conical drum, beaten with a stick in the shape of a half-moon.

CHARGE OF THE HORSEMEN AT THE FÊTE OF MAHOMET.

There were eight of them—big, black, and shining like ebony, with nothing on them but a long white shirt, bound round the waist by a thick green cord. Seven of them held each other's hand in a ring, while the eighth was in the middle, and all danced together, or rather accompanied the music, without moving from their places, but with a certain indescribable movement of the hips, and that satyr-like grin, that expression of stupid beatitude and bestial voluptuousness, which is peculiar to

Negro Dancers.

the black race. Whilst I stood looking on at this scene, two boys, about ten years of age, among the spectators, gave me a taste of the ferocity of Arab blood. They suddenly—and for some unknown reason—fell upon each other, and, clinging together like a couple of young tigers, bit, clawed, and scratched, with a fury that was horrible to see. Two strong men had as much as they could do to separate them, and they were borne off all bloody and torn, and struggling to attack each other again.

The fencers made me laugh. They were four, fencing in couples, with sticks. The extravagance and awkwardness of this performance is not to be described. In other cities in Morocco I afterwards saw the same thing, so it is evidently the native

E

school of fencing. The leaps, contortions, attitudes, and waving
of arms, were beyond words, and all done with a self-satisfied air
that was enough to make one fall upon them with their own
sticks and send them flying. The Arab spectators, however,
stood about with open mouths, and frequently glanced at me,
as if to enjoy my wonder and admiration, while I, willing to
content them, affected to be much delighted. Then some of
them drew aside that I might see them better, and I presently
found myself surrounded and pressed on all sides by the Arabs,
and was able to satisfy in full my desire to study the race in all
its more intimate peculiarities. A soldier of the Italian Legation,
seeing me in these straits, and thinking me an involuntary
prisoner, came to my rescue, rather against my will, with fists
and elbows.

The circle of the story-teller was the most interesting, though
the smallest of all. I arrived just at the moment when he had
finished the usual inaugural prayer, and was beginning his narrative. He was a man of about fifty, almost black, with a jet-
black beard and gleaming eyes, wearing, like all of his profession
in Morocco, an ample white robe, bound round the waist with a
camel's-hair girdle, giving him the majestic air of an antique
priest. He spoke in a high voice, and slowly, standing erect
within the circle of listeners, while two musicians with drum and
hautboy kept up a low accompaniment. I could not understand
a word, but his face, voice, and gestures were so expressive that
I managed to gather something of the meaning of his story.
He seemed to be relating a tale of a journey. Now he imitated
the action of a tired horse, and pointed to a distant and immense
horizon ; then he seemed to seek about for a drop of water, and
his arms and head dropped as if in complete exhaustion. Suddenly he discovers something at a distance, appears uncertain,
believes, and doubts the evidence of his senses—again believes, is
re-animated, hastens his flagging steps, arrives, gives thanks to
Heaven, and throws himself on the earth with a long breath of
satisfaction, smiling with pleasure, in the shade of a delightful

oasis. The audience meanwhile stood without breath or motion, suspended on the lips of the orator, and reflecting in their faces his every word and gesture. The ingenuousness and freshness of feeling that are hidden under their hard and savage exterior became plainly visible. As the story-teller became more fervent in his narrative, and raised his voice, the two musicians blew and beat with increasing fury, and the listeners drew closer together in the intensity of their interest, until, finally, the whole culminated in one grand burst; the musicians threw their instruments into the air, and the crowd dispersed, and gave place to another circle.

There were three performers who had drawn a large audience about them. One played on a sort of bagpipes, another on a tambourine with bells, and the third on an extraordinary instrument compounded of a clarinet and two horns, which gave forth most discordant sounds. All three men were bandy-legged, tall, and with backs bent into a curve. Wrapped in a few rags, they stood side by side close together as if they had been bound one to the other, and, playing an air which they had probably played for fifty years or more, they marched around the square. Their movement was peculiar—something between walking and dancing—and their gestures so extraordinary, made as they were with mechanical regularity and all together, that I imagine them to have expressed some idea founded in some characteristic peculiarity of the Arab people. Those three, streaming with heat from every pore, played and marched about for more than an hour in the fashion I have described, with unalterable gravity, while a hundred or so of lookers-on stood, with the sun in their eyes, giving no outward sign either of pleasure or of weariness.

The noisiest circle was that of the soldiers. There were twelve, old and young, some with white caftans, some in shirts only, one with a fez, another in a hood, and all armed with flint muskets as long as lances, into which they put the powder loose, like all their fellows in Morocco, where the

cartridge is not in use. An old man directed the manœuvres.
They ranged themselves in two rows of six each, facing one
another. At a signal, all changed places with each other,
running and putting one knee to the ground. Then one of
them struck up, in a shrill falsetto voice, a sort of chant, full
of trills and warblings, which lasted a few minutes, and was
listened to in perfect silence. Then suddenly they all bounded
to their feet in a circle, and with an immense leap and a

Dance of the Soldiers.

shout of joy, fired off their guns muzzle downwards. The
rapidity, the fury, and something madly festive and diaboli-
cally cheerful in the performance, is not to be described.
Among the spectators near me was a little Arab girl about
ten years old, not yet veiled, one of the prettiest little faces
I saw in Tangiers, of a delicate pale bronze in colour, who,
with her large blue eyes full of wonder, gazed at a spectacle
much more marvellous to her than that of the soldiers' dance :
she saw me take off my gloves, which Arab boys believe to
be a sort of second skin that Christians have on their hands,
and can remove at pleasure without inconvenience or pain.

I hesitated about going to see the serpent charmers, but curiosity overcame repugnance. These so-called magicians belong to the confraternity of the Aissawa, and pretend to have received from their patron Ben Aissa the privilege of enduring uninjured the bite of the most venomous beasts. Many travellers, in fact, most worthy of belief, assert that they have seen these men bitten severely, until the blood flowed, by serpents that a moment before had shown the fatal effect of their venom upon some animal. The Aissawa whom I saw gave a horrible but bloodless spectacle. He was a little fellow, muscular, with a cadaverous and stern countenance, the air of a Merovingian king, and dressed in a sort of blue shirt that came down to his heels. When I drew near he was engaged in jumping grotesquely about a goat-skin spread on the ground, upon which was a sack containing the serpents; and as he jumped he sang, to the accompaniment of a flute, a melancholy song that was perhaps an invocation to his saint. The song finished, he chattered and gesticulated for some time, trying to get some money thrown to him, and then, kneeling down before the goat-skin, he thrust his arm into the sack and drew out a long greenish snake, extremely lively, and carried it round, handling it very carefully, for the spectators to see. This done, he began to twist it about in all directions, and generally use it as if it had been a rope. He seized it by the neck, he suspended it by the tail, he bound it round his head like a fillet, he hid it in his bosom, he made it pass through the holes in the edge of a tambourine, he threw it on the ground and set his foot upon it, he stuck it under his arm. The horrible beast erected its head, darted out its tongue, twisted itself about with those flexible odious abject movements that seem the expression of perfidious baseness; and all the rage that burned in its body seemed to shoot in sparkles from its small eyes; but I could not see that it ever once attempted to bite the hand that held it. After this, the Aissawa seized the serpent

by the neck, and fixed a small bit of iron in its mouth, so
as to keep it open and display the fangs to the spectators;
and then, taking its tail between his teeth, he proceeded to
bite it, while the beast went through violent contortions; and
I left the place in horror and disgust.

At that moment our *chargé d'affaires* appeared in the Soc.
The Vice-Governor beheld him from the hill, ran to meet
him, and conducted him under the tent, where all the members
of the future caravan, myself included, speedily assembled.
Then came soldiers and musicians, and an immense semi-
circle of Arabs formed itself in front of the tent, the men in
front, the gentle sex in groups behind; and then began a
wild concert of songs, dances, yells, and gunshots, which lasted
for more than an hour, in the midst of dense clouds of smoke,
the sounds of barbaric music, the enthusiastic shouts of the
women and children, the paternal satisfaction of the Vice-
Governor, and our great amusement. Before it was over, the
charge d'affaires put some coins into the hand of an Arab
soldier, to be given to the director of the spectacle, and the
soldier presently returning, delivered the following odd form
of thanks, translated into Spanish :—"The Italian Ambassador
has done a good action; may Allah bless every hair of his
beard!"

The strange festival lasted until sunset. Three water-
sellers were sufficient to satisfy the needs of all that crowd,
exposed all day to the rays of the sun of Africa. One *marengo*
was perhaps the utmost of the sum that circulated in that
concourse of people. Their only pleasures were to see and
hear. There was no love-making, no drunkenness, no knife
play; nothing in common with the holidays of civilisation.

The country about Tangiers is not less curious to see than the
city. Around the walls extends a girdle of gardens, belonging
for the most part to the Ministers and Consuls, and rather neg-
lected, but rich in luxuriant vegetation. There may be seen long
files of aloes, like gigantic lances bound up in sheaves of enor-

mous curved dagger blades, for such is the shape of their leaves. The points, with the fibre attached, are used by the Arabs to sew up wounds. There is the Indian fig—in the Moorish tongue, *kermus del Inde*—very tall, with leaves of extraordinary thickness, and growing so thickly as to obstruct the paths; the common fig, under whose shadow ten tents could be erected; oaks, acacias, oleanders, and shrubs of every sort, that interlace their branches with those of the highest trees, and with the ivy, the vine, the cane, and the thorn, form a tangled mass of verdure under which ditch and footpath are entirely concealed. In some places one has to grope one's way, and pass from one enclosure to another through thick, thorny hedges, over prostrate fences, in the midst of grass and flowers as high as one's waist, and no living creature to be seen. A small white house, and a well, with a wheel by means of which the water is sent flowing through little trenches dug for the purpose, are the only objects which indicate the presence of property and labour. Sometimes, if the Captain of the staff, who was a clever guide, had not been with me, I should have lost my way in the midst of that wild vegetation; and we often had to call out, as in a labyrinth, to prevent our losing each other. It was a pleasure to me to swim amid the greenery, opening the way with hands and feet, with the joyous excitement of a savage returned from slavery to his native forest.

Beyond this girdle of gardens there are no trees, or houses, or hedges, or any indication of boundaries ; there are only hills, green valleys, and undulating plains with an occasional herd of cattle pasturing and without any visible herdsman, or a horse turned loose. Once only did I see any tilling of the ground. An Arab was driving an ass and a goat, harnessed to a very small plough, of a strange shape, such as might have been in use four thousand years ago, and which turned up a scarcely visible furrow in the stony, weedy earth. I have been assured that it is not unusual to see a donkey and a

woman ploughing in company, and this will give an idea of
the state of agriculture in Morocco. The only attempt at
manuring is to burn the straw left after the grain is gathered;
and the only care taken not to exhaust the earth is to leave it
every third year to grow grass for pasture, after having grown
grain, and buckwheat or maize, in the two preceding years.
In spite of this, however, the ground becomes impoverished
after a few years, and then the husbandman leaves it, and

A Moorish Husbandman.

seeks another field, returning, after a time, to the old one; and
so but a very small part of the arable land is under cultivation
at one time, whereas if it were even badly cultivated, it would
return a hundredfold the seed thrown in it.

The prettiest excursion we made was that to Cape Spartel,
the *Ampelusium* of the ancients, which forms the north-western
extremity of the African continent, a mountain of grey stone,
about three hundred mètres in height, rising abruptly from the
sea, and opening underneath into vast caverns, the larger of
which were consecrated to Hercules: *Specus Herculi sacer.*
Upon the summit of this mountain stands the famous lighthouse

erected a few years ago, and maintained by contributions from
most of the European States. We climbed to the top of the
tower, where the great lantern sends its beneficent rays to a
distance of five-and-twenty miles. From thence the eye
embraces two seas and two continents. There can be seen the
last waters of the Mediterranean and the horizon of the
Atlantic—the sea of darkness, *Bar-el-Dolma*, as the Arabs call

Excursion to Cape Spartel.

it—beating at the foot of the rock; the Spanish coast, from
Cape Trafalgar to Cape Algesiras; the African coast, from the
Mediterranean to the mountains of Ceuta, the *septem fratres*
of the Romans; and far in the distance, faintly outlined,
the enormous rock of Gibraltar—eternal sentinel of that port
of the old continent, mysterious terminus of the antique
world, become the " *Favola vila ai naviganti industri.*"

In this expedition we encountered but few persons, for
the most part Arabs on foot, who passed almost without
looking at us, and sometimes a Moor on horseback, some

personage important either for his wealth or his office, accompanied by a troop of armed followers, who looked contemptuously at us as they passed. The women muffled their faces even more carefully than in the city, some muttering, and others turning their backs abruptly upon us. Here and there an Arab would stop before us, look fixedly at us, murmur a few words that sounded as if he were asking a favour, and then go on his way without looking back. At first we did not understand, but it was explained that they were asking us to pray to God for some favour for them. It seems that there is a superstition much in vogue among the Arabs that the prayers of a Mussulman being very grateful to God, He generally delays granting what they ask for, in order that He may prolong the pleasure of hearing the prayer; whilst the prayer of an infidel dog, like a Hebrew or a Christian, is so hateful to Him that He grants it at once, *ipso facto*, in order to be rid of it. The only friendly faces we saw were those of some Jewish boys who were scampering about on donkeys, and who threw us a cheerful " *Buenos dies, Caballeros !* " as they galloped by.

In spite, however, of the new and varied character of our life at Tangiers, we were all impatience to leave it, in order to get back in the month of June, before the great heats began. The *chargé d'affaires* had sent a messenger to Fez to announce that the embassy was ready; but ten days at least must pass before he could return. Private notices informed us that the escort was on its way, others that it had not yet started. Uncertain and contradictory rumours prevailed, as if the longed-for Fez were distant two thousand miles from the coast, instead of about one hundred and forty miles; and this, from one point of view, was rather agreeable, because our fifteen days' journey thus assumed in our fancy the proportions of a long and adventurous voyage, and Fez seemed mysteriously attractive. The strange things, too, which were related by those who had been there with

former embassies, about the city, its people, and the dangers
of the expedition, all combined to excite our expectations.
They told how they had been surrounded by thousands of
horsemen, who saluted them with a tempest of shots, so near
as almost to scorch their skins and blind them, and that
they could hear the balls whistle by their ears; that in all
probability some of us Italians would be shot in the head by
mistake by some ball directed against the white cross in our
flag, which would no doubt seem an insult to Mahomet in
Arab eyes. They talked of scorpions, serpents, tarantulas, of
clouds of grasshoppers and locusts, of spiders and toads of
gigantic size that were found on the road and under the tents.
They described in dismal colours the entrance of the embassy
into Fez, in the midst of a hostile crowd, through tortuous,
dark streets, encumbered with ruins and the carcases of
animals; they prophesied a mountain of troubles for us
during our stay at Fez—mortal languors, furious dysenteries
and rheumatisms, musquitoes of monstrous size and ferocity,
compared with which those of our country were agreeable
companions, and, finally, home-sickness; apropos of which,
they told us of a young Belgian painter who had gone to
Fez with the embassy from Brussels, and who, after a week's
stay, was seized with such a desperate melancholy that the
Ambassador was obliged to send him back to Tangiers by
forced marches, that he might not see him die under his eyes;
and it was true. But all this only increased our impatience
to be off, and our delight can be easily imagined when Signor
Soloman Affalo, the second dragoman of the Legation, one
day presented himself at the door of the dining-room, and
announced, in a sonorous voice—"The escort from Fez has
arrived."

With it came horses, mules, camels, grooms, tents, the route
laid down for us by the Sultan, and his permission to start at
once. Some days, however, had to be allowed for men and
beasts to take a little rest.

The animals were sheltered at the Casba. The next day we
went to see them. There were forty-five horses, including those
of the escort, about twenty mules for the saddle, and more than
fifty for baggage, to which were afterwards added others hired
at Tangiers; the horses small and light, like all Morocco horses,
and the mules robust; the saddles and packs covered with

The Animals of the Caravan.

scarlet cloth; the stirrups formed of a large plate of iron bent
upwards at the two sides, so as to support and enclose the whole
foot, and serving also as spurs, as well as defences. The poor
beasts were almost all lying down, exhausted more from hunger
than from fatigue, a large part of their food having, according
to custom, found its way, in the shape of coin, into the pockets
of the drivers. Some of the soldiers of the escort were there,
who came about us, and made us understand by signs and words
that the journey had been a very fatiguing one, with much

suffering from heat and thirst, but that, thanks to Allah, they
had arrived safe and sound. They were blacks and mulattoes,
wrapped in their white capotes, tall, powerful men, with bold
features, sharp white teeth, and flashing eyes, that made us
consider whether it would not be well to have a second escort
placed between them and ourselves in case of necessity. Whilst
my companions coversed in gestures, I sought among the mules

Tents of the Soldiers of the Escort.

one with a mild expression of generosity and gentleness in its
eyes, and found it in a white mule with a crupper adorned with
arabesques. To this creature I decided to confide my life and
fortunes, and from that moment until our return the hope of
Italian literature in Morocco was bound to her saddle.

From the Casba we proceeded to the Soc-de-Barra, where the
principal tents had been placed. It was a great pleasure to us to
see these canvas houses where we were to sleep for thirty nights
in the midst of unknown solitudes, and see and hear so many
strange things : one of us preparing his geographical maps,
another his official report, another his book, a fourth his picture ;

forming altogether a small Italy in pilgrimage across the empire of the Scheriffs. The tents were of a cylindrical conical form,

The Commander of the Escort.

some large enough to contain about twenty persons, all very high, and made of double canvas bordered with blue, and ornamented on the top with a large metal ball. Most of them belonged to the Sultan; and who knows how often the beauties of the seraglio had slept under them on their journeys from Fez to Meckïnez and Morocco! In one corner of the encampment was a group of foot-soldiers of the escort, and in front of them a personage unknown, who was awaiting the arrival of the Minister. He was a man of about thirty-five, of a dignified appearance, a mulatto, and corpulent, with a great white turban, a blue capote, red drawers, and a sabre in a leathern sheath with a hilt of rhinoceros-horn. The Minister, arriving in a few moments, presented this gentleman to us as the Commandant of the escort, a general of the imperial army, by name Hamed Ben

Kasen Buhamei, who was to accompany us to and from Fez back to Tangiers, and whose head answered to the Sultan for the safety of ours. He shook hands with us with much grace and ease of manner, and his visage and air reassured me completely with regard to the eyes and teeth of the soldiers whom I had seen at the Casba. He was not handsome, but his countenance expressed mildness and intelligence. He must know how to read, write, and cipher—be, in fact, one of the most cultured generals in the army—since he had been chosen by the Minister of War for this delicate mission. The distribution of tents was now made in his presence. One was assigned to painting ; among the largest, after that of the Ambassador, was the one taken possession of by the commander of the frigate, the Captain of the staff, the Vice-Consul, and myself, which afterwards became the noisiest tent in the encampment. Another very large one was set aside as a dining-room ; and then came those of the doctor, the interpreters, cooks, servants, and soldiers of the Legation. The commander of the escort and his soldiers had their tents apart. Other tents were to be added on the day of departure. In short, I foresaw that we should have a beautiful encampment, and already felt within me the beginnings of descriptive frenzy.

On the following day the *chargé d'affaires* went with the Commandant of the frigate and the Captain to pay a visit to the representative of the imperial Government, Sidi-Bargas, who exercises what may be called the office of Minister of Foreign Affairs in Tangiers. I begged permission to accompany them, being very curious to see a Minister of Foreign Affairs who, if his salary has not been increased within the last twenty years (which is not probable), receives from his Government the sum of seventy-five francs or fifteen dollars a month, which includes the fund for the expenses of representation—a magnificent stipend, nevertheless, compared with that of the Governors, who receive only fifty francs. And it is not to be said that their charge is a sinecure, and may be entrusted to the first comer. The famous Sultan Abd-er-Rahman, for instance, who reigned

from 1822 to 1859, could find no man so well adapted for it as one
Sidi-Mohammed el Khatïb, merchant in coffee and sugar, who
continued while he was Minister to traffic regularly between
Tangiers and Gibraltar. The instructions which this Minister
received from his Government, although very simple, are such
as to embarrass the most subtle of European diplomatists. A
French Consul has set them down for us with much precision—
viz., to respond to all demands of the Consuls with promises; to
defer to the very latest moment the fulfilment of these promises;
to gain time; to raise difficulties of every kind against com-
plaint; to act in such a way that the complainants will get
tired, and desist; to yield, if threatened, as little as possible; if
cannon are introduced, to yield, but not until the latest moment.
But it must be acknowledged that after the war with Spain, and
especially under the reign of Muley-el-Hassan, things have very
much changed.

We went up to the Casba where the Minister lives; a
line of soldiers kept guard before the door. We crossed a
garden and entered a spacious hall, where the Minister and
the Governor of Tangiers came to meet us. At the bottom
of the hall was a recess or alcove, with a sofa and some
chairs; in one corner a modest bed; under the bed a coffee-
service; the walls white and bare; the floor covered with
matting. We seated ourselves in the alcove.

The two personages before us formed an admirable contrast. One, Sidi-Bargas, the Minister, was a handsome old
man, with a white beard and a clear complexion, eyes of
extraordinary vivacity, and a large smiling mouth, display-
ing two rows of ivory-white teeth; a countenance which
revealed the finesse and marvellous flexibility demanded of
him by the very nature of his office. His eye-glasses and
snuff-box, together with certain ceremonious airs of head and
hands, gave him something of the look of a European diploma-
tist. Plainly a man accustomed to deal with Christians;
superior, perhaps, to many of the prejudices and superstitions

of his people; a Mussulman of large views; a Moor varnished with civilisation. The other, the Caid Misfiui, seemed the incarnation of Morocco. He was about fifty years of age, with black beard and bronze complexion, muscular, sombre, and taciturn; a face that looked as if it had never smiled. He held his head down, his eyes fixed on the ground, his brow bent; his expression was one of strong repugnance. Both men wore large muslin turbans and long ample robes of transparent stuff.

The Author's Interview with the Minister and Governor of Tangiers.

The *chargé d'affaires* presented to these two personages through the interpreter the Commandant of the frigate and the Captain. They were two officials, and their introduction required no comment. But when I was presented, a few words of explanation as to the office which I filled were necessary; and the *chargé d'affaires* expressed himself in rather hyperbolical terms. Sidi-Bargas stood a moment silent, and then said a few words to the interpreter, who translated—

"His Excellency demands why you have such ability with your hand. Your lordship wears it covered; your lordship will please remove your glove that the hand may be seen."

F

The compliment was so new to me that I was at a loss for a reply.

"It is not necessary," observed the *chargé d'affaires*, "because the faculty resides in his mind, and not in his hand."

One would have thought this settled the question; but when a Moor gets hold of a metaphor, he does not leave it so easily.

"True," replied his Excellency, through the interpreter; "but the hand being the instrument is also the symbol of the faculties of the mind."

The discussion was prolonged for a few minutes. "It is a gift of Allah," finally concluded Sidi-Bargas.

The conversation continued for some time, and the journey was discussed. There was a long citation of names of Governors, of provinces, of rivers, valleys, mountains, and plains, that we should find upon our route; names that resounded in my ear as so many promises of adventure, and set my fancy to work. What was the Red Mountain? What should we find on the banks of Pearl River? What sort of a man could that Governor be who was called "Son of the Mare?" Our *chargé* made numerous inquiries as to distances, water, and shade. Sidi-Bargas had it all at the points of his fingers, and in this direction was certainly greatly beyond Visconti Venosta, who could not for his life have given information to a foreign Ambassador as to how many springs of water and how many groups of trees there were between Rome and Naples. Finally, he wished us a pleasant journey, with the following formula :—"May peace be in your path!" and accompanying the Ambassador to the entrance, shook hands with us all with an air of great cordiality. The Caid Misfiui, always mute, put out the tips of his fingers, without raising his eyes. "My hand—yes," I thought, as I gave it, "but not my head!"

"Start on Monday!" called out Sidi-Bargas, as we took leave.

The Ambassador asked why Monday rather than Sunday.
"Because it is a day of good omen," he answered, with gravity;
and with another deep salutation, he left us.

I learned later that Sidi-Misfiui is accounted a man of
great learning among the Moors; he was tutor to the reigning
Sultan, and is, as his face shows, a fanatical Mussulman.
Sidi-Bargas enjoys the more amiable reputation of being a
very fine chess-player.

Three days before our departure the street before the
Legation was thronged with curious lookers-on. Ten tall
camels, which were to carry to Fez, in advance of us, a part
of our provision of wine, came one after the other, kneeled
down to receive their load, and departed with their guard of
soldiers and servants. Within the house all was bustle, and
the servants who had come from Fez were added to those
already on the spot. Provisions arrived at every hour in the
day. It was feared, at one moment, that we should not be
able to get off on the appointed day. But on the Sunday
evening, 3rd of May, everything was ready, including the
lofty mast of an immense tricoloured flag which was to float
in the midst of our encampment; and in the night the baggage
mules were loaded so that they should start early on Monday
morning, several hours before us, and arrive in the evening in
time to have everything ready for us at the encampment.

I shall always remember with a pleasant emotion those last
moments passed in the court of the Legation just before our
departure. We were all there. An old friend of the *chargé
d'affaires* had arrived the evening before to join us, Signor
Patot, formerly Minister from Spain to Tangiers, and also
Signor Morteo, a Genoese, and consular agent for Italy to
Mazagan. There was the doctor of the caravan, Miguerez, a
native of Algiers; a rich Moor, Mohammed Ducali, an Italian
subject, who accompanied the embassy in the quality of writer;
the second dragoman of the Legation, Soloman Affalo; two
Italian sailors, one orderly to Commander Cassone, and the

F 2

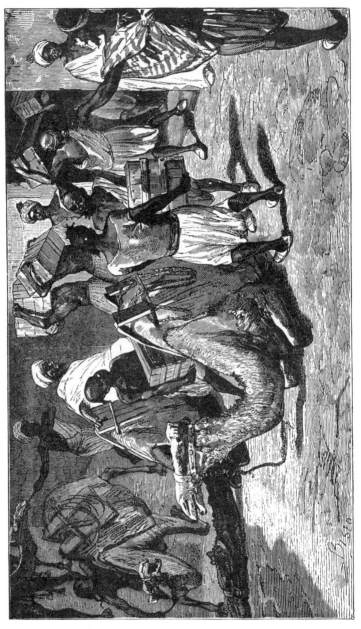

LOADING THE CAMELS.

other belonging to the *Dora ;* the soldiers of the Legation in holiday dress; cooks, workmen, and servants, all persons unknown to me, whom two months of life in common in the interior of Morocco were to render familiar to me, and whom I prepared myself to study from that moment, one by one, and to make move and speak in a book that I had in my head.

On the Road to Fez.

Every one of them had some peculiarity of dress, which gave the whole a singularly picturesque appearance. There were plumed caps, white mantles, gaiters, veils, wallets, and blankets of every colour. There were enough pistols, barometers, quadrants, albums, and field-glasses to have set up a bazaar. We might have been setting off on an expedition to the Cape of Good Hope, and every one of us was quivering with impatience, curiosity, and pleasant anticipation. To crown all, the weather was exquisite, and a delightful sea breeze was blowing. Mahomet was with Italy.

At five o'clock exactly the Ambassador mounted his horse, and the flags on the terrace of the Legation rose in salute. Preoccupied as I was with my white mule, and in all the confusion and uproar of departure, I remember but little of the crowd that encumbered the street, the handsome Jewish women peering from their terraces, and an Arab boy, who exclaimed, with a strange accent, as we issued from the gate of the Soc-de-Barra, " *Italia!* "

At the Soc we were joined by the representatives of the other Legations, who were to accompany us, according to custom, a few miles beyond Tangiers; and we took the road to Fez, a numerous and noisy cavalcade, before which waved the green folds of the banner of the Prophet.

The Encampment

CHAPTER II.

HAD-EL-GARBIA.

A THRONG of Ministers, Consuls, dragomans, secretaries, clerks, a great international embassy, representing six monarchies and two republics, and composed for the most part of people who had been all over the world. Among others, there was the Spanish Consul, dressed in the graceful costume of the province of Mercia, with a poignard in his girdle; the gigantic figure of the United States Consul, once a colonel in a cavalry regiment, towering a whole head above the rest of the troop, and riding a beautiful Arab horse with Mexican saddle and accoutrements; the dragoman of the Legation of France, an athletic man, mounted upon an enormous white horse, with which he presented, in certain points

DEPARTURE OF THE CARAVAN FOR FEZ.

of view, the image of a centaur; English, Andalusians, and
Germans were there, and as every one spoke in his own
tongue, mingled with laughter, the humming of songs, and
the neighing of beasts, the effect may be imagined. Before
us rode the banner-bearer, followed by two soldiers of the
Italian Legation; behind came the escort, led by the mulatto
General, with his rifle erect, one end resting on the saddle;
on either side a crowd of Arabs on foot. All this motley
company, gilded by the rays of the setting sun, presented a
spectacle so splendidly picturesque that each one of us wore
an air of complacency at the thought that we formed part of
the picture.

Little by little, those who had accompanied us from Tangiers took their leave and turned back; only America and
Spain remained with us. The road so far was not bad; my
mule seemed the most docile of mules; what remained for
me to desire? But there is no perfect felicity on this earth.
The Captain drew near and gave me a most unpleasing piece
of news. The Vice-Consul, Paolo Grande, our tent companion,
was a somnambulist. The Captain himself had met him the
night before on the stairs of the Legation, wrapped in a sheet,
with a lamp in one hand and a pistol in the other. The
servants, being questioned, confirmed the tale. To sleep with
him in the same tent was dangerous. The Captain entreated
me, as I was more intimate with the Vice-Consul than he, to
induce him to give up his arms for the night. I promised to
do my best. "I leave it in your hands," said he, as he
turned away, "and I speak in the name of the Commandant
also." "Here's a fine business!" thought I, as I went in
search of the Vice-Consul. He came to meet me. With one
cautious question and another I succeeded in discovering that
he carried with him a small arsenal, what with fire-arms and
cutting weapons, comprising an ugly Moorish poignard that
seemed expressly made for cutting a hole in my own person.
After turning it over in my mind, I decided to wait until

the hour for going to bed arrived, and for the rest of the
way the teasing thought pursued me.

We were moving now in a great curve over an undulating
country, green and solitary. The road, if road it could be
called, was formed of a large number of parallel paths crossing
each other here and there, winding through stones and bushes,
and sunken, like the beds of streams. A few palms and aloes
showed their dark outlines upon the golden sky, which, above
our heads, began to glitter with stars. No person was to be
seen far or near. Once we heard some gunshots: it was a
group of Arabs on the top of a hill, saluting the Ambassador.
After three hours' travelling it was dark night, and we began
to wish for the encampment. Hunger in some and fatigue in
others made us silent. Nothing was heard but the horses'
feet and the panting breath of the servants running beside
us. Suddenly there was a shout from the Caid. On a height
to the right lights were glittering, and we hailed with a
unanimous shout our first encampment.

I cannot express the pleasure I felt in dismounting among
the tents. Had it not been for my dignity as the representative of Italian literature, I think I should have indulged
in a sort of jig. It was a little city, illuminated, and full
of noise and people. Kitchen fires blazed on every side. Servants, soldiers, cooks, sailors, went to and fro, exchanging
questions in all the tongues of the Tower of Babel. The
tents were arranged in a large circle, with the Italian banner
in the midst. Behind the tents were ranged the horses and
mules. The escort had its own small encampment apart.
Everything was in military order. I recognised at once my
own habitation, and ran to take possession. There were four
camp-beds, mats and carpets, lanterns, candlesticks, small tables,
folding chairs, wash-basins striped with the Italian colours,
and a great Indian fan. It was a princely establishment, in
which one might willingly spend a year. Our tent was placed
between those of the Ambassador and the artists.

One hour after our arrival we were seated at dinner in the
tent consecrated to Lucullus. I think that was the merriest
dinner that ever took place within the confines of Morocco
since the foundation of Fez. We were sixteen, comprising the
American Consul with his two sons, and the Spanish Consul,
with two *attachés* from the Legation. The Italian *cuisine*
carried off a solemn victory. It was the first time, I be-

Dining in the Tent.

lieve, that in that desolate country the fumes of macaroni with
gravy and *risotto alla Milanese* ever rose to the nostrils of
Allah. The fat French cook, come from Tangiers for that night
only, was clamorously called before the footlights. Toasts went
off one after the other in Italian, in Spanish, in verse, in prose,
in music. The Spanish Consul, a handsome Castilian of the
antique stamp, large-bearded, broad-shouldered, and deep-hearted,
declaimed, with one hand on his dagger-hilt, the dialogue of
Don Juan Tenorio with Don Luis Mendia, in Zorilla's famous
drama. There were discussions upon the Eastern Question,
upon the eyes of Arab women, upon the Carlist war, upon

the immortality of the soul, and upon the properties of the terrible *cobra di capello*—the aspic of Cleopatra—which the charlatans of Morocco allow to bite them with impunity. Some one, in the midst of the clamour of conversation, whispered in my ear that he would be grateful to me for life if I would mention, in my future book on Morocco, that he had killed a lion. I seized the occasion to request my fellow-guests to give me each a note as to the particular ferocious beast which he had conquered. The Spanish Consul, out of gratitude, improvised a verse in honour of my mule, and all singing it to a tune from the "Italiana in Algieri," we issued forth, and sought our different sleeping-places.

The encampment was immersed in profound slumber. In front of the tent of the Ambassador, who had retired before us, watched the faithful Selam, first soldier of the Legation. In the distance paced like a shadow, among the tents, the form of the Caid of the escort. The sky was all sparkling with stars. What a blessed night, if I had not had that thorn inserted in my pillow!

I had no sooner entered my tent than the Captain repeated his advice, and I determined to attack the subject after we should be in bed. It was unavoidable, but it was very unpleasant. The Vice-Consul might take it badly, and I should be very sorry. He was so agreeable a companion. Like a true Sicilian, full of fire, he talked of the most insignificant things with the accent and style of an inspired preacher. He made use of the most terrible adjectives—immense, divine, and so on—on the slightest occasion. His quietest and least expressive gesture was to shake his hands wildly above his head. To see him discuss any question, with his eyes flying out of his head, and his aquiline nose that seemed to defy the world, was to judge him an irascible and imperious man, whereas he was in reality the kindest and gentlest person conceivable.

"Come, courage!" whispered the Captain, when we were all in bed.

" Signor Grande," I began, " are you in the habit of getting up in the night ? "

He seemed much astonished at my question. " No," he answered ; " and I should be very sorry to think that any one had such a habit."

" That's queer," I thought. " Then," said I, " you recognise that it is a dangerous habit ? "

He looked at me. " Excuse me," he said, after a moment's silence ; " I don't suppose you mean to joke on such a subject."

" Excuse *me*," I answered ; " I have not the least intention of joking. It is not my custom to jest on serious subjects."

" Serious indeed ; and it will be for you to guard against the consequences."

" Well, this is fine ! Do you imagine that I shall go and sleep in the middle of the camp ? "

" Of the two, it seems to me that you should go, rather than I."

" That is an impertinence ! " cried I, sitting up in bed with a jump.

" Oh, a new idea ! " shouted the Vice-Consul, bouncing up in his turn ; " an impertinence, not to risk being murdered ! "

A shout of laughter from the other two broke up the discussion, and before they spoke we understood that we had been the victims of a joke. They had told him that *I* was in the habit of wandering about in the night wrapped in a sheet, and with a pistol in my hand.

The night passed without disturbance, and I woke at dawn. The camp was still immersed in slumber ; only among the tents of the escort a few persons were in motion. The sky in the east was of a brilliant rose-colour. I went out among the tents, and stood in contemplation before the spectacle that lay in front of me.

The camp was placed on the side of a hill covered with

grass, aloes, the prickly pear, and some flowering shrubs.
Near the Ambassador's tent rose a tall palm-tree, gracefully
inclined towards the east. In front of the hill extended an
immense plain, undulating and covered with verdure, closed
in the distance by a chain of dark-green mountains, behind
which appeared other blue heights almost lost in the limpid
sky. In all that space there was no house, nor curl of smoke,
nor tent, nor cattle, to be seen. It was like an immense
garden where no living thing was admitted. A fresh and
perfumed breeze rustled the branches of the palm, and made
the only sound that broke the silence. Suddenly, as I turned
I beheld ten dilated eyes fixed on mine. Five Arabs were
seated upon a mass of rock at a few steps from me—labourers
from the country, come in in the night to see the encampment. They seemed sculptured out of the rock on which
they sat. They looked at me without winking, without the
least sign of curiosity, or sympathy, or embarrassment, or
malevolence; the whole five motionless and impassive, their
faces half hidden in their hoods, like personifications of the
solitude and silence of the fields. I put one hand in my
pocket, and the ten eyes followed it; I took out a cigar, and
the ten eyes fixed themselves upon it; they followed every
motion that I made. Little by little I discovered other
figures farther off, seated in the grass two by two and three
by three, motionless and hooded, and, like the first, with their
eyes fixed on me. They seemed to have risen from the earth,
dead men with their eyes open, appearances rather than real
persons, which would vanish under the first beams of the sun.
A long and tremulous cry, coming from that part of the camp
where the escort lay, disturbed me from my contemplation
of these beings. A Mussulman soldier was announcing to his
fellows the first of the five canonical hours of prayer which
every Mussulman must follow. Some soldiers came out of
the tents, spread their mantles on the earth, and knelt down
upon them, their faces towards the east. Three times they

rubbed their hands, arms, head, and feet with a handful of earth, and then began to recite their prayers in a low voice, kneeling, rising to their feet, prostrating themselves face downwards, lifting their open hands to a level with their ears, and crouching on their heels. Soon the commander of the escort issued from his tent, and was followed by his servants, then the cooks. In a few minutes the greater part of the population of the camp was afoot. The sun, scarcely above the horizon, was scorching.

When I went back to my tent, I made the acquaintance of several odd personages to whom I shall have frequently to allude.

The first to appear was one of the Italian sailors, orderly to the Captain of the frigate, a Sicilian, born at Porto Empedocle, Ranni by name—a young fellow of twenty-five, very tall, and of herculean build and strength—good-tempered, grave as a magistrate, and endowed with the singular virtue of never being astonished at anything, except, perhaps, the astonishment of others. For him, Porto Empedocle, Gibraltar, Africa, China, the moon itself, had he been in it, were all the same.

"What do you think of this way of living?" asked the Captain, while Ranni helped him to dress.

"What am I to say?" was the response.

"Why, the journey, the new country, all this confusion—do they make no impression upon you?"

He was silent a moment, and then answered ingenuously, "No impression at all."

"But the encampment—that at least is new to you."

"Oh no, Signor Commandant."

"When did you ever see one before?"

"I saw this one last evening."

The Commandant looked at him, repressing his irritation. Then he said, "Well, last evening—what impression did it make then?"

"Well," answered the sailor with candour, "the same impression, you know, that it made this morning."

The Commandant hung his head with an air of resignation.

Soon after there entered another not less curious personage. He was an Arab from Tangiers, who was in the Vice-Consul's service for the time of the journey. His name was Ciua; but his master called him Civo, for greater facility of pronunciation. He was a large and tall young fellow, rather given to practical joking, but good-natured and willing—a big, ingenuous boy, who laughed and hid his face when you looked at him. He had no other garment than a long, wide, white shirt, without a girdle, which floated about him when he walked, and gave him a ridiculous resemblance to a cherub. He knew about thirty Spanish words, and with these he managed to make himself understood, when constrained to speak ; but he usually preferred to converse in pantomime. To look at him, you would judge him to be about five-and-twenty ; but it is easy to make a mistake in an Arab's age. I asked him how old he was. He covered his face with one hand, thought a moment, and answered, " *Cuando guerra España—año y medio.*" In the time of the war with Spain, which was in 1860, he was a year and a half old, consequently he was then seventeen.

The third personage was the Ambassador's cook, who brought us our coffee—an unadulterated Piedmontese from Turin, who had dropped from the clouds one day into Tangiers, and had not yet recovered his wits. The poor man was never tired of exclaiming, " What a country ! What a country ! "

I asked him if before leaving Turin they had not told him what sort of a place Morocco was. He answered, yes, they had told him, " Take care ; Tangiers is not Turin." And he had thought, " *Pazienza !* it will be like Genoa or Alexandria ;" and instead he had found himself in the midst of savages. And they had given him two Arab assistants who could not understand a word he said. And then to make a two months' journey through the *deserts of Egypt !* He knew he should never get back alive.

"But at any rate," I said, " you will have something to tell when you get back to Turin."

"Ah!" he answered, turning away with an air of profound depression, " what can I tell about a country where one cannot find a single leaf of salad ? "

Breakfast over, the Ambassador gave the order to break up the encampment. During that long operation, in which not less than one hundred persons were concerned, I noticed a singular trait of Arab character—the insatiable passion for command.

Striking the Tents.

There was no need of any indication to recognise at once in that crowd of figures the head muleteer, the head porter, the head tent-servant, the chief of the soldiers of the Legation. Each of these was invested with an authority, and he made it felt and heard, with hand and voice and eye, with or without occasion, and with all the strength of his soul and body. Those who had no authority resorted to all sorts of pretexts for giving orders, and seeming to be something a little above their fellows. The most ragged wretch among them gave himself imperious airs. The simplest operation, such as tying a cord or lifting a box, provoked an exchange of thundering yells, lightning glances, and gestures worthy of an angry sultan. Even Civo, the modest

G

Civo, domineered over two country Arabs who allowed themselves to glance at his master's trunks from a distance.

At ten in the morning, under a burning sun, the long
caravan began slowly to descend into the plain. The Spanish
Consul and his two companions had been left behind ; of foreigners
none remained with us now but the American Consul and his
two sons.

From the place where we had passed the night, called in
Arabic Ain-Dalia, which signifies fountain of wine, because of
the vines that once were there, we were to go that day to Had-
el-Garbia, beyond the mountains that shut in the plain.

For more than an hour we journeyed over a gently undulating
plain, among fields of barley and millet, through winding paths
forming at their crossings many little islets of grass and flowers.
We met no one, and no figure was visible in the fields. Only
once we encountered a long file of camels led by two Bedouin
Arabs, who muttered as they passed the common salutation
" Peace be on your way."

I felt a great pity for the Arab servants who accompanied us
on foot, loaded with umbrellas, field-glasses, albums, clocks, and
a thousand objects of name and use unknown to them ; constrained to follow our mules with rapid step, suffocated by dust,
scorched by the sun, half fed, half clothed, subject to every one,
possessing nothing in the world but a ragged shirt and a pair of
slippers ; running afoot from Fez to Tangiers, only to go back
again ; and then, perhaps, to follow some other caravan from
Fez to Morocco, and so to go on throughout their lives, without
other recompense than just not to die of hunger, and to repose
their bones under a tent at night ! I thought as I looked at
them of Goethe's " Pyramid of Existence." There was among
them a boy of thirteen or fourteen years old, a mulatto, handsome and slender, who constantly fixed on us his large dark eyes
full of a pensive curiosity, seeming to speak confusedly of many
things, and dumbly demanding sympathy. He was a foundling,
the fruit of no one knew what strange amours, who, beginning

this fatiguing life in the Italian Embassy, would probably never
cease until he should fall dying in some ditch.   Another, an old
man all skin and bones, ran with his head down, his eyes closed,
and his hands clenched, with a sort of desperate resignation.
Some talked and laughed as they panted on.   Suddenly one
darted from the ranks, passed before us, and disappeared.   Ten
minutes afterwards we found him seated under a fig-tree.   He
had done a half-mile at top speed, in order to gain upon the
caravan and enjoy five minutes' rest and shade.

Meantime we arrived at the foot of a small mountain,
called in Arabic the Red Mountain, because of the colour
of its earth ; steep, rocky, and still bristling on its lower part
with the remains of a felled wood.   This climb had been
announced to us at Tangiers as the most difficult part of
our road.   " Mule," said I to my beast, " I desire you to
remember my contract with my editor," and I pushed forward in a bold and reckless manner.   The path rose winding
among great stones that seemed to have been placed there
on purpose to bring me to grief by some personal enemy ; at
every doubtful movement of my mule I felt a whole chapter
of my future book fly away out of my head—twice the poor
beast came down on her knees, and launched my soul upon
the confines of a better world—but at last we reached the
summit, safe and sound, where to my amazement I found
myself in presence of the two painters, who had gone on
ahead in order to see the caravan climbing up.   The spectacle
was well worth the fatigue of the rapid ascent.

The caravan stretched back for more than a mile from
the side of the mountain into the plain.   First came the
principal members of the Embassy, among whom shone con-
spicuous the plumed hat of the Ambassador and the white
turban of Mohammed Ducali, and on either side came a
troop of servants on foot and on horseback, picturesquely
scattered among the rocks and shrubs of the ascent.   Behind
these, in couples and groups of three or four, wrapped in
G 2

their white and blue mantles, and bending above their scarlet
saddles, the horsemen of the Moorish escort looked like a
long procession of maskers ; and behind them came the endless file of mules and horses carrying trunks, furniture, tents,
and provisions, flanked by soldiers and servants, the last of
whom appeared like white and red points among the green

The Caravan ascending the Red Mountain.

of the fields. This many-coloured and glittering procession
animated the solitary valley, and presented the strangest and
gayest spectacle that can be imagined. If at that moment I
had had the power to strike it motionless, so that I could
contemplate it at my leisure, I think I could not have
resisted the temptation. As I turned to resume my road,
I saw the Atlantic Ocean lying as blue and tranquil as a
lake at a few miles distance. There was but one ship in view,
sailing near the coast, and towards the strait. The Com-

mandant, observing her with his glass, discovered her to be Italian. What would we not have given to have been seen and recognised by her!

From the Red Mountain we descended into another lovely valley, carpeted with red, white, and lilac flowers. There was not a house, nor tent, nor human being, to be seen. The Ambassador deciding to halt here, we dismounted and sat down under the shade of some trees, while the baggage-train went on.

Around us, at the distance of a few steps, the servants were grouped, each holding a horse or mule. The artists drew forth their sketch-books, but it was of no use. Scarcely did one of the vagabonds perceive that he was an object of observation than he hid himself behind a tree, or drew his hood over his face. Three of them, one after the other, got up and went grumbling off, to sit down about fifty paces further on, dragging their quadrupeds with them. They did not even wish the animals to be sketched. In vain the vexed artists prayed, and coaxed, and offered money; it was all useless waste of breath. They made signs of no with their hands, pointing to the sky and smiling cunningly, as if to say, " We are not such fools as you think us." Not even the mulatto boy, or the Legation soldiers, who were familiar with Europeans, and knew the two artists, would permit their persons to be profaned by a Christian pencil. The Koran, as we know, prohibits the representation of the human figure, as well as that of animals, as a beginning of and temptation to idolatry. One of the soldiers was asked, through the interpreter, why he would not consent to stand and have his portrait taken. " Because," he answered, " in the figure which he will make the artist cannot put a soul. What is the purpose of his work then? God alone can create living beings, and it is a sacrilege to pretend to imitate them." The mulatto boy answered, laughing, " Have my portrait taken! Yes, while I am asleep; then it does not matter, and I am not in fault; but never, if I know it, shall it be done."

Then Signor Biseo began to draw one who was asleep.
All the others, grouped about, stood turning their eyes, now
on the painter, now on their sleeping companion.   Presently
the latter awoke, looked about him, made a gesture of
displeasure, and went off grumbling, amid the laughter of
his fellows, who seemed to be saying, "You are done for
now."

After an hour more on the road, we saw the white tents

Signor Biseo's Sketch of the Sleeping Arab.

of the encampment, and a troop of horsemen, sprung from we
knew not where, came towards us, yelling and firing off their
guns.   At about ten paces off they stopped, their chief shook
hands with the Ambassador, and his men joined our escort.
They proved to be soldiers of a species of *landwehr* belonging to
the place where our camp was pitched, and forming part of the
army of Morocco.   Some had turbans, some a red handkerchief
bound round the head, and all wore the white caftan.

The encampment was placed this time upon a barren spot;
in the distance on one side there was a chain of blue mountains,
on the other verdant hills.   At about half a mile from the

THE CHIEF AND THE AMBASSADOR.

tents were two groups of huts built of stubble, and half hidden among prickly-pear bushes.

We had hardly seated ourselves in the tent when a soldier came running, and, planting himself before the Ambassador, said, joyfully, "The *muna*." "Let them come in," said the Ambassador, rising. We all rose to our feet.

A long file of Arabs, accompanied by the chief of the escort, the soldiers of the Legation, and servants, crossed the encampment, and, ranging themselves before our tent, deposited at the feet of the Ambassador a great quantity of coal, eggs, sugar, butter, candles, bread, three dozen of hens, and eight sheep.

This tribute was the *mona* or *muna*. Besides the heavy tax they pay in money, the inhabitants of the country are obliged to furnish all official personages, the soldiers of the Sultan, and all envoys passing by, with a certain quantity of provisions. The Government fixes the quantity, but the local authorities demand whatever they please, without reference to the quantity received, although it may be more than is required, and it is always a small portion of that which has been extorted the month before, or will be extorted in the following month after the presentation.

An old man, who appeared to be the head of the deputation, addressed, through the interpreter, some obsequious words to the Ambassador. The others, who were all poor peasants clothed in rags, looked at us, our tents, and their tribute—the fruit of their labour lying at our feet—with an air of mingled astonishment and depression which betrayed a profound resignation.

A division having been quickly made of the things, between the Ambassador's larder and that of the escort, muleteers, and soldiers, Signor Morteo, who had that morning been named Intendant-General of the camp, rewarded the old Arab, who made a sign to his companions, and all silently departed as they had come.

Then began, what was to take place every day from that

time forth, a great squabbling among the servants, muleteers, and soldiers over the sharing of the *muna*. It was a most amusing scene. Two or three of them went up and down with measured steps, carrying each a sheep in his arms, invoking Allah and the Ambassador; others yelled out their discontent and enforced their reasoning by beating the ground with their fists; Civo fluttered about in his long white shirt with the profound conviction that he was very terrible; the sheep baa-d, the hens ran here and there, the dogs yelped. Suddenly up rose the Ambassador, and all was still.

The only one who continued to grumble was Selam.

Selam was a great personage. In reality there were two of the Legation soldiers who bore that name, both belonging to the special service of the Ambassador; but, as when we say Napoleon we mean the first of that name, so when we said Selam we meant one, and one only.

He was a handsome young fellow, tall and slender, and full of cleverness. He understood everything at a glance, did everything with all his might, walked in a series of leaps, spoke with a look, and was in motion from morning until night. Everybody came to him, about the baggage, the tents, the kitchen, the horses, and he had an answer for all. He spoke Spanish badly and knew a few words of Italian, but could have made himself understood in Arabic, so speaking and picturesque was his pantomime. To indicate a hill, he made the gesture of a fiery colonel pointing out to his men a battery that is to be assaulted. To reprove a servant, he fell upon him as if he were about to annihilate him. He always reminded me of Salvini in "Othello," or "Oromanes." In whatever attitude he presented himself, whether pouring water on the Ambassador's spine, or galloping by on his chestnut horse, nailed to his saddle, he was always the same bold, graceful, and elegant figure. The two painters were never tired of looking at him. He wore a scarlet caftan and blue drawers, and was easily distinguished from one end of the camp to another. His name was in every mouth all

over the encampment. When he was angry he was a savage;
when he laughed, a child. *Il Signor Ministro* was for ever in
his mouth and in his heart, for he placed him after Allah and
the Prophet. Ten guns levelled at his breast would not have

Selam pointing out a Hill.

paled his cheek, and an undeserved rebuke from the Ambassador
made him cry. He was about five-and-twenty.

When he had done grumbling, he came near me and began
opening a box. As he stooped, his fez fell off, and I saw a large
blood-mark on his head. In answer to my question, he said that
he had been wounded by a loaf of sugar. "I threw it up in the

air," he said, with gravity, "and it came down on my head."
I looked amazed, and he explained—"I do it," he said, "to
harden my head. The first time I fell down insensible, but now
it only draws a little blood. A time will come when it will not
break the skin. All the Arabs do it. My father broke bricks
as thick as two fingers on his head as easily as I would break a
loaf of bread. A true Arab," he concluded, with a haughty air,
striking his head a blow with his fist, "should have a head of
iron."

The encampment that evening presented a very different
aspect from that of the preceding days. Everybody had fallen
into their own habits of passing the time. The artists had
erected their easels and were hard at work in front of their tent.
The Captain had gone to observe the ground, the Vice-Consul to
collect insects; the ex-Spanish Minister to shoot partridges; the
Ambassador and the Commandant were playing chess in the
dining-tent; the servants were playing leapfrog; the soldiers of
the escort conversed sitting in a circle; of the rest some walked
about, some read, some wrote; one would have thought we had
been there a month. If I had had a small printing-press I could
have found it in my heart to edit a newspaper.

The weather was exquisite; we dined with the tent open,
and during dinner the horsemen of Had-el-Garbia shouted, and
fired off their guns, while the sun went down in splendour.

Opposite to me at table sat Mohammed Ducali. For the
first time I was able to observe him attentively. He was a true
type of the wealthy Moor—supple, elegant, and obsequious; I
say wealthy, because he possessed, it was said, more than thirty
houses at Tangiers, although at that time his affairs were supposed to be in some confusion. He might have been about forty
years of age, was tall of stature, with regular features, fair, and
bearded; he wore a small turban, twisted in a *caic* of the finest
of the fabrics of Fez, which fell down over a purple embroidered
caftan; he smiled to show his teeth, spoke Spanish in a feminine
voice, and had the languid air of a young lover. In former

THE DINNER.

days he had been a merchant; had been in Italy, in Spain, London, and Paris, and had returned to Morocco with some ideas of European customs. He drank wine, smoked cigarettes, wore stockings, read romances, and related his gallant adventures. The principal reason for his going to Fez was a debt owed him by the Government, which he hoped to get paid through the good offices of the Ambassador. He had brought with him his own tent, servants, and mules. His glance gave one to understand that he would have brought his wives also had that been possible, but upon my hazarding a question in that direction he modestly dropped his eyes, and made no reply.

After dinner I satisfied a desire which I had nourished ever since leaving Tangiers, and went out to see the camp at night. I waited until every one had entered his tent, wrapped myself in a white mantle, and went out. The sky was studded with stars; the lights were all out, except the lantern that was attached to the flag-staff; a profound silence reigned throughout the camp. Very quietly, and avoiding a stumble over the tent-cords, I moved to the left, and had not made ten steps when an unexpected sound stopped me short. Some one appeared to be tuning a guitar, in a closed tent that I had never visited, and which stood about thirty paces outside of the circle of the camp. I approached and listened. The guitar accompanied a soft and very sweet voice singing an Arab ditty full of melancholy. Could there be a woman in this mysterious tent? It was closed on every side, so I lay down on my face and tried to peep underneath. Almost at the same moment a soft voice beside me said, " *Quien es?* " (Who is there?) " Allah protect me!" I thought, "there *is* a woman here." I answered, aloud, " An inquisitive person," with the most pathetic voice I could assume at the moment. A laugh responded, and a male voice said in Spanish, " Bravo! Come in and take a cup of tea!" It was the voice of Mohammed Ducali. He opened a little door, and I found myself within the tent, which was hung with some rich flowered stuff, ornamented with small arched windows, lighted by a

Moorish lantern, and perfumed in a way to do honour to the
fairest odalisque of the Sultan's harem.   And there, luxuriously
stretched upon a Persian carpet, with his head on a rich cushion,
lay a young Arab servant lad, of gentle and pensive aspect, with a

Mohammed Dulcali.

guitar in his hands.   In
the middle of the tent there
was a tea-service, and on
one side smoked a perfume-
burner.   I explained to
Ducali how I came to be
so near his tent, took a
cup of tea, listened to an
air sung by the Arab
musician, and taking my
leave, resumed my wan-
derings. Avoiding another
tent where more of Ducali's
servants were sleeping, I
turned towards that of the
Ambassador.

Before the door lay
Selam, stretched on his blue
mantle, with his sabre by
his side.   "If I wake him,
and he does not recognise
me at once," I thought,
"it is all over with me!
Let me be prudent." I advanced on tip-toe, and peeped
into the tent.   It was divided in the middle by a rich curtain:
on one side was the reception-room, with a table covered with
a cloth, and writing materials, and a few gilded chairs; on
the other side slept the Ambassador and his friend, the ex-
Minister from Spain.   I thought I would leave my card on
the table, and advanced a step, when a low growl arrested

me. It was Diana, the Ambassador's dog. Almost at the same moment the master's voice called out, "Who's that?"

"An assassin!" answered I.

He knew my voice, and called out, "Strike!" I explained the motive of my visit, at which he laughed, and, giving me his hand in the darkness, wished me success in my undertaking. Coming out I stumbled over something which proved to be a tortoise, and as I struck a match to examine him, I discovered

Selam sleeping before the Tent of the Ambassador.

a monstrous toad sitting looking at me. For a moment I thought I would give up my enterprise, but, curiosity overcoming disgust, I went on.

I reached the tent of the intendant. As I bent down to listen, a tall white figure rose between me and the door, and said in sepulchral accents, "He sleeps." I started back as at the apparition of a phantom, but recovered myself immediately. It was an Arab servant of Morteo's, who had been with him for several years, and spoke a little Italian, and who, in spite of my white hood, had recognised me instantly. Like Selam, he had been stretched before the door of his master's tent,

with his sabre by his side. I wished him good night, and
went on my way.

In the next tent were the doctor and Solomon the dragoman. An acute odour of drugs pervaded the neighbourhood,
and there was a light inside. The doctor was seated at his
table, reading; the dragoman was asleep. This physician,
young, highly cultivated, and of very gentlemanlike manners
and appearance, had a very singular peculiarity. Born in Algeria
of French parents, he had lived many years in Italy, and had
married a Spanish wife. Not only did he speak the languages
of the three countries with equal facility, but he partook of
the characteristics of the three nations, loved all three countries alike, and was, in short, a sort of Latin three in one,
who was equally at home in Rome, in Madrid, and in Paris.
He was, besides, gifted with a most delicate and acute sense
of the ridiculous; so that, without speaking, with one furtive
glance, or slight movement of the lip, he could throw into
relief the ridiculous side of a person or thing in a way to
make one burst with laughter. At the sight of me he guessed
at once the reason of my presence, offered me a glass of wine,
and, raising his arm, whispered, " Success to your expedition ! "
" With the aid of Allah ! " I rejoined, and left him to his
reading.

Passing before the empty dinner-tent, I turned to the left,
came out of the circle of the encampment, walked between
two long rows of sleeping horses, and found myself among
the tents of the escort. Listening, I could hear the breathing
of the soldiers as they slept. Guns, sabres, saddles, shoulder-
belts, poignards, were scattered about before the tents, together
with the banner of Mahomet. I looked abroad, across the
country; not a soul was visible. Only the two groups of
cabins appeared like black and formless blots.

I turned back, passed between the American Consul's tent
and that of his servants, both close-shut and silent, crossed a
little space of ground where the kitchen had been planted, and,

stepping over a barricade of pots and saucepans, reached the little tent of the cook. With him were the two Arabs who served him as scullions. All was black within; I put in my head and called, "*Gioanin!*"

The poor fellow, afflicted by the non-success of an omelet, and perhaps worried by the neighbourhood of his two "savages," was not asleep. "Is that you?" he asked. "It is I."

He was silent a moment, and then, turning restlessly on his bed, exclaimed, "*Ah, che pais!*" (Ah, what a country!")

"Courage!" I said; "think that in ten days we shall be before the walls of the great city of Fez."

He muttered some confused words in which I could only distinguish the name of his native city in Italy; and, respecting his grief, I silently withdrew.

In the adjoining tent were the two sailors—Ranni, the Commandant's orderly, and Luigi, from the *Dora*, a Neapolitan, and such a kind, pleasant, handy young fellow, that in two days he had gained the good-will of all. They had a light, and were busy eating something. Lending an ear, I could hear some portions of their dialogue, which was very curious. Luigi inquired for whom were intended the crayon sketches which the two artists made in their albums. "Why, for the king, of course," said Ranni. "What, without any colour, like that?" demanded the other. "Oh, no! when they get back to Italy, first they will colour them, and then they will send them." "Who knows how much the king will pay for them?" "Oh, a great deal, of course! Perhaps as much as a *scudo* (five francs) a leaf. Kings think nothing of money."

Once more I left the circle of the encampment, and wandered for a minute or two among long rows of horses and mules, among which I recognised with emotion the white companion of my journey, apparently sunk in profound contemplation; and I next found myself before the tent of M. Vincent, a Frenchman residing at Tangiers, one of those mysterious personages who have been all over the world, speak

II

all tongues, and understand all trades—cook, merchant, hunter, interpreter, reader of ancient inscriptions—and who, having, with his own tent and horse, attached himself to the Italian Embassy in the capacity of high director of the kitchen, was now going to Fez to sell to the Government French uniforms bought in Algeria.

I looked in at him through a crack. He was seated on

M. Vincent.

a box, in a meditative attitude, with a great pipe in his mouth, by the light of a small candle stuck in a bottle. But what a strange figure! He reminded me of those old alchemists in the Dutch pictures, musing in their studies, their faces illuminated by the fire of an alembic. Meagre, bent, and bony, he looked as if every episode of his life had been written in the wrinkles of his visage and in the angles of his form. Who knows what he was thinking about? What memories of adventurous journeys, strange meetings, mad undertakings, and odd personages, were mingling in his head? Perhaps, after all, he was only thinking of the price of a pair of *Turco* breeches, or about his scanty provision of tobacco. Just as I was going to speak he blew out his light with a puff, and vanished into the darkness like a magician.

A few paces further on were the tents of the Commandant of the escort, that of his first officer, and that of the chief of the horsemen of Had-el-Garbia. I was in the act of looking into one of these when a light step came behind me, and a hand of steel closed upon my arm. I turned, and found myself face to face with the mulatto General. He withdrew his hand at once, and with a laugh, said, in a tone of apology, " Salamu alikum! salimu alikum!" ("Peace be with you!") He had taken me for a thief. We shook hands in token of amity, and I went on.

In a few moments I saw before me what appeared to be a hooded figure seated on the ground with musket in hand and concluded that this must be a sentinel. About fifty paces further on there was another, and then a third; a chain of them all around the encampment. I learned later that this vigilance was from no fear of violence, but simply to guard the tents from thieves, who abound there, and are extremely clever at their trade, having much practice among the tribes who live in tents. Fortunately the frankness of my movements aroused no suspicion, and I was allowed to finish my excursion.

I passed by Malek and Saladin, the envoy's two fiery steeds, stumbled over another tortoise, and stopped before the tent of the footmen. They were lying on a little straw, one upon the top of the other, and sleeping so profoundly that they seemed like a heap of corpses. The boy with the great black eyes lay with half his body outside of the tent, and I narrowly missed stepping on his face. I felt so sorry for him that, wishing to give him a little comfort in the morning when he should wake, I placed a piece of money in his hand that lay open on the grass, palm upwards, as if begging charity from the spirits of the night.

A murmur of merry voices drew me away to a neighbouring tent, where were the soldiers and servants of the Embassy; they appeared to be eating and drinking. I perceived the odour

of kif, and recognised the voices of Selam the Second, Abd-el-
Rhaman, and others; it was an Arab orgie in full swing. The
poor fellows had well earned a little diversion after the fatigues
of the day, and I passed on without disturbing their merriment
by my presence. In a few moments I reached the artists' tent,
which completed the circle of the encampment, and my nocturnal excursion was over.

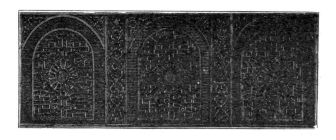

CHAPTER III.

TLETA DE REISSANA.

THE next morning we started before sunrise in a thick wet fog, which chilled us to the bone and hid us from each other· The horsemen of the escort had their cowls over their heads, and their guns slung across their shoulders. We were all wrapped in cloaks and mantles; it seemed like autumn in the Low Countries. In front of me I could discern nothing distinctly save the white turban and blue cloak of the Caid; all the others were confused shadows lost in the grey mist. We went onward in silence over the rough ground covered with dwarf palms, broom, and wild plums, and fennel, in groups compact or scattered according to the crossing or forking of the road. The sun, appearing in the horizon, gilded our left side a moment, and again vanished. The mist presently grew thinner, and we could catch glimpses of the country. It was a succession of green valleys, into which we descended and came up again almost unconsciously, so gradual were the slopes. The banks were covered with the aloe and the wild olive. The olive, which grows prodigiously here, is left almost everywhere in its wild state, and the inhabitants

use the fruit of the *argan* for light and food. We saw no
signs of habitation, neither houses nor tents. We seemed to
be travelling through a virgin country. From valley to valley,
from solitude to solitude, after about three hours' journeying
we finally reached a point where the larger trees and wider
paths, and a few scattered cattle here and there, gave token of
an inhabited place. One after the other our mounted escort
spurred their horses and galloped away over a height, others
darted off in another direction, the rest arranged themselves in
close order. Presently we found ourselves in front of the
opening of a gorge formed by low hills, upon which stood some
huts. A few ragged Arabs of both sexes looked curiously at us
from behind the hedge. As we rode into the gorge the sun
shone out, and, turning an abrupt angle, we found ourselves in
front of a wonderful spectacle.

Three hundred horsemen, dressed in all the colours of the
rainbow, and scattered in a sort of grand disorder, came
towards us at full speed, with their muskets held aloft, as if
they were rushing to the assault. It was the escort from the
province of Laracce, preceded by the Governor and his officials,
coming to relieve the escort of Had-el-Garbia, which was to
leave us on the confines of the province of Tangiers, a point
that we had now reached.

The Governor of Laracce, a dignified old man with a great
white beard, stopped the advance of his horsemén with a sign of
his hand, saluted the envoy, and then, turning to the troop, who
seemed boiling over with impatience, made a vigorous gesture, as
if to say, " Break loose ! " Then began one of the most splendid
lab-el-baroda (or powder-plays) that could be desired.

They charged in couples, by tens, one by one, in the bottom
of the valley, on the hills, in front and at the sides of the
caravan, forwards and backwards, firing and yelling without
cessation. In a few minutes the valley was as full of the smoke
and smell of powder as a battle-field. On every side horses
pranced, arms glittered, mantles floated, and red, yellow, green,

LAB-EL-BARODA OF THE ESCORT OF THE GOVERNOR OF LARACCE.

blue, and orange caftans mingled with the shine of sabres and poignards. One by one they darted by, like winged phantoms, old and young, men of colossal proportions, strange and terrible figures, erect in their stirrups, with heads thrown back, hair streaming in the wind, and muskets held aloft; and each as he discharged his piece gave a savage cry, which the interpreter translated for us:—" Have a care !" "Oh, my mother!" "In the name of God !" "I kill thee !" "Thou art dead !" "I am avenged!" Some dedicated the shot to a special purpose or person : "To my master !" "To my horse !" "To my dead !" "To my sweetheart!" They fired up and down, and behind, bending and twisting as though they had been tied to the saddle. Here and there one would lose his turban or his mantle, and he would turn in full career and pick it up with the point of his musket. Some threw their guns up in the air and caught them as they fell. Their looks and gestures were like those of men mad with drink, and risking their lives in a sort of joyful fury. Most of the horses dripped blood from their bellies, and the feet and stirrups, and extremities of the mantles of the riders, were all bloody. Some faces in that multitude impressed themselves upon my memory from the first. Among others, a young man with a Cyclopean head and an immense pair of shoulders, dressed in a rose-coloured caftan, and who emitted a succession of roars like those of a wounded lion ; a lad of fifteen, handsome, bare-headed, and all in white, who passed three times, crying, "My God! my God !" a long, bony old man, with a most ill-omened visage, who flew by with half-shut eyes and a satanic grin upon his face, as if he carried the plague behind him ; a black, all eyes and teeth, with a monstrous scar across his forehead, who writhed furiously about in his saddle, as if to free himself from the clutch of some invisible hand.

In this fashion they accompanied the march of the caravan, ascending and descending the heights, forming groups, dissolving and re-forming, with every combination of colour, till they seemed like the fluttering of a myriad of banners.

At a short distance from the end of the gorge the Ambassador stopped, and we all dismounted to enjoy a little repose and refreshment under the shade of a group of olive-trees, but the escort from Laracce continued its exercises before us. The baggage train went on towards the spot selected for the camp.

We had reached the *Cuba* of Sidi-Liamani.

In Morocco they give the name of *Cuba* (or cupola) to a

The Cuba of Sidi-Liamani.

small square chapel, with a low dome, in which a saint lies buried. These *Cube*, very frequent in the southern part of the empire, placed in general near a spring and a palm-tree, and visible by their snowy whiteness from a great distance, serve as guides to the traveller, are visited by the faithful, and are for the most part in charge of a descendant of the saint, heir to his sanctity, who inhabits a hut close by, and lives by the alms of pious pilgrims. The *Cuba* of Sidi-Liamani was posted upon a little eminence at a few paces distant from us. Some Arabs were seated before the door. Behind them protruded the head of a decrepit old man—the saint—who looked at us with stupid wonder.

In a few minutes our kitchen fires were lighted and we were breakfasting; while an empty sardine box, thrown away by the cook, and picked up by the Arabs, was carried to the *Cuba* for examination, and made the object of a long and animated discussion. Meantime, the *lab-el-baroda* being over, the horsemen had dismounted, and were scattered all about the valley; some of them were resting, some pasturing their horses, while others, seated in their saddles, remained to keep watch as sentinels upon the heights.

As I walked about with the Captain, I then for the first time observed the horses of Morocco. They are all small, so much so that, upon my return to Europe, after having become accustomed to them, even middle-sized horses seemed at first enormous to me. They have brilliant eyes, the forehead a little flattened, very wide nostrils, the cheek-bone very prominent, the whole head beautiful; the shin-bone and tibia slightly curved, which gives a peculiar elasticity of movement; the crupper very sloping, rendering them more able to gallop than to trot, indeed, I do not remember ever to have seen a horse trot in Morocco. Seen in repose, or merely walking past, even the finest of them makes no show; but put to a gallop, they are quite changed, and become superb. Although they have much less food, and are more heavily caparisoned than ours, they bear fatigue much better. Also the manner of riding is different. The stirrups are very short, and the reins very long. The rider sits with his knees almost at a right angle, and the saddle, extremely high before and behind, holds him in a way that makes it almost impossible for him to be thrown. The horsemen wear heelless boots of yellow leather. Most of them have no spurs, but use instead of them the angle of the stirrup; some wear a small iron point in the shape of a dagger, fastened to the heel by a metal band and chain. Wonderful things are told of the great love of an Arab for his horse, the animal of the Prophet's predilection.

He is said to consider him as a sacred being ; that every morning at sunrise he places his hand upon his steed's head, and murmurs, *Bismillah!* (in the name of God), and then kisses the hand, which has been sanctified by the touch ; and that he is prodigal of cares and caresses. It may be all true. But as far as I could see, the Arab's great affection for his horse did not prevent him from lacerating his sides in a quite unnecessary way, or from leaving him in the sun when he could have put him in the shade, or from taking him a long distance to drink, with his legs hobbled, or from exposing him a dozen times a day to the danger of breaking his limbs, out of pure mischief, or finally, from neglecting his trappings in a way that would put him in prison for six months if he belonged to a European cavalry regiment.

The heat being very great we remained some hours at our resting place, but no one could sleep by reason of the insects. It was the first warning of the great battle that was to be waged, growing hotter every day, until the end of the journey. Hardly had we stretched ourselves upon the ground when we were assaulted, stung, and tormented on every side, as if we had chosen a bed of nettles. Caterpillars, spiders, monstrous ants, hornets and grasshoppers, big, impudent, and determined, swarmed about us. The Commandant, who had taken upon himself to raise our spirits by always exaggerating the perils of the way, now assured us that these creatures might be considered microscopic compared with the insects that we should encounter at Fez and later in the summer; and he declared that so little would be left of us upon our return to Italy that our best friends would not know us. The cook listened to these remarks with a forced smile, and became pensive. Close by there was a monstrous spider's web, spread over some bushes like a sheet hung out to dry. The Commandant exclaimed that everything in that country was gigantic, formidable, miraculous ! and insisted that the spider which had made that web *must* be as large as a horse. But we could not discover him. The only ones of us who slept were the Arabs, curled up in the burning sun with a procession of creeping things marching over them. The two artists tried to sketch, surrounded by a cloud of ferocious flies, which drew from Ussi a whole rich litany of Florentine oaths.

The heat becoming less, the escort from Had-el-Garbia, the American Consul, and the Vice-Governor of Tangiers, took leave of the Ambassador and turned back, while we pursued our way, accompanied by the three hundred horsemen from Laracce.

Vast undulating plains, covered here with corn and there with barley, further on with yellow stubble or with grass and flowers; here a few black tents and the tomb of a saint; now and then a palm-tree; from mile to mile three or four horsemen coming to join our escort; an immense solitude, a sky of perfect purity, a burning sun; such are the notes I find in my note-book as to the march of May 5th.

The encampment was at Tleta de Reissana. We found the tents pitched as usual in a circle, in a deep and shell-shaped gorge so overgrown with tall grass and flowers that they almost impeded our steps. It seemed like a great garden. Beds and boxes in the tents were almost hidden by tall flowers of every form and colour. Close to the tent of the two painters rose two enormous aloes in blossom.

The Italian Consular Agent from Laracce met us here. He was Signor G——, an old Genoese merchant, who had lived for forty years on the Atlantic coast, jealously preserving the accent of his native town; and towards evening arrived, from no one knew where, an Arab who wished to consult the doctor of the Embassy.

He was a poor old man, lame and bent. Signor Miguerez, who spoke Arabic, questioned him about his ailments, and searched in the portable medicine chest for a remedy. Not finding the right one, he sent for Mohammed Ducali, and made him write down a prescription in Arabic, by means of which the sick man was to be treated when he got back to his family and friends. It was a medicine much in use among the Arabs. Whilst Ducali wrote, the old man muttered prayers; and when it was ready, the paper was handed to him.

Instantly, before there was time to say one word, he crammed it into his mouth with both hands. The doctor called out—"No! no! Spit it out! spit it out!" But it was of no use. The poor old fellow chewed the paper with the avidity of a starving creature, swallowed it, thanked the doctor, and turned to go away. They had all the pains in the world to persuade him that the virtue of the medicine did not reside in the paper, and that another prescription must be written.

The incident cannot surprise any one who knows what the science of medicine is in Morocco. It is almost exclusively exercised by quacks, necromancers, and "saints." Some juices of herbs, blood-letting, sarsaparilla for certain diseases, the dry skin of a serpent or chameleon for intermittent fevers, a hot iron for wounds, certain verses from the Koran written upon the medicine bottles, or on bits of paper worn round the sick man's neck; these are the principal remedies. The study of anatomy being forbidden by their religion, it is easy to imagine to what a pass surgery is reduced. Amputation is held in abhorrence. The few Arabs who are within reach of the aid of European surgeons would prefer to die in atrocious spasms rather than submit to the cut that would save their lives. It follows that though cases of injury to a limb are frequent in Morocco, especially from the explosion of fire-arms, there are very few mutilated persons; and those few are for the most part poor wretches whose hands have been cut off by the executioner with a dull knife, and the hemorrhage stopped by the application of boiling pitch. These violent remedies, however, especially the red-hot iron, sometimes obtain admirable effects; and they apply them themselves brutally, boldly, without any aid. Either by reason of small nervous sensibility, or from their souls having been hardened in a fatalistic faith, they resist the most

horrible pain with tremendous force of will. They go through
the operation of cupping with an earthen pot and enough fire
to roast the spine; they open boils with their daggers, driving
them in at the risk of cutting an artery; and they will apply
fire to an open wound on their own arm, blowing away the
smoke of the frizzling flesh without a groan. The maladies
that are most prevalent are fevers, ophthalmia, scald-head,
elephantiasis, and dropsy; but the most common of all is
syphilis, handed down from generation to generation, altered
and reproduced in strange and horrid forms, with which whole
tribes are infected, and of which a large proportion die; and the
mortality would no doubt be even greater but for their ex-
treme sobriety in eating, to which both their poverty and the
exigencies of the climate compel them. European physicians
there are none, excepting in the cities of the coast; in Fez itself
there are none, unless some renegade quack who has fled from
Algeria or the Spanish garrisons may be counted such. When
the Emperor, or a Minister, or a rich Moor falls ill, he sends for
a European doctor from the coast. But this is never done
except in cases of extremity, and they hide their infirmities for
years, so that when the physician does arrive, it is often only to
see his patient die. They have great faith in the skill of
European doctors; the sight of the drugs, the chemical preparations, the surgical instruments, give them an immense
idea of the power of science ; they promise themselves prodigies,
following the first prescriptions with the docility and cheer-
fulness of people quite certain of a prompt cure. But if the cure
is not immediate, they lose all faith, and go back to their quacks.

The evening passed without any event worth noting, beyond the discovery of a monstrous scorpion of preternatural
blackness on the pillow of my bed. I was seized with a
momentary terror, and carefully threw the light upon him as I
approached with cautious steps ; whereupon I was able to read
upon his back the following reassuring inscription :—*Ceasar
Biseo made it—May 5th*, 1875.

At dawn in the morning we left for the city of Alkazar. The weather was dark. The gorgeous colours of the soldiers of our escort shone out with marvellous force against the grey sky and the dark green of the country. Hamed Ben Kasen Buhamei planted himself upon a height above the road and looked complacently down upon the brilliant cavalcade as they filed by in close order, silent, grave, with eyes fixed upon the horizon, like the advance guard of an army on the morning of a

Evolutions of the Soldiers of Alkazar.

battle. For some time we rode among olive-trees and high bushes; then we entered a vast plain all covered with flowers, violet and yellow, where the escort scattered to go through the *lab-el-baroda*. It would be impossible to convey an idea of the strange beauty of the spectacle upon that flowery plain, under the threatening sky. I can scarcely believe that they had any rule by which they grouped themselves and dissolved again to form new combinations, but that morning I fancied it. One would have sworn that their movements were directed by a ballet-master. In the midst of a group of blue mantles there would appear, as if sent on purpose, one in a white cloak; and a

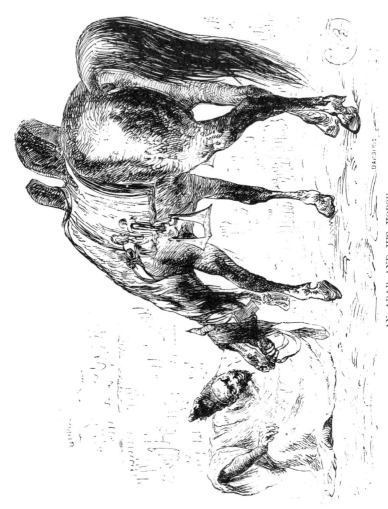

AN ARAB AND HIS HORSE.

company of white caftans surrounded a figure in brilliant rose-colour, looking as if made by the stroke of an artist's brush. Harmonious colours followed, met, and mingled for the space of a moment, and then dissolved to form new harmonies. The three hundred seemed multiplied into an army; they were everywhere, wheeling and swooping like a flock of birds; and the two painters were driven to despair by them.

" Ah, *canaglie!*" exclaimed one, " if I only had you in my clutch at Florence! "

CHAPTER IV.

ALKAZAR-EL-KIBIR.

AT a certain point the Ambassador made a sign to the Caid, and the escort came to a stand, while we, accompanied by a few soldiers, went a short distance beyond to visit the ruins of a bridge. The place was worthy of the silent respect with which we stood and viewed the little that remained of what was once a bridge. Three hundred years ago, on the fourth of August, over those flowery fields, fifty cannon and forty thousand horsemen thundered and charged under the command of one of the greatest captains of Africa, and the youngest, the most adventurous, the most unfortunate of European monarchs. On the shores of that river were put to death—by the implacable scimitars of Arabs, Turks, and Berbers—the flower of the Portuguese nobility, courtiers, bishops, Spanish soldiers, and soldiers of William of Orange, Italian, German, and French adventurers. Six thousand Christians fell that day. We stood upon the field of that terrible battle of Alkazar, which spread consternation throughout Europe, and sent a shout of joy from Fez to Constantinople. Over that bridge passed at that time the road to Alkazar. Near it was the camp of Muley Moluk, Sultan of Morocco. Muley Moluk came from Alkazar, the King of Portugal from Arzilla. The battle was fought upon that plain, and along the shores of the river. Beyond the ruins of the bridge there was not a stone or a sign to record it. From which side had the cavalry of the Duke of Riveiro made

The Alkazar Band.

its first victorious charge? Where had Muley Ahmed fought, the brother of the Sultan, the future conqueror of the Soudan, a captain suspected of cowardice in the morning, a victorious monarch in the evening? At what point on the river was drowned Mohammed the Black, the discrowned fratricide, and provoker of the war? At what angle of the field had King Sebastian received those death-wounds that killed with him the independence of Portugal and the last hopes of Cameons?

I 2

THE ALKAZAR ESCORT.

And where stood the litter of Sultan Moluk when he expired among his officers, with his finger on his lip ? Whilst these thoughts were passing through our minds, the escort stood afar off, motionless on that famous field, like a handful of Muley Ahmed's cavalry brought to life by the noise of our passage. And yet very likely not one among those soldiers knew that this had been the battle-field of three kings, the glory of their ancestors ; and when we resumed our march, they glanced about with curious eyes, as if seeking among the grass and flowers for the reason of our halt.

We crossed the Mkhacem and the Uarrur, two small affluents of the Kus, or Lukkos, the *Lixos* of the ancients, which from the mountains of the Rif, where it is born, throws itself into the Atlantic at Laracce, and continued our way towards Alkazar over a succession of arid hills, meeting only an occasional camel with his driver.

At last, we thought as we rode along, we shall arrive at a city ! It was three days since we had seen a house, and every one felt a wish to get away for a day from the monotony of desert life. Besides, Alkazar was the first of the towns of the interior that we should reach, and our curiosity was very lively. The escort fell into order as we approached the place. We almost unconsciously ranged ourselves in two ranks, with the Ambassador in front flanked by his two interpreters. The weather had cleared up, and a cheerful impatience animated the whole caravan.

Suddenly, from the top of a hill, we saw in the plain below, surrounded by gardens, the city of Alkazar, crowned with towers, minarets, and palms, and at the same moment there burst forth the cracking of musketry and the sound of a most infernal din of music.

It was the Governor coming to meet us with his staff, a company of foot-soldiers, and a band of music. In a few minutes we met.

Ah ! he who has not seen the Alkazar band, with its ten pipers, and horn-players, old men of a hundred years and boys of ten, all mounted on donkeys about as large as dogs, ragged and half naked, with their shaven heads, their satyr-like gestures, their mummy faces, has not seen, I think, the

Entering Alkazar.

most sadly comic spectacle that can be witnessed under the wide sky.

Whilst the aged Governor was giving welcome to our

chief, the soldiers fired their muskets in the air, and the band continued to play. We advanced to within half a mile of the city, to an arid field where the tents were to be pitched.

The band accompanied us, still playing. The dinner tent was pitched and made ready, and we entered it while the escort fired their muskets.

Meanwhile the band, ranged before the tent, continued to blow with increasing ferocity, but a supplicating gesture from the Ambassador silenced it at last. Then we assisted at a curious scene.

Almost at the same moment there presented themselves to the Ambassador, one on the right and the other on the left, a black man and an Arab. The black, handsomely dressed in a white turban and a blue caftan, deposited at his feet a jar of milk, a basket of oranges, and a dish of *cùscùssù;* the Arab, poorly attired in the usual burnouse, placed before him a sheep. This done, the two darted lightning glances at each other. They were two mortal enemies. The Ambassador, who knew them, and expected them, called the interpreter, sat down, and began to question them.

They had come to ask for justice. The black was a sort of factor or steward of the old Grand Scheriff Bacali, one of the most powerful personages at the court of Fez, proprietor of much land in the neighbourhood of Alkazar. The Arab was a countryman. Their dispute had been going on for some time. The black, strong in the protection of his master, had several times imprisoned and fined the Arab, accusing him, and supporting his accusation with many proofs, of having stolen horses, cattle, and goods. The Arab, who insisted that he was innocent, finding no one willing to take up his defence against his persecutor, had abandoned his village one fine day, and, going to Tangiers, had there inquired who among the foreign Ambassadors was most just and generous. Being told that it was the Minister from Italy, he had cut the throat of a sheep before the gate of the Legation, asking in this sacred form, to which no refusal was

possible, for protection and justice. The Ambassador had listened
to his story, had intervened through the agent at Laracce, and
had called upon the authorities at Alkazar to see to it; but his
own distance, the intrigues of the black, and the weakness of the
authorities had all combined to put the poor Arab in a worse
condition than at first; and he was indeed again accused, and

Justice at the Ambassador's Tent.

subjected to new persecutions. Now the presence of the Ambassador was to undo the knot. Both individuals were admitted to
tell each his own story: the interpreters rapidly translating.

Nothing more dramatic can be imagined than the contrast
between the figures and the language of the two men.

The Arab, a man of about thirty years of age, of a sickly
and suffering aspect, spoke with irresistible fervour, trembling,
shivering, invoking God, striking the earth with his fists, cover-

ing his face with his hands with a gesture of despair, fulminating
at his enemy with glances that no words can describe. He
declared that the other had suborned witnesses, intimidated the
authorities, that he had imprisoned him, the speaker, solely to
extort money, that he had cast many others into prison in order
to possess their wives, that he had sworn his death, that he was
the scourge of the country, an accursed of God, an infamous
being; and as he spoke, he showed the marks of the fetters
upon his naked limbs, and his voice was choked with anguish.
The black, whose every feature confirmed one, at least, of these
accusations, listened without looking, answered quietly, smiled
slightly with the edge of his lip, impassive and sinister as a
statue of Perfidy.

The discussion had lasted for some time, and seemed yet far
from a conclusion, when the Ambassador cut it short by a decision
that was received favourably by both parties. He called Selim,
who appeared upon the instant with his great black eyes shining
and ordered him to mount his horse and gallop to the Arab's
village, distant an hour and a half from Alkazar, and there
gather from the inhabitants information concerning the persons
and the facts. The black thought:—"They are afraid of me;
they will either be silent, or speak in my favour." The Arab
thought, and he was quite right, that interrogated by a soldier
of the Embassy, they would have courage to speak the truth.

Selim darted off like an arrow; the two disputants vanished
and were seen no more. We heard afterwards that the village
people had all testified in favour of the Arab, and that the black
had been condemned, through the intervention of the Ambassador, to restore to his victim the money he had extorted from
him.

Meantime the tents had been pitched, the usual poor wretches
had brought the usual *muna*, and a few of the inhabitants of the
city had come into the encampment.

As soon as it began to grow cooler, we proceeded towards
Alkazar on foot, preceded, flanked, and followed by an armed force.

We saw from a distance, in passing, a singular edifice, between the camp and the town, all arches and cupolas, with a court in the midst, like a cemetery. It proved to be one of those *zania*, now fallen into disuse, which, when Moorish civilisation flourished, contained a library, a school of letters and sciences, a hospital for the poor, an inn for travellers, besides a mosque and a sepulchral chapel; they belonged, and belong still in general, to the religious orders.

We approached the gates of the city. It is surrounded by old battlemented walls; near the gate by which we entered were some tombs of saints surmounted by green domes. Hearing a great noise over our heads, we looked up, and found it proceeded from some large storks, erect upon the roofs of the houses, which were clattering their bills together, as if to give warning of our coming. We entered a street; the women rushed into their houses; the children took to flight. The houses are small, unplastered, without windows, and divided by dark and dirty alleys. The streets look like the beds of torrents. At some of the corners lie entire carcases of donkeys and dogs. We trudge through the dirt, among great stones, and deep holes, stumbling and jumping. The inhabitants begin to gather upon our track, looking at us with amazement. The soldiers make way for us with their fists and the butts of their muskets, with a zeal which the Ambassador hastens to restrain. A throng of people now follow and precede us. When one of us turns suddenly round, all stop, some run away, and others hide themselves. Here and there a woman slams her door in our faces, and a child utters a yell of terror. The women look like bundles of dirty rags; the children are in general quite naked; boys of ten or twelve have nothing on but a shirt, tied round the waist with a cord. Little by little the people about us grow bolder. They look curiously at our trousers and boots. Some boys venture to touch the skirts of our coats. The general expression of the faces is far from benevolent. A woman, in full flight, throws some words at the Ambassador which the interpreter translates—" God confound thy race!" A young man cries out—"God grant us a good day of victory over these!" We reach a small square, so steep and stony that we can with difficulty climb it, and pass a line of horrible old women almost completely naked, seated on the ground, with bread and other matters before them which they appear to be selling. In the streets through which we pass there is at every hundred paces a great arched door, which is closed at night. The houses are everywhere naked, cracked, gloomy. We enter a bazaar, roofed with canes and branches of trees that are falling down on every side. The shops are mere niches; the shopmen wax figures; the merchandise rubbish offered in joke and hopeless of a purchaser. In every corner are crouched sad, sleepy, stupid-looking figures; children with scald-heads; old women with no semblance of humanity. We seem to be wandering in the halls of a hospital. The air is full of aromatic odours. Not a voice is heard. The crowd accompanies us in spectral silence. We come out of the bazaar. We meet Moors on horseback, camels with their burthens, a fury who shakes her fist at the Ambassador, an old saint crowned with a laurel wreath, who laughs in our faces. At a certain point we began to see men dressed in black, with long hair, their heads covered with a blue handkerchief, who looked smilingly at us, and made humble salutations. One of these, a ceremonious old gentleman, presently came forward and invited the Ambassador to visit the *Mellà*, or Jews' quarter, called by the Arabs by that insulting name, which signifies accursed ground. The Ambassador accepting, we passed under a vaulted door or gateway, and engaged in a labyrinth of alleys more hideous, more wretched, and more fetid than those of the Arab city, between houses that seemed mere dens, across small squares like stable-yards, from which could be seen courts like sewers; and from every side of this dirt-heap emerged beautiful women and girls, smiling and murmuring—*Buenos dias!—Buenos dias!* In some places we were obliged to stop our noses and pick our way on the tips of our toes. The Ambassador was indignant. "How is it possible," said he to the old Jew, "that you can live in such filth?"

"It is the custom of the country," he replied.

"The custom of the country! It is shameful! And you ask the protection of the Legations, talk of civilisation, call the Moors savages! You, who live worse than they, and have the face to pride yourselves upon it!" The Hebrew hung his head and smiled, as if he thought—"What strange ideas!"

As we came out of the Mellà the crowd again surrounded us. The Vice-Consul patted a child on the head, and there were signs of astonishment; a favourable murmur arose; the soldiers were obliged to drive back the boys who crowded in upon us. We went with quickened pace up a deserted street, leaving the crowd gradually behind us, and coming outside the walls into a road bordered by enormous cactus and tall palm-trees, felt, with a long breath of relief, that we were free of the city and its people.

Such is the city of Alkazar, commonly called Alkazar-el-Kebir, which signifies the great Palace. Tradition says that it was founded in the twelfth century, by that Abou-Yussuf Yacoub-el-Mansur, of the dynasty of the Almoadi, who conquered Alonzo IX. of Castile at the battle of Alarcos, and who built the famous tower of the *Giralda* at Seville. It is related that one evening he lost his way while hunting, and that a fisherman sheltered him in his hut. The Caliph in gratitude built for him on the same spot a great palace with some other houses, around which clustered gradually the city. It was once a flourishing and populous place; now it has about five thousand inhabitants, between Moors and Jews, and is very poor, although it draws some advantages from being on the road of the caravans that traverse the empire from north to south.

Passing near one of the gates we saw an Arab boy of about twelve years old walking stiffly and with difficulty, with his legs wide apart in the most awkward attitude. Other boys were following him. When he came near we saw that he had a great bar of iron about a foot in length fixed between his legs by two rings around his ankles. He was a lean and

Entering a Bazaar at Alkazar.

dirty lad, with an ill-favoured countenance. The Ambassador questioned him through the interpreter.

" Who put that bar upon you ? "

" My father," answered the boy, boldly.

" For what reason ? "

" Because I will not learn to read."

We did not believe him, but a town Arab who was present confirmed what he had said.

" Have you worn it long ? "

" Three years," he answered, smiling bitterly.

We thought it all a lie. But the Arab again confirmed it, adding that the boy slept with the bar upon him, and that all Alkazar knew him. Then the Ambassador, moved with compassion, made him a little speech, exhorting him to study, to get rid of that shame and torture, and not to dishonour his family; and when the interpreter had repeated it, he was asked what his answer was.

" My answer is this," replied the boy, " that I will wear the iron all my life, but that I will never learn to read, and that I will die before I yield."

The Ambassador looked fixedly at him, but he sustained his glance with unflinching eye.

" Gentlemen," said the Ambassador, turning to us, " our mission is over." We returned to the camp, and the boy with his iron bar re-entered the city.

" A few years more," said a soldier, " and there will be another head over the Alkazar gate."

CHAPTER V.

BEN-AUDA.

Hamed.

THE next morning, at sunrise, we forded the river Kus, on the right bank of which the city of Alkazar is situated, and again advanced over an undulating, flowery, solitary country, whose confines stretched beyond our sight. The escort was scattered in a number of detached groups, looking like so many little *cortéges* of a Sultan. The artists galloped here and there, sketch-book and pencil in hand, sketching horses and riders. The rest of the members of the Embassy talked of the invasion of the Goths, of commerce, of scorpions, of philosophy, eagerly listened to by the mounted servants who came behind.

Civo lent particular attention to a philosophic discussion; Hamed listened to his master, who was telling about a wild boar hunt, in which he had risked his life. This Hamed was, after Selim, the most notable personage in the whole category of servants, soldiers, and grooms. He was an Arab of about thirty years old, very tall, bronzed, muscular, strong as a bull; but he had also a beardless face, the softest dark eyes a voice, a smile, a grace in all his movements, which made the most marked contrast with his powerful person. He wore a white turban, a blue jacket, and Zouave trousers; spoke Spanish, knew how to do everything, and

BALLARINI

Civo.

pleased everybody, so that the vain-glorious Selim was jealous of him. The others also were all more or less handsome young fellows, attentive, and full of obsequious solicitude. When one of us looked back, he encountered their big eyes asking whether he needed anything. "What a pity," thought I, "that we should not be attacked by a band of robbers, so that we might see all these nimble fellows put to the proof!"

We had ridden about two hours when we began to meet people. The first was a black horseman, who held in his hand one of those little sticks with an inscription in Arabic, called *herrez*, which the monks give to travellers to preserve them from robbers and illness. Then came some ragged old women,

A Postman.

bearing great bundles of wood upon their shoulders. Oh, power of fanaticism! Bent as they were, tired, breathless, they still found strength to launch a curse at us. One murmured, " God curse these infidels! " Another, " God keep us from the evil spirit! " About an hour later we met a courier, a poor lean Arab, bearing letters in a leathern bag slung about

J

his neck. He stopped to say that he came from Fez, and was going to Tangiers. The Ambassador gave him a letter for Tangiers, and he hastened on his way.

Such, and no other, is the postal service of Morocco, and nothing can be more wretched than the lives of these couriers. They eat nothing on their journey but a little bread and a few figs; they stop only at night for a few hours to sleep, with a cord tied to the foot, to which they set fire before going to sleep, and which wakens them within a certain time; they travel whole days without seeing a tree or a drop of water; they cross forests infested with wild boar, climb mountains inaccessible to mules, swim rivers, sometimes walk, sometimes run, sometimes roll down declivities, or climb ascents on feet and hands, under the August sun, under the drenching autumn rains, under the burning desert wind, taking four days from Tangiers to Fez, a week from Tangiers to Morocco, from one extremity of the empire to the other, alone, barefooted, half-naked; and when they have reached their journey's end, they go back! And this they do for a few francs.

At about half-way from Alkazar to our destination the road began to ascend very gradually until we reached a height from whence we saw another immense plain covered with vast tracts of yellow, red, and white flowers, looking like stretches of snow, striped with gold and crimson. Over this plain there came galloping to meet us some two hundred horsemen, with muskets resting on their saddle, led by a figure all in white, which Mohammed Ducali recognised and announced in a loud voice to be the Governor of Ben-Auda.

We had reached the confines of the province of Seffian, called also Ben-Auda, from the family name of the Governor, which signifies *son of a mare*—a name which had taken my fancy before leaving Tangiers.

We descended into the plain, and the two hundred of

Seffian having drawn up in a line with the three hundred of Laracce, the Governor Ben-Auda presented himself to our chief.

If I live to be a hundred years old I shall never forget that countenance. He was a lean old man, with savage eyes, a forked nose,* a lipless mouth cut in the form of a semi-circle turned downwards. Arrogance, superstition, Venus, *kif*, idleness, and satiety were written upon his visage. A big turban covered his forehead and ears. A curved dagger hung from his girdle.

The Ambassador dismissed the commander of the escort from Laracce, who at once withdrew with his horsemen at a gallop; and we went on with the new escort, and the usual accompaniment of charging and firing.

Their faces were blacker, their robes more gaudy, their horses finer, their yells more extraordinary, their charges and manœuvres more wildly impetuous than any we had yet seen. The further we advanced, the more apparent became the local colour of all things.

In all that multitude, twelve horsemen, dressed with un-usual elegance and mounted on beautiful horses, were con-spicuous, even in the eyes of the Arabs. Five of them were colossal young men, who appeared to be brothers; all had pale bronzed faces and great black brilliant eyes under enor-mous turbans. These five were the sons, and the other seven nephews, of the Governor of Ben-Auda.

The firing and charging went on for about an hour, at which time we reached a garden belonging to the Governor, where we dismounted to rest and refresh ourselves.

It was a grove of orange and lemon trees, planted in parallel rows, and so thickly as to form an intricate green roof, under which one enjoyed the coolness, shade, and per-fume of paradise.

The Governor dismounted with us, and presented his sons;

* *Naso forcuto*, a favourite expression with the author.

five as handsome, dignified, and amiable faces as are often to
be seen.   One after the other pressed our hands, with a
slight bow, casting down his eyes with an air of boyish shy-
ness.

We were all presently seated in the garden, upon a beautiful carpet from Rabat, where we were served with breakfast.
The Governor of Ben-Auda sat upon a mat at twenty paces

Breakfast with the Governor of Ben-Auda.

from us, and also breakfasted, waited upon by his slaves.
Then ensued a curious exchange of courtesies between him
and the Ambassador.   First, Ben-Auda sent a vase of milk as
an offering; the Ambassador returned it with a beefsteak.
The milk was followed by butter, the beefsteak by an omelet;
the butter by a sweet dish, the omelet by a box of sardines;
the whole accompanied by a thousand coldly ceremonious gestures—hands clasped upon the breast, and eyes turned up to
heaven with a comical expression of gastronomic enthusiasm.
The sweet dish, by the way, was a species of tart made of
honey, eggs, butter, and sugar, of which the Arabs are ex-

tremely fond, and about which they have an odd superstition
—that if while the woman is cooking it a man should happen
to enter the room, the tart goes wrong, and even if it could
be eaten it would not be prudent to do so. " And wine ? "
some one asked; " should we not offer him some wine ? "
There was some discussion. It was asserted that Governor
Ben-Auda was in secret devoted to the bottle; but how could
he drink in the presence of his soldiers ? It was decided not
to send any. To me,
however, it seemed
that he cast very soft
glances at the bottles,
much softer than those
with which he favoured
us. During the whole
time that he sat there
on his mat, except when
he was giving
thanks for gifts,
he maintained a
frowning expres-
sion of pride and
anger that made

The Governor of Ben-Auda.

me wish to have under my orders our forty companies of
*bersaglieri,** that I might parade them under his nose.

Mohammed Ducali meantime was relating to me a notable
episode in the history of Ben-Auda, in which family the
government of Seffian has been for ages. The people of this
province are brave and turbulent; and they are said to have
given proof of their valour in the late war with Spain, when,
at the battle of Vad-Ras, in March, 1861, Sidi Absalam Ben-
Abd-el-Krim Ben-Auda, then Governor of the whole province
of Garb, was killed. To this Absalam succeeded his eldest son,
Sidi Abd-el-Krim. He was a violent and dissipated man, who

* *Bersaglieri*, Italian riflemen.

despoiled his people by taxation, and tormented them with a capricious ferocity. One day he intimated to one Gileli Ruqui that he desired a large sum of money. The man excused himself on the plea of poverty. He was loaded with chains and cast into prison. The family and friends of the prisoner sold all they had and brought the desired sum to Sidi Abd-el-Krim. Gileli came out of prison, and, having assembled all his friends, they took a solemn oath to kill the Governor. His house was situated at about two hours' ride from the garden where we were. The conspirators attacked it in the night in force. They killed the sentinels, broke into the hall, strangled and poignarded Sidi Abd-el-Krim, his wives, children, servants, and slaves; sacked and burned the house, and then threw themselves into the open country, raising the cry of revolt. The relatives and partisans of Ben-Auda gathered themselves together and marched against the rebels; the rebels dispersed them, and rebellion broke out all over the Garb. Then the Sultan sent an army; the revolt, after a furious resistance, was put down, and the heads of the leaders hung from the gates of Fez and Morocco; the land of the *Benimalek* was divided from the province; the house of Ben-Auda was rebuilt; and Sidi-Mohammed Ben-Auda, brother of the murdered man, and guest of the Italian Embassy, assumed the government of the land of his fathers. It was a passing victory of desperation over tyranny, followed by a harder tyranny than before; in these words may be summed up the history of every province of the empire, and, perhaps, at that very moment there was a predestined Gileli Ruqui for Sidi-Mohammed Ben-Auda.

Before sunset we reached our encampment, which was not very far off, on a solitary plain, at the foot of a small eminence on which was a *Cuba* flanked by a palm-tree.

The Ambassador had hardly arrived, when the *muna* was brought and deposited as usual before his tent, in the presence of the intendant, the Caid, the soldiers, and servants. Whilst they were busy making the division, I saw, as I raised my

eyes towards the *Cuba,* a man of tall stature and strange
aspect coming down with long strides towards the encampment. There was no doubt about it : here was the
hermit, the saint, coming to make a
disturbance. I said not a word, but
waited. He skirted the camp on the
outside, so as to appear suddenly
before the Ambassador's tent. He

The Saint Cursing the Ambassador.

moved on the tips of his toes : a sepulchral figure, covered with
black rags, disgusting to behold. All at once he broke into a run,
dashed into the midst of us, and, recognising our chief by
his dress, rushed upon him with the howl of one possessed.

But he had scarcely time to howl. With lightning rapidity
the Caid seized him by the throat and dragged him furiously
into the midst of the soldiery, who in a second had him out
of the camp, stifling his roars with a mantle. The interpreter
translated his invectives as follows : " Let us exterminate all
these accursed Christian dogs, who go to the Sultan and do
what they please, while we are dying with hunger ! "

A little after the presentation of the customary *muna* there
arrived at the camp about fifty Arabs and blacks, bearing in
single file great round boxes, with high conical covers of
straw, and containing eggs, chickens, tarts, sweets, roast
meats, *cùscùssù*, salads, etc., enough to satisfy an entire tribe.
It was a second *muna*, spontaneously offered to the Ambassador by Sidi-Mohammed Ben-Auda, perhaps to do away with
the effect of his threatening visage in the morning.

That personage himself presently appeared on horseback,
accompanied by his five sons and a crowd of servants. The
Ambassador received them in his tent, and conversed with them
through the interpreters. He asked one of his sons if he had
ever heard of Italy. The young man answered that he had
heard it mentioned several times. One of them asked whether
England or Italy was farthest from Morocco; how many
cannons we had, what was the name of our chief city, and
how the king was dressed. As they spoke, they all examined
curiously our neckties and our watch-chains. The Ambassador
then asked the Governor some questions about the extent and
population of his province. Either he knew nothing, or did
not choose to tell; anyhow, it was not possible to get any
information out of him. I remember he said that the exact
number of the population could not be known. " But about
what number ? " was asked. Not even about the number
could be known. Then he questioned us again. " How did
we like the city of Alkazar ? What did we think of the
country ? The water was good, was it not ? Should we like
to stay in Morocco ? Why had we not brought our wives ? "

They drank tea with us, and, after many salutations and genu-flexions, remounted their horses and spurred away—or, rather, disappeared; for, as there was not a village or a house within eyeshot, all those who came and went made the effect of people who had risen out of the ground, or vanished into thin air.

This, like every other day, closed with a splendid sunset, and a noisy, merry dinner. But the night was one of the most disturbed that we had had throughout the journey; per-haps because it was necessary in the land of Seffian that the Ambassador should be more carefully guarded than in other places, the night sentinels kept each other awake by singing every quarter of an hour a verse from the Koran. One in-toned the words, and all the others responded in chorus, in loud voices, accompanied by the neighing of steeds and the barking of dogs. We had hardly dropped asleep when we were aroused again, and could not succeed in closing an eye. By way of addition, a little after midnight, in one of the in-tervals of silence, a wild harsh voice arose out in the fields, and never ceased until dawn. Sometimes it approached, then seemed to recede, then approached again very near, taking a tone of menace, or lamenting, despairing, and bursting out now and then in piercing cries or yells of laughter that chilled one's bones. It was the saint, wandering about the confines of the camp, and calling down God's malediction on our heads. In the morning, when we issued forth from our tents, there he was, erect like a spectre, in front of his solitary *Cuba*, bathed in the first rose tints of dawn, and pouring out curses in a harsh voice, waving his skeleton arms above his head.

I went in search of the cook, to see what he thought of this awful personage; but I found him so busy making coffee for an impatient crowd, who were all attacking him at once, that I had not the heart to torment him. Some were talking Arabic, Ranni spoke Sicilian, the *Calefato* Neapolitan, Hamed Spanish, and M. Vincent French.

" *Ma*, I can't understand a word you say, gallows-birds that you are ! " screamed the cook in despair.

" *Ma*, this is Babylon ! Let me breathe ! Do you want to see me die ? *Oh che pais, mi povr'om !* Oh, what a country for a poor man to be in ! They all talk together, and no one understands the other ! "

When he had recovered his breath a little, I pointed out the howling saint, and asked him, " Well, what do you think of that piece of impudence ? "

He raised his eyes to the *Cuba*, looked steadily at the saint for a few moments, and then, with a gesture of profound contempt, answered in Piedmontese accent, " *Guardo e passi !* " * and withdrew with dignity into his tent.

* " *Non ragionam di lor, ma guarda e passa.*"—*Dante.*

CHAPTER VI.

WE struck our camp and moved on in the usual order, amid the cries and musket-shots of the escort, arriving in two hours' time at a small water-course which marked the confines of Seffian. Here we were met by a large company of horsemen, led by the Governor of the province which extends from Seffian to the large river Sebù. The escort from Ben-Auda turned and disappeared; we forded the stream, and were instantly surrounded by the new-comers.

Bu-Bekr-Ben-el-Abbassi, an elegant and graceful personage, pressed warmly the hand of our chief, saluted amicably Ducali, his former school companion, and welcomed the rest with a dignified and graceful gesture. We rode on, and for some time not one of us could take our eyes off the new-comer. He was the most interesting of all the Governors we had seen. Of middle height, and slender figure, dark, with soft penetrating eyes, aquiline nose, and a full black beard, through which, when he smiled, gleamed two rows of beautiful teeth. He was wrapped in a fine snow-white mantle, with the hood drawn over his turban, and mounted on a jet-black horse with sky-blue

MEETING OF THE AMBASSADOR AND BU-BEKR-BEN-EL-ABBASSI.

housings.   He looked like a generous, beloved, and happy man.
Either my fancy misled me, or the aspect of the two hundred
horsemen from Karia-el-Abbassi reflected the benignity of the
Governor.   They appeared to me to have the open and con-

Bu-Bekr-Ben-el-Abbassi.

tented expression of men who had for years enjoyed the
miraculous grace of a humane government.

   This appearance, together with the huts, that began to be
more frequent in the country, and the serene weather, refreshed
by a perfumed breeze, gave me for a time the delusion that the

province was an oasis of prosperity and peace in the midst of the
miserable empire of the Schereifs.

We passed through a village, composed of two rows of
camel-skin tents, held together with canes and sticks; every
tent having a tiny enclosure surrounded by a cactus hedge.
Beyond the tents cows and horses were feeding; in front, upon
our road, were some groups of half-naked children come to look
at us; ragged men and women peeped at us over the hedges.

Village of Camel-skin Tents.

No one shook his fist at us, no one cursed us. Hardly had we
passed the village when they all came out of their huts, and we
beheld a crowd of some hundreds of black, hideous, famine-
stricken wretches, who might have risen from some grave-yard.
Some ran behind us for a while; others vanished among the
irregularities of the ground.

The configuration of the country through which we were
passing gave rise to a wonderful variety of picturesque effects
as the escort and caravan proceeded. It was a succession of
deep valleys, parallel to each other, formed by great earth waves,
and all covered with flowers like a garden. Passing from one

valley to another we would lose sight of the escort for a
moment ; then on the top of the height behind us would appear,
first the muzzles of the muskets, then fezes and turbans, then
faces, and finally the figures of men and horses, rising apparently
out of the earth.   Looking back from a height we could see the
two hundred scattered along the valley amid the smoke and
re-echoing noises of their shots, and far along behind, the servants, soldiers, horses, and mules, appearing for an instant, and
then plunging into the depths and lost to sight.   Seen in that
way the caravan appeared interminable, and presented the
grandiose aspect of an expeditionary army or an emigrating
people.

Karia-el-Abbassi was made up of the Governor's house and
a group of huts shaded by a few fig and wild olive trees.
We accepted the Governor's invitation to rest at his house,
and the caravan went on to the spot selected for the camp.

Crossing two or three courts enclosed between bare white
walls, we entered a garden, upon which opened the principal
gate of the mansion : a little white house, windowless, and
silent as a convent.   A few mulatto slaves showed us into a
small ground-floor room, also white, with no aperture except
the door by which we entered, and another little door in a
corner.   There were two alcoves, three white mattresses on the
mosaic floor, and some embroidered cushions.   It was the first
time we had been within four walls since our departure from
Tangiers ; we stretched ourselves voluptuously in the alcoves,
and awaited with curiosity the continuation of the spectacle.

The Governor came in wrapped in a snowy *caic* that reached
from his turban to his feet.   He threw off his yellow slippers,
and sat down barefooted on the mattress between Ducali and
the Ambassador.   Slaves brought jars of milk and plates of
sweetmeats, and Ben-el-Abbassi himself made the tea, and
poured it out into beautiful little cups of Chinese porcelain,
which his favourite servant—a young mulatto with his face
tattooed in arabesques—carried round.   The grace and dignity

TAKING TEA WITH THE GOVERNOR OF KARIA-EL-ABBASSI.

of our host in all that he did are not to be described, and
seemed amazing in a man who was probably very ignorant,
who governed a few thousands of tented Arabs, and never in
all his life, perhaps, had seen fifty
civilised persons. In the most aris-
tocratic *salon* in Europe not the
least fault could have been found
in his manners. His dress was
fresh, neat, and fragrant as that of
an odalisque just come from the
bath. As he moved, his *caic* showed
beneath gleams of the splendid and
varied colours of his costume, in-
spiring in the spectator an ardent
wish to tear off the veil and see
what was hidden under it.   He
spoke in quiet tones, and without
the slightest appearance of curiosity,
as if he had seen us the day before.
He had never been out of Morocco,
and said that he should like much
to see our railways and our great
palaces ; and he knew that there
were in Italy three cities which were
called Genoa, Rome, and Venice. As
he conversed, the little door opened
behind him, and the head of a
pretty little mulatto girl was thrust
out, which rolled around two large
astonished and startled eyes, and
vanished. She was the Governor's

The Governor's Daughter.

daughter by a black woman. He was aware of the apparition,
and smiled. There followed a long interval of silence. In
the middle of the chamber rose the fumes of burning aloes
from the perfume-burners ; before the door stood a group of

K

curious slaves; behind the slaves were palm-trees; and over all smiled the clear blue sky of Africa. It all seemed so unreal that I found myself thinking of my little room in Turin, and of its sometime occupant as of another person.

On our way to the encampment, which was about half a mile from the Governor's house, upon a high plain covered with dry grass, we for the first time felt the scorching power of the sun. It was only the 8th of May, and we were not a hundred miles from the Mediterranean coast, and we had yet to cross the great plain of the Sebù!

Notwithstanding the heat, our camp was enlivened towards evening by an unusual concourse of people. On one side a long row of Arabs, seated on the ground, watched the manœuvres of the cavalry escort; on the other, some were playing ball; a little farther on, a group of women, huddled in their coarse *caics*, observed us with gestures of astonishment, and a throng of children ran about everywhere. The population seemed really less savage than those we had left behind.

Biseo and I went to look at the ball-players, who immediately left off, but, after some consulting glances, resumed their game. There were fifteen or twenty of them—tall fellows, big and athletic, with nothing on but shirts bound round the waist, and a kind of mantle made of coarse and dirty stuff, wound round the body like a *caic*. Their play was different from that at Tangiers. One struck the ball into the air with his foot; all the others rushed to catch it as it fell, leaping up into the air as if they were about to fly; and the one who caught it struck it up again in his turn. Often, in the mêlée, one would fall; and, others falling over him, and others again on them, the whole would roll about together, kicking and screaming, and with small regard for modesty. More than one thus turned upside down displayed a curved dagger at his girdle, or a little purse hung from his neck, containing probably some verses from the Koran, as a charm against illness. Once the ball fell at my feet, and I seized it, placed it on my open palm, made some necromantic gestures over it, and launched it into the air. For a few moments not one of the players dared to touch it. They came near it, looked at it, touched it with a foot timidly; and it was not until they saw me laugh and make signs that it was a joke, that they ventured to pick it up and go on with their play.

Meantime, nearly all the boys who were running about had gathered around us. There might have been fifty of them, and all the clothing they possessed among them would not have brought tenpence at the rag-shop. Some were very handsome, some had scald heads, most of them were coffee-coloured, and the rest had a greenish-yellow tint, as if they were plastered over with some vegetable substance. A few had tails like the Chinese. At first they stood about ten paces off, looking suspiciously at us, and exchanging observations in whispers. Then, seeing that we did nothing hostile, they came a little nearer, and began to get upon tiptoe, and bend themselves about in order to see us on every side, as we do in looking at statues. We stood immovable. One of them touched my shoe with the tip of his finger, and snatched it away as if it had burnt him; another smelled at my sleeve. We were surrounded, and smelt all sorts of exotic odours: we felt as if they were plotting something. "Come," said Biseo, "it is time to free ourselves. I have an infallible method;" and he pulled out sketch-book and pencil, and made as if he were about to copy one of their faces. In a moment they were all gone, like a flight of birds.

A little later some women approached. "Wonderful!" said we. "It is to be hoped that they are not coming to give us a dagger-thrust in the name of Mahomet!" But they were only poor sick people, who had scarcely strength to walk, or hold up their arms to cover their faces. Among them there was a young girl, whose groans moved our compassion, and who showed only one blue eye, full of tears. We understood that they were seeking the doctor, and pointed out his tent.

K 2

One, helping her words with gestures, asked if there would
be anything to pay. We said no, and they tottered towards
the doctor's quarters. We followed, to assist at the consultation.
" What do you feel ? " asked Signor Miguerez, in Arabic, of
the first one. " A great pain here," pointing to her shoulder.
" I must see it," said the physician; "take off your mantle
a moment." The woman did not move. This is the great
point! Not one of them—not even a woman of ninety—will
let herself be seen, and all pretend that the doctor can divine
what is the matter. " Come, will you, or will you not, unveil yourself ? " said Miguerez. No reply. " Well, let me hear
the others," and he questioned them, while the first withdrew,
sadly enough. The others had no need to unveil, and the
doctor distributed pills and potions, and sent them away " with
God." Poor creatures! Not one of them was more than
thirty years old, and already youth was over for them, and
with its departure had come the fatigue, brutal treatment, and
contempt which make an Arab woman's old age horrible : instruments for man's pleasure up to twenty, beasts of burthen until
death.

The dinner was made gay by a visit from Ben-el-Abbassi,
and the night was disturbed by a frightful invasion of insects.
Already during the heat of the day I had foreseen the coming
terrors in the unusual buzzing and swarming which was apparent
among the grass. The ants were making long black lines,
beetles were in bunches, and grasshoppers as thick as flies ; and
with them a great number of other insects unseen until now,
which did not inspire me with confidence. Captain de Boccard,
the professor of entomology, named them for me. There,
among others, was the *Cicindela campestris,* a living trap, which
closes the opening of its den with its own large head, and drops
down into the depths the incautious insects that pass over it ;
there was the *Pheropsophus Africanus,* which darts at its pur-
suing enemy a puff of corrosive vapour from its tail ; the *Meloe
majalis,* dragging along its enormous dropsical belly swollen

with grass and eggs; the *Carabus rugosus,* the *Pimelia scabrosa,* the *Cetonia opaca,* the *Cossyphus Hoffmannseghi,* animated leaf, of which Victor Hugo gives a fanciful description enough to chill one's blood. And a great number of big lizards, enormous spiders, centipedes six inches long, crickets as big as my thumb, and green bugs as big as pennies, that came and went as if they were preparing by common accord some warlike expedition. As if these were not enough, I had scarcely seated myself at table and stretched out my hand to take my glass, when there appeared over the edge of it the head of a monstrous locust,

A Scorpion.

which, instead of flying away at my threatening gesture, continued to look at me with the utmost impudence. And finally, by way of climax, Hamed appeared with the face of one who has escaped a great danger, and laid before us, stuck in a cleft stick, nothing less than a tarantula, a *Lycosa tarentula,* the terrible spider, that *" cuando pica á un hombre,* when it stings a man," said he, " Allah help him! The unfortunate one begins to laugh and cry, and sing and dance, and nothing but good music, very good music! the music of the Sultan's band, can save him." The reader can imagine with what courage I went to my bed. Nevertheless, my three companions and I had been in bed for some little time, the lights were out, and silence prevailed, when suddenly the Commandant sprang

into a sitting position, and cried out:—" I am populated ! "
(*Io mi sento popolato !*)   Then we too began to feel something.
For a time there were furtive touches, timid punctures, ticklings
and slight provocations of explorers and advanced sentinels that
were not worthy of notice.   But soon the big patrols began
to arrive, and a vigorous offensive resistance became necessary.
The struggle was ferocious.   The more we fought the hotter
grew the attack.   They came from the head, from the foot,
and dropped from the curtains of the bed.   They seemed to be
carrying on the assault under the direction of some great insect
of genius.   It was evidently a religious war.   Briefly, we
could resist no longer.   " Lights ! " roared the Vice-Consul.
We all jumped out of bed, lighted our candles and prepared
for strategy.   The common soldiers were slaughtered on the
spot; the leaders, the big bugs, first classified by the Captain,
and sentenced by the Commandant, were roasted by the Vice-
Consul, and I composed a funeral eulogium in prose and verse
which will be published after my death.   In a few minutes
the ground was strewn with wings and claws, legs and heads ;
the survivors dispersed, and we, weary of carnage, reciprocally
named each other knights of various orders, and retired once
more to bed.

The following morning at sunrise Governor Ben-el-Abbassi
presented himself to escort us to the confines of his province.
We descended from the high table-land on which our tents were
pitched, and saw spread before our eyes the immense horizon of
the plain of the Sebù.

This river, one of the largest in the Magreb, descends from
the western flank of the mountain chain that stretches from
the upper Atlas towards the Straits of Gibraltar, and in a
course of about two hundred and forty kilomètres, swelled
by many affluents, goes in a vast curve to throw itself into
the Atlantic Ocean, near Mehedia, where the accumulation of
sand, common to the mouths of all the rivers of Morocco on
that side, prevents the entrance of vessels, and produces great

inundations at certain seasons. The valley of the Sebù, which embraces at its commencement all the space lying between the two cities of Laracce and Salé, and touches at its upper extremity the high basin of the Muluia (the great river which marks the eastern boundary of Morocco), opens to Europeans, by the shore and by Teza, the way to the city of Fez; comprising, besides Fez, the large city of Mechinez, the third capital; which gathers to itself, it may be said, all the political life of the Empire, and is the principal seat of the wealth and power of the Schereifs. The Sebù, it may be noted, marks in the north the confines which the Sultan never oversteps, except in case of war, the three cities, Fez, Morocco, and Mechinez, lying south of the river. In these three cities he sojourns alternately. There is also the double city of Salé-Rabatt, through which he passes in going from Fez to Morocco. He takes this road in order not to have to cross the mountains that shut in the valley of the Sebù to the south, their slopes being inhabited by the Zairi, a mixed Berber race, who have the reputation of being, with the Beni-mitir, the most turbulent and indomitable of the tribes of those mountains.

The Sebù reminded me of the Tiber in the Roman Campagna. At the point where we struck it it is about a hundred yards in width, of a muddy colour, turbulent and rapid, shut in between two high arid banks, which are almost vertical, and at whose feet extend two zones of miry ground.

Two antediluvian barks, rowed by eight or ten Arabs, approached the shore. These boats alone, if there were nothing else, would suffice to show what Morocco is. For hundreds of years Sultans, Pashas, caravans, and embassies have crossed the river on such hulks as these, with their feet in mud and water, sometimes in danger of drowning; and when the hulks—as often happens—are full of holes, caravan and embassy, Sultan and Pasha, wait on the shore while the boatmen stop the holes with mud or something else, sometimes for several hours in rain or scorching sun; and for hundreds of years horses, mules, and

THE PASSAGE OF THE SEBÙ.

camels, for want of a piece of plank a couple of yards long, run the risk of breaking their legs, and do break them, in jumping from the shore into the boats; and no one has ever conceived the idea of constructing a bridge of boats, and no one has ever thought of bringing down a piece of plank two yards long; and if any one reproves them for these things, they look at him with an air of stupefaction as if he had suggested a prodigy.

In many places they cross the rivers upon rafts made of cane, and their armies cross on floating bridges made of skins blown up with air and covered with earth and branches.

We dismounted, and went down a steep pathway to the river, when we Italians crossed in the first boat, and then looked on from the opposite shore at the passage of the caravan. What a picture it was! In the middle of the river came a great boat filled with the Moors and camels of a caravan of merchandise, and a little beyond another bringing the horses and men of the escort from Fez, from the midst of which floated the banner of the Prophet, and shone the black visage and snowy turban of the Caid. On the opposite shore, in the midst of a great confusion of horses, mules, servants, and baggage, which encumbered the bank for a long distance, appeared the white and gracious figure of the Governor Ben-el-Abbassi, seated upon a rising ground, his officers grouped behind him, and his fine black horse with its sky-blue trappings standing near. Upon the top of the bank, which rose like the wall of a fortress, and upon which sat a long row of country Arabs with dangling legs, were ranged the two hundred horsemen of the Governor, who, seen thus against the blue background of the sky, looked like giants. Some black servants, as naked as they were born, were plunging and re-plunging into the river, screaming and shouting. A few Arabs, according to Moorish custom, washed their rags, bobbing up and down over them like so many puppets; and some crossed the river swimming. Above our heads passed flights of storks; far away on the shore rose the smoke from a group of Bedouin tents; the boatmen chanted in chorus a prayer to the Prophet

for the good result of the enterprise; the water sent up golden
sparkles in the sun, and Selam, standing at a little distance in
his famous caftan, made in the midst of this barbaric and festive
picture the most harmonious red point that could be imagined by
a painter.

The passage occupied several hours, and as each party reached
the shore, it resumed its march with the caravan.

When the last horse had crossed, Governor Ben-el-Abbassi
mounted and joined his soldiers in the heights opposite. The
Ambassador and his suite all raised their hands in salute. The
escort of Karia-el-Abbassi answered with a storm of musket-
shots, and vanished; but for a moment or two the fine white
figure of the Governor was visible amid the smoke, with his arm
stretched towards us in token of amity and farewell.

Accompanied only by our Fez escort, we now entered upon
the sadly famous territory of the Beni-Hassan.

CHAPTER VII.

BENI-HASSAN.

FOR more than an hour we travelled through fields of barley, from which showed here and there a black tent, the head of a camel, or a cloud of smoke. In the paths we traversed, scorpions, lizards, and snakes were numerous. Our saddles were so heated by the sun that we could scarcely hold our hands upon them. The light blinded our eyes, the dust choked us, and everything around was still as death. The plain which stretched before us like an ocean seemed awful to me, as if the caravan were doomed to go on for ever. But at the same time my curiosity to see the proud Beni-Hassan, of whom I had heard so much, kept up my drooping spirits. "What kind of people are they?" I asked of the interpreter. "Thieves and murderers," answered he; "faces from the other world; the worst crew in Morocco." And I scanned the horizon with anxiety.

The faces from another world were not long in coming. We saw in advance a great cloud of dust, and in a few minutes were surrounded by a throng of three hundred mounted savages, in green, yellow, white, violet, and scarlet, ragged, dishevelled, and panting, as if they had just come out of a fray. In the midst of the thick dust they raised we could discern their Governor, a long-haired, black-bearded giant, who, followed by two hoary Vice-Governors, all armed with muskets, approached the Ambassador, pressed his hand, and then disappeared. Immediately the usual charging, firing, and yelling began. They seemed frantic. They fired between the legs of our mules, over our heads, and close to our shoulders.

The Governor Abd-Alla.

Seen from a distance they must have looked like a band of assassins assailing us. There were formidable old men, with long white beards, all skin and bone, but looking as if they might live for centuries; and young men with long locks of black hair flying like manes. Many had their chests, arms, and legs bare, turbans in tatters,

and red rags twisted round the head ; *caics* torn, saddles broken,
bridles made of cord, old sabres and poignards of strange forms.
And such faces ! " It is absurd," said the Commandant, " to
suppose that these people will be capable of the self-sacrifice of
not killing us." Every one of those faces told a story of blood.
They looked at us as they passed, out of the corner of their
eyes, as if to hide the expression of their glance. One hundred
came on the right, one hundred on the left, one hundred behind
us, stretched out in open order. This guard on the flank was
new to us ; but we were not long in perceiving its necessity.
As we advanced, the tents became more frequent in the open
country, so that we finally passed through real villages surrounded by cactus and aloe hedges. From all these tents came
Arabs running, dressed in a single garment or shirt, in groups,
on foot, on horseback, on the cruppers of donkeys—two, and
sometimes three on the same animal ; women with children hung
to their shoulders, old men supported by boys, all breathless,
wild to see us, and perhaps not to see us only. Gradually a
veritable people had gathered about us. Then the soldiers of the
escort began to disperse them. They darted among them at a
gallop, here and there and everywhere, yelling, striking, over-
turning beast and rider, and raising a tempest of cries and curses.
But the scattered groups formed again, and continued to accompany us at a run. Through the smoke and powder, broken by
the lightning of the shots, we saw over those vast fields, in the
distance, tents, horses, camels, droves of cattle, groups of aloes,
columns of smoke, crowds of people turned towards us motionless,
in an attitude of amazement. We had at last reached an
inhabited land ! It did exist, then, and was not a fable, this
blessed population of Morocco ! After an hour's rapid riding
we were again in the solitude of the country, with no one save
our escort, and soon came to our camp, which was pitched upon
the bank of the Sebù, a thick chain of sentinels, on foot and
armed with muskets, being extended all around the encampment.
The country then was really dangerous ! If I had been able to

doubt it, I should have been more than persuaded by what I afterwards heard.

The Beni-Hassan are the most turbulent, the most audacious, the most quarrelsome, and the most thievish tribe in all the valley of the Sebù. Their last performance was a sanguinary revolt which broke out in the summer of 1873

Dispersing the Crowd.

(when the reigning Sultan came to the throne), which began with the sack of the Governor's house, and the carrying off of his women. Theft is their principal profession. They gather together in bands, armed and mounted, and make raids beyond the Sebù, or in other neighbouring lands, stealing all that they can drag or carry off, and killing, by way of precaution, all persons whom they encounter. They have their chiefs, their statutes, discipline, and rights recognised,

in a certain sense, even by the Government, which sometimes makes use of them to get back stolen property. They
rob in the way of forced imposts. The people who are despoiled by them, instead of losing their time in seeking their
property, protect what is left to them by paying a certain
stipulated sum to the chief of the robbers. As for the boys
especially, it is admitted as a most natural thing that they
should all steal. If they get a ball in the ·back, or a skull
fractured by a stone, so much the worse for them; no one
will be robbed if he can help it, and there is no rose without
its thorn. Their fathers say ingeniously—a boy of eight years
old makes little, one of twelve much more, one of sixteen
a great deal. Every thief has his own peculiar branch of the
profession : there is the corn thief, the cattle thief, the horse
thief, the merchandise thief, the thief of the *duar* (or Arab
encampment), the street thief. In the streets they assault
particularly the Jews, who are forbidden to carry arms. But
the commonest kind of larceny is that at the expense of
the *duar*. In this they are incomparable artists, not only
among the Beni-Hassan, but all over Morocco. In stealing
on horseback the great art consists in the lightning-like
rapidity with which they act; they pass, seize, and disappear
before any one can recognise them. They rob also on foot,
and in a masterly manner. They creep into the *duar* naked,
because dogs will not bark at a naked man; they soap themselves all over, so as to be able to slip out of the hands of
any one who might seize them, and carry a branch in their
arms, so that horses, taking them for bushes, may not be
frightened. Horses are the most coveted prey. They seize
them round the neck, stretch their legs under the belly, and
away like an arrow. Their audacity is incredible. There is
no encampment of a caravan, be it that of a Pasha or Ambassador, where they will not penetrate in spite of the
strictest watch. They glide upon the ground like snakes,
covered with grass, with straw, with leaves, dressed in sheep-

skin, disguised as beggars, as madmen, as saints, as soldiers.
They will risk their lives for a chicken, and go ten miles for
a dollar.   They will even steal a bag of money from under
the head of a sleeping man.   And that very night, in spite
of the chain of sentinels, they stole a sheep that was tied to

The Horse Stealer.

the cook's bed, who, when he discovered his loss in the
morning, stood half-an-hour motionless, with folded arms,
before the door of his tent, his eyes fixed upon the horizon,
exclaiming, ever and anon: "Ah! holy Madonna! what a
country!—what a country!—what a country!"

I have spoken of the *duar:* Morocco cannot be understood without a description of them, and with what I saw,

and what Signor Morteo, who has lived twenty years among them, told me, I can venture to describe them.

The *duar* is in general made up of ten, fifteen, or twenty families, who are related to each other, and each family has a tent. The tents are disposed in two parallel rows, distant from each other about thirty paces, forming thus a sort of square open at both ends. The tents are almost all of equal size, and consist of one great piece of black or chocolate-brown stuff, woven of the fibre of the dwarf palm, and of camels' and goats' hair, which is sustained by two poles or thick canes upholding a cross-piece of wood. Their shape is still that of the habitations of Jugurtha's Numidians, which Sallust compares to a boat with its keel in the air. In the winter and autumn the cloth is stretched to the ground and securely fastened by cords and pegs, so that wind and water cannot enter. In summer, a large aperture is left all round for the circulation of air, protected by a little hedge of reeds, canes, and dried brambles. By these means the tents are cooler in summer, and better closed against the rain and wind than even the Moorish houses in the cities, which have neither doors nor windows. The greatest height of a tent is two mètres and a half, the greatest length ten mètres; those that exceed these measurements belong to some opulent sheik, and are rare. A reed partition divides the tent into two parts, in one of which the father and mother sleep, while the other is occupied by the children and the rest of the family.

One or two straw mats; a gaily painted and arabesqued wooden chest for clothes; a little round mirror from Trieste or Venice; a high tripod made of cane, which is covered with a *caic*, under which they wash themselves; two large stones for grinding grain; a weaver's loom, such as was in use in Abraham's time; a rusty tin lamp, a few earthen jars, a goat-skin or two, a plate or two, a distaff, a saddle, a musket, a poignard, comprise the furniture of such a tent. In a corner there is generally a hen with her brood of

L

A DUAR IN BENI-HASSAN.

chickens; in front of the tent door, an oven composed of two bricks; on one side a little kitchen garden, beyond two or three round pits lined with stones and cement, in which they keep their corn.

In almost all the great *duars* there is a tent appropriated to the schoolmaster, who receives from the community five francs a month and his food. All the little boys are sent to him to recite a hundred thousand times the same verses from the Koran, and to write them, when they know them by heart, upon a wooden tablet. The greater part of them leave school before they know how to read, to go and work for their parents, forgetting in a short time the little they have learned. The few who have the will and power to study, continue until twenty years of age, after which they go to some city to complete their studies, and become *taleb,* which signifies notary or scrivener, and is equivalent to being a priest, because among the Mahometans the civil and religious law is identical. Life in the *duar* is of the utmost simplicity. Everybody rises at dawn; they say their prayers, feed the cows, make the butter, and drink the buttermilk that remains. For drinking vessels they make use of shells and *patelle* which they buy from the people of the coast. Then the men go to labour in the fields and do not return until evening. The women fetch wood and water, grind the corn, weave the coarse stuffs of their own and their husbands' dress, twist cords for the tents out of the fibre of the dwarf palm, send food to their husbands, and prepare the *cùscùssù* for the evening meal. The *cùscùssù* is a mixture of beans, squash, onions, and other green stuff; sometimes it is sweetened, peppered, and flavoured with the juice of meat; on feast days it is eaten with meat. When the men come home there is supper, and in general bed at sundown. Sometimes after supper an old man will tell a story in the midst of a circle of listeners. During the night the *duar* remains immersed in silence and darkness; here and there a family will keep a small lamp burning before the tent, to serve

L 2

as a guide to wandering travellers. The dress of the men and
women consists of a cotton shirt, a mantle, and a coarse *caic*.
The mantles and *caics* are only washed two or three times a
year, on the occasion of solemn festivals, and in consequence
they are generally of the same colour as the wearer's skin, and

Type of Native of Beni-Hassan.

often blacker. The cleanliness of the body is better cared
for, since without the ablutions prescribed by the Koran,
no one can pray. The women for the most part wash all over
every morning, hiding themselves under the tripod covered
by a *caic*. But working as they do, and sleeping as they
sleep, they are always dirty, more or less, even although, for
a wonder, they make use of soap. In their leisure hours many
play at cards, and when not playing, one great amusement of the

men is to lie on the ground and play with their children; for whom, however, they care less when they get older. Many of these children of the *duar* arrive at the age of ten or fourteen years without ever having seen a house, and it is curious to hear an account of their behaviour when taken into the service of Moors or Europeans in the cities; how they feel the walls, stamp on the floors, and with what intense emotion they look out of a window, or run down a staircase. The principal event in these wandering villages is a marriage. The parents and friends of the bride, with a great noise of firing of muskets and shouting, bring her seated on a camel to the husband's *duar*. She is wrapped in a white or blue mantle, perfumed, with her nails tinted with henna and her eyebrows blackened with burnt cork, and is generally fattened for the occasion by the use of a herb called *ebba*, much in vogue among young girls. The husband's *duar* meantime has invited the neighbouring *duars* to the festival, and from a hundred to two hundred men, mounted and armed, respond to the invitation. The bride dismounts from her camel before the door of her husband's tent, and, seated on a seat decorated with flowers and fringes, looks on at the festival; whilst the men go through the *powder play*, the women and girls, disposed in a circle before her, dance to the music of a fife and drum, around a cloth spread upon the ground, into which every guest in passing throws a coin for the newly married pair, and a sort of crier announces the amount of the offering in a loud voice, with good wishes for the donor. Towards evening, the dancing and firing over, every one sits down on the ground, and great dishes of *cùscùssù*, roast chickens, sheep on the spit, tea, sweetmeats, and fruits are carried round; the supper being prolonged up to midnight. The next day, the bride, dressed in white, with a red scarf bound over her mouth and a hood upon her head, goes, accompanied by her friends and relations, to the neighbouring *duars* to collect more money. This done, the husband goes back to his labour, the wife to hers, and

love takes to flight. When any one dies, the dances are
repeated. The relations nearest to the defunct record his
virtues; the rest, crowded about him, dance with gestures and
attitudes of grief, cover themselves with dust, tear their hair,
and scratch their faces. After which they wash the corpse,
wrap it in a piece of new cloth, carry it on a bier to the
cemetery, and bury it, lying on the right side, with its face
turned to the east. These are their customs and usages, as one
may say, patent to all the world; but who knows their more
private doings? Who can follow the clue by which life in
a *duar* is ordered? Who can say how first love speaks, how
slander is disseminated, in what strange forms, by what strange
accidents, adultery, jealousy, envy are produced; what virtues
shine, what sacrifices are consummated, what abominable and
perverted passions are rife under the shadow of those tents?
Who can trace the origin of their monstrous superstitions?
Who can clear up the odd mingling of Pagan and Christian
traditions in their religious rites: the sign of the cross made
on the skin, the vague belief in satyrs where forked elm-trees
are found, the image carried in triumph at the budding of
the grain, the name of Mary invoked for the help of women
in childbirth, the circular dances resembling those of the
worshippers of the sun? One thing only is certain and
manifest: their poverty. They live on the scant produce of
ill-cultivated ground, borne down by heavy and often changing
taxes, collected by the sheik or head of the *duar*, elected by
themselves, but directly under the orders of the governor of the
province. They pay the governor, in money or produce, the
tenth part of the harvest, and one franc a head for cattle.
One hundred francs a year is paid for every tract of land
corresponding to the labour of a yoke of oxen. The Sultan,
at the principal festivals of the year, exacts a " present "
equivalent to five francs per tent. They pay money or furnish
provisions at the order of the governors whenever the Sultan,
or a Pasha, or an ambassador, or a body of soldiers passes by.

Besides this, any one who has money is exposed to the extortions of the governor, veiled or excused by no pretext whatever, but practised with insolence and violence. To be esteemed rich is a misfortune. Whoever has a small sum laid by, buries it, spends in secret, feigns poverty and hunger. No one accepts a blackened coin in payment, even when he knows it to be good, because it may look as if it had been buried in the ground, and cause the suspicion of hidden treasure. When a rich man dies, the heirs, in order to avoid ruin, offer a present to the governor. Presents are offered to secure justice, to prevent persecution, to avoid being reduced to die of hunger. And when at last hunger has them by the throat and despair blinds them, they strike their tents, seize their muskets, and raise the signal of revolt. What happens then? The Sultan unchains three thousand mounted fiends and sows death throughout the rebellious district. His soldiers cut off heads, lift cattle, carry off women, burn grain fields, reduce the land to a desert and strew it with ashes slaked in blood, and then return to announce the extinction of the rebellion. If the rebellion extends, and the armies and arts of the Government are vain, what advantage do the rebels gain beyond a few short days of warlike liberty, bought by thousands of lives? They can elect another Sultan, and provoke a dynastic war between province and province, behind which lurks a worse despotism than before; and so it goes on from century to century.

On the morning of the tenth the caravan resumed its march, escorted by the three hundred of Beni-Hassan and their chief, Abd-Allah—*servant of God.*

All that morning we travelled over a plain covered with fields of barley, wheat, and buck-wheat, interspersed with large tracts of wild fennel and flowers, and dotted with groups of trees and black tents, which last resembled in the distance those heaps of charcoal that are seen on the Tuscan *maremma.* We met more cattle, horses, camels, and Arabs than on the preceding days. Far away in front extended a mountain chain

LAB-EL-BARODA IN THE CAMP OF THE ITALIAN EXPEDITION.

of a most delicate grey tint, and in the middle distance glimmered two white *cube*—the first illuminated by the sun, the second hardly visible. They were the tombs of the saints Sidi-Ghedar and Sidi-Hassem, between which lie the confines of the land of Beni-Hassan. Our camp was to be pitched near the last.

Some time, however, before arriving at that point, Governor Sidi-Abd-Allah, who, from the moment of our departure, had seemed anxious and thoughtful, drew near to the Ambassador, and signified his wish to speak. Mohammed Ducali came up quickly. "The Ambassador from Italy will pardon me," said the haughty chief, "if I venture to ask permission to turn back with my men."

The Ambassador demanded why.

"Because," answered Sidi-Abd-Allah, contracting his black brows, "my own house is not secure."

Is that all? thought we. Only two miles away too! What an agreeable existence must be that of a Governor of Beni-Hassan!

The Ambassador consented; the chief took his hand and pressed it to his breast with an energetic expression of gratitude. This done, he turned his horse, and in a few minutes the many-coloured, ragged, and terrible crew was nothing but a cloud of dust upon the horizon.

CHAPTER VIII.

SIDI-HASSEM.

THE province we were about to enter was a kind of colony, divided into farms among a large number of soldiers' families, in each of which military service is obligatory for all the sons; thus every boy is born a soldier, serves, as he can, from his very infancy, and receives a fixed pay before he is able to handle a musket. These military families are also exempt from taxes, and their property is inalienable as long as male descendants exist. They thus constitute a regular militia, disciplined and faithful, by means of which the Government can *devour*—according to the popular expression—any rebellious province, without fear that the tool will fly off the handle. They may be called a militia of collectors of revenue, paying the Government more than they cost; for in Morocco the army is a servant of the finances, and the principal tool of the administrative machine is the sword.

We had scarcely passed the boundaries of Beni-Hassen when we saw in the distance a troop of horsemen galloping towards us, preceded by a green banner. Contrary to custom, they were spread out in two long lines, one behind the other, with their officers in front.

At about twenty paces off they stopped abruptly. Their Commandant—a big old man with a white beard, a benevolent aspect, and a lofty turban—came forward and took the Ambassador's hand, saying, "You are welcome! you are welcome!" And then to us, "Welcome! welcome! welcome!"

We resumed our march. The new horsemen were very different from the Beni-Hassen. They had clean garments and shining arms; almost all wore yellow boots embroidered with red; their sabres had handles of rhinoceros hide, their mantles were blue, their caftans white, with green girdles. Many of them were old—those petrified old men for whom eternity seems to have begun. Some were very young—two in particular not more than ten years old, handsome and full of life, looking at us with a smiling air, as though they were thinking, "Come, you are not such scarecrows as we had expected to see." There was one black old man of such tall stature that if he had taken his feet out of the stirrups they would have touched the ground. One of the officers wore stockings.

In about half-an-hour we met another company with a red banner, commanded by an old *Caid,* who joined themselves to the first; and from time to time other groups of four, eight, fifteen horsemen, each with its banner, who came to swell our escort. When all had arrived, the usual firing and charging went on.

It was evident that they were regular soldiers; they manœuvred with more regularity and order than any we had seen. They had a new play. One would dart forward at full speed, another behind him, *ventre à terre.* Suddenly, the first would rise in his stirrups, turn and fire right into the chest of the pursuer, who at the same instant discharged his musket into the first one's side; so that, had they been firing with ball, both would have fallen dead at the same moment. The horse of one who was flying in full career fell, and threw his rider to such a distance that we thought he must be killed; but

MANŒUVRES OF THE CAVALRY.

in a moment he was up and in the saddle, and rushing about
with more fury than ever.   Each one had his cry.   "Take
care!—take care!   Bear witness all!   It is I!   Here comes
death!   Place for the barber!" (he was the soldiers' barber).
And one shouted, to the manifest amusement of his companions, "*Alla mia depinta!*"   The interpreters explained that
he meant, "To my lady, who is as beautiful as a picture"—
odd enough for one of a people who have portraiture in horror,

The Two Brothers.

and who cannot even have a clear idea of it.   The two
little lads fired and shouted together, "Place for the brothers!"
pointing their muskets downwards, and bending to the
saddle-bow.

In this manner we arrived near the *cuba* of Sidi-Hassem,
where our camp was to be pitched.

Poor Hamed Ben-Kasen Buhammei!   Until now I have
but glanced at him; but, remembering how I saw him that
morning—he, General of the armies of the Schereef—helping
to plant the supports of the Ambassador's tent, I feel the need

of expressing my admiration and gratitude towards him.   What
a good fellow of a General!   From the moment of our departure he had not bastinadoed soldier or servant; had never
shown ill-temper; always the first to rise, and the last to go
to bed; never had allowed to transpire, even to the most prying
eye, that his stipend of forty francs a month might seem a
trifle scanty; had not a particle of self-conceit; helped us to
mount, saw that our saddles were secure, gave a passing blow
with his stick to our restive mules; was always ready for
everything and everybody; rested, crouched like an humble
mule-driver, near our tents; smiled when we smiled; offered
us *cùscùssù*; sprang to his feet at a sign from the Ambassador,
like a puppet on wires; prayed, like a good Mussulman, five
times a day; counted the eggs of the *muna*, presided at the
killing of sheep, looked over the artists' sketch-books without
blenching; was, in short, *the* man of all others whom his
Imperial Majesty should have chosen for that mission among
all the crew of barefooted Generals.   Hamed Ben-Kasen often
related with pride that his father had been a General in the
war with Spain, and sometimes spoke of his sons, who were
with their mother at Mechinez, his native city.   "It is three
months," he would say, with a sigh, "since I have seen
them."

That day, after having witnessed the presentation of the
muna, when there was ·a monstrous dish of *cùscùssù* that took
five men to carry it, we took refuge, as usual, in our tents, to
endure, also as usual, the forty degrees centigrade which lasted
from noon until four o'clock, during which time the camp was
immersed in profound silence.   At four life woke again.   The
artists took their brushes, the doctor received the sick, one went
to bathe, another to fire at a mark, another to hunt, another to
walk, another to visit a friend in his tent, to see the escort
charge, to visit the cook in his struggle with Africa, to go to
the nearest *duar*, and thus every one at dinner-time had something to tell, and conversation burst forth like a firework.

At sunset I went with the Commandant to see the escort at
their usual exercises, in a vast field near the camp. There we
found about a hundred Arabs sitting in a row along the edge of
a ditch looking on. As soon as they discovered us they rose and
came in groups to follow us. We pretended not to see them.
For a few minutes not one of them spoke ; then one said something that set the others laughing. Then another, and a third

spoke, and everybody
laughed as before. They
were evidently laughing
at us, and we were
not long in discovering
that their laughter cor-
responded with our move-
ments and the inflections
of our voices. It was the
most natural thing in the
world ; to them we were
ridiculous. We were cu-
rious to know what they
were saying, and as one
of the interpreters was
passing, made a secret
sign for him to come and
translate, which he did.
Presently one made

The Cùscùssù Dish.

an observation which was received with a burst of laughter.
" He says," said Morteo, " that he does not know what the
skirts of your coats are for, unless to hide your tails." Again,
" He says that the parting up the back of your head is the
road where certain insects make the *lab-el-baroda.*" A third
speech, and a third shout of laughter. " He says that these
Christians are strange creatures ; that in their ambition to seem
tall they put vases on their heads and two props under their
heels."

At this point a dog from the camp came and lay down at our feet. There was a remark and a loud yell of laughter. "This is rather too much!" said Morteo; "he says that a dog has come to lie down with the other dogs. I will teach them——" As he spoke, he turned abruptly to the Arabs and said something in a tone of menace. It was like a flash of lightning. In one instant they had all vanished.

Poor fellows, let us be just! they were not so far wrong after all! Ten times a day, while they skirmished about us on their superb horses, we remarked to each other : " Yes, we are civilised, we are the representatives of a great nation, we have more science in our heads, we ten men, than exists in the whole empire of the Schereefs ; but planted on our mules, dressed in these clothes, with these hats, in these colours, among them, Goodness knows, we are hideous ! " And it was true. The last among those ragged figures on horseback was more noble, more dignified, handsomer, more worthy of a lady's glance, than all the dandies of Europe in a bunch.

At table that evening there was another curious little scene. The two oldest of the Caids of the escort came in and sat down, one on each side of the Ambassador. He asked them whether they had ever heard of Italy. Both together, eagerly making the sign of " no " with the hand, replied, in the tone of those who wish to dissipate a suspicion, " Never ! never ! " The Ambassador, with the patience of a master, gave them some geographical and political information respecting our mysterious country. They listened with wide-open eyes and gaping mouths, like children.

" And how many people live in your country ? " one asked.

" Twenty-five millions," answered the Ambassador.

They gave a sign of astonishment. " And Morocco," asked the other, " how many millions has it ? "

" Four," replied the Ambassador, feeling his ground.

" Only four ! " they exclaimed ingenuously, looking at each other. Evidently these two brave Generals knew no more about

Morocco than they did about Italy; and perhaps as little about their own province in Morocco.

Signor Morteo showed them a photograph of his wife, saying, "Allow me to present my wife."

They looked and looked at it with much complacency, and then asked in one voice, "And the others?" Either they did not know, or had forgotten, that we unhappy Christians are limited to one.

That night there was no possibility of sleep. The hens clucked, the dogs barked, the sheep bleated, the horses neighed, the sentinels sang, the water-sellers tinkled their bells, the soldiers quarrelled over the *muna*, the servants tumbled over the tent cords; the camp was like a market-place. But we had only four more days to travel, and—a magic word of consolation —Fez!

M

CHAPTER IX.

ZEGUTA.

A Locust.

WE started for Zeguta at an early hour in the morning, cheered by the thought that that day we should see the mountains of Fez. A light autumnal breeze was blowing, and a slight mist veiled the prospect. A throng of Arabs, muffled in their mantles, looked on as we left the camp; the soldiers of the escort kept together in a compact body; the children of the *duar* watched us with sleepy eyes over the hedges and from the tents. But soon the sun shone out, the horsemen scattered, the air resounded with shots and yells, everything became full of colour, light, and animation, and immediately, as happens in that country, to the chill of autumn succeeded the ardent heat of summer.

Among my notes of that morning I find one which says, laconically, "Locusts." I remember to have noticed a distant field which appeared to be moving, and perceived that the appearance was produced by a vast number of green grasshoppers which were advancing towards us in great jumps. Selim, who was riding at my side, gave me an admirably picturesque description of the invasion of these formidable insects, and I remember it word for word; but I cannot render the effect of his gesture, voice, and look, which were more expressive than his words. " It is a terrible thing, sir! They come from there (pointing towards the south). A black cloud. You can hear the noise from afar off. They advance, and advance, and they have their Sultan, the Sultan Jeraad, who guides them. They cover roads and fields, houses, *duars*, and woods. The cloud grows and grows, and comes and comes and comes, and eats and eats and eats, passes rivers, passes walls, passes fires; destroys grass, flowers, leaves, fruit, grain, bark of trees, and goes and goes. Nothing stays it, neither the tribe with fire, nor the Sultan with all his army, nor all the people of Morocco gathered together. Heaps of locusts dead; forward the living locusts! Ten die, a hundred are born! A hundred die, a thousand are born! Roads covered; gardens covered; sea shore covered; all green, all in motion, alive, dead, smell, plague, famine, the curse of heaven!" So indeed it is. The horrid smell that emanates from myriads of dead locusts sometimes produces contagious fevers, and, to cite one example, the terrible pestilence that depopulated in 1799 the cities and country of Barbary broke out after one of their invasions. When the advance guard of their devastating army appears, the Arabs go to meet it in squads of four or five hundred with sticks and fire; but they succeed only in turning it a little from its road, and it often happens that one tribe turning it aside towards the territory of another, war against the locusts is suddenly turned into civil war. The only force that can liberate the country from this scourge is a favourable wind which drives them into the sea, where they are drowned, and are thrown afterwards in heaps upon the coast; and the only comfort the inhabitants can take when the favourable wind is wanting, is to eat their enemies, which they do,

M 2

THE CAMEL CONVEYANCE.

before they have deposited their eggs, boiled, and seasoned with salt, pepper, and vinegar. They have the flavour of shrimps, and as many as four hundred can be eaten in a day.

At about two miles from the camp we rejoined a part of the caravan that was carrying to Fez the presents from Victor Emanuel.* There were camels in pairs, one behind the other, with two long poles suspended from the crupper, on which the cases were carried. Some Arabs on foot, and mounted soldiers, accompanied them. At the head of the caravan was a cart drawn by two bullocks; the first cart we saw in Morocco! It was made at Laracce on purpose, after the pattern, I believe, of the first vehicle that ever appeared upon the earth—a heavy deformed body, upon two wheels all of one piece, without spokes; the strangest and most ridiculous affair that can be imagined. But to the natives, the most of whom had never seen a cart, it was a wonder. They came from all sides to see it, pointed it out to one another, followed and preceded it, and talked about it with excited gestures. Meantime our mules, unused to such an object, gave signs of surprise, and planting themselves on their four legs refused to pass it. Selim himself regarded it with complacency, as if he said to himself, " It was made in our country." And he was excusable, since in all Morocco there exist about as many carts as pianofortes, which latter, if I may believe the assertion of the French Consul, are about a dozen ; and also it seems that there is in that country a national anti-pathy against every kind of vehicle. The authorities of Tangiers, for example, prohibited Prince Frederic of Hesse Darmstadt, who was in that city in 1839, from going out in a carriage. The Prince wrote to the Sultan, offering to pave the principal street at his own expense, if he would permit what the authorities denied him. " I permit it," answered the Sultan, " and wil-lingly ; but on one condition—that the carriage shall be without wheels ; because, being protector of the faithful, I cannot expose my subjects to be crushed by a Christian." And the Prince, in

* The then King of Italy. Died in 1878.

CONVEYING THE PRESENTS FOR THE SULTAN TO FEZ.

order to make the thing ridiculous, availed himself of the permission with the conditions,
and there are still at Tangiers persons who remem-
ber having seen him going
about the city in a carriage
without wheels, suspended
between two mules.

We arrived at last at
those blessed hills which we
had been looking forward
to for three days with impatient longing. After a
long climb we entered a
narrow gorge, called in
Arabic Ben-Tinca, where
we were obliged to pass
one by one, and came out
upon a beautiful flowery
valley, quite solitary, where
the escort scattered gaily,
filling the air with songs
and cries of joy.

At the bottom of the
valley we met another escort
from the territory of the
military colonies, which took
the place of the former one.

They were about one
hundred horsemen, some
very old and some very
young, black, and hairy;
some were mounted on stu-

One of the Escort of Abu-Ben-Gileli.

pendous horses, caparisoned with great pomp. The Caid, Abu-Ben-
Gileli, was a robust old man, of severe aspect and reserved manners.

At a certain moment the Ambassador and the Captain, accompanied by Hamed Ben-Kasen and a few soldiers, left the caravan to ascend a mountain called Selfat, a few miles distant; the rest of us continued on the regular route.

A short time after their departure there came towards us an Arab boy of sixteen or eighteen years of age, and almost naked, driving two unwilling oxen before him with a whip.

The Caid, Abu-Ben-Gileli, stopped his horse, and called

A Pair of Oxen.

him. We learned afterwards that this boy was to attach his oxen to the cart that we had seen, and was several hours behind his time.

The poor lad, all trembling, presented himself before the Caid. The latter asked some questions, to which the boy replied, stammering, and pale as a corpse.

Then the Caid turned towards the soldiers and said, coldly, "Fifty *bastonate*."

Three robust men sprang from their horses. The poor young fellow, without a word, without even lifting his eyes to the face of his judge, threw himself face downwards on the ground, according to the custom, with arms and legs stretched out.

It all happened in a moment. The stick was yet in the air, when the Commandant and others had sprung forward, and declared that the brutal punishment could not be permitted. The Caid bowed his head. The lad rose from the

Punishment of the Bastinado.

ground, pale and convulsed, looking with an expression of astonishment and terror from his preservers to the Caid.

"Go," said the interpreter; "you are free!"

"Oh!" he cried, with an indescribable accent, and vanished. We resumed our march. I have seen a man killed, but never have I experienced so profound a feeling of horror as that which assailed me at the sight of that half-naked boy stretched on the ground to receive his fifty blows with a stick. And after the horror, my blood rushed to my face with indig-

nation against the Caid, the Sultan, Morocco, and barbarism.
But it is true that second thoughts are best. After a moment,
I thought—And we, how many years is it since we abolished
the stick? How many since it was in use in Austria, in Prussia,
and in others of the European States? This reflection calmed
my anger, and left me only a sentiment of bitterness. If any
one wants to know in what fashion the bastinado is carried on in
Morocco, it is enough to say that sometimes, the operation over,
the victim is carried to the cemetery.

From thence to Zeguta the caravan passed from hill to hill,
from valley to valley, through fields of grain and barley, and
verdant plains surrounded by aloes, cactus, wild olive, dwarf
oaks, arbutus, myrtle, and other flowering shrubs. We saw no
living soul nor any tents. The country was solitary, silent, and
all overgrown, like an enchanted garden. Coming to a rising
ground, we saw the blue summits of the mountains of Fez suddenly appearing, as if they had thrust up their heads to
look at us; and at the hottest time in the day we reached
Zeguta.

It proved to be one of the most beautiful of the places we
had yet seen. The tents were pitched on the slope of a hill in a
large rocky cavity, in the form of an amphitheatre, around the
sides of which the accidents of the ground and the passage of
men and animals had formed something resembling rows of seats
or steps, which at that time were swarming with Arabs seated in
a semicircle, as if looking on at a spectacle. In front a broad
valley of a shell-like form opened with all its lovely variety of
colour, according to the cultivation, in squares of green, yellow,
red, violet, and white, like a great chessboard made of silk and
velvet. With the glass could be seen, on the more distant hills,
here a string of tents, there a white *cuba* among aloe plants;
beyond, a camel, a crouching Arab, cattle, a group of women—a
life so still and scattered that it threw into relief the profound
peacefulness of the scene better than complete solitude could
have done. And over all this beauty was spread a white and

burning sky that dazzled the eyes and obliged one to stand with drooping head.

But I remember the encampment at Zeguta less for its beauty than for an experiment we made there with the famous *kif*.

Kif, for those who do not know it, is the leaf of a kind of hemp, called *hashish,* known all over the East for its intoxicating quality.   It is much in use in Morocco, and it may be said that all those Moors and Arabs who are met in the streets of the cities dragging themselves about, and looking with a dull stupefied expression, like men who have just had a blow on the head, are victims of this deleterious drug.   The greater part of them smoke it, mixed with a little tobacco, in small clay pipes; others eat it in the form of a sweatmeat called *madjun,* made of butter, honey, nutmeg, and cloves.   The effects of it are most curious. Doctor Miguerez, who had tried it, often told me about it, saying, among other things, that he had been seized with a fit of irresistible laughter, and that he imagined himself to be lifted from the ground, so that passing under a lofty archway, he had stooped his head for fear of striking it.   Stimulated by curiosity, I had more than once asked him to give me a dose of *madjun*—a little, not enough to make me lose my wits, but enough to let me experience at least one or two of the wonders that he related.   The good doctor at first excused himself, declaring that it was better to try it at Fez ; but he yielded at last to my entreaties, and the experiment was made at Zeguta, where, much against his will, he finally presented me with the wished-for morsel on a small plate.   We were at table, and if I am not mistaken the two artists shared it with me, but I do not remember how it affected them.   It was a soft paste of a violet colour, and smelt like pomatum.   For about half an hour, from the soup to the fruit, I felt nothing, and chaffed the doctor for his timidity. But he only said, " Wait a bit ! " and smiled.   Presently I was conscious of a feeling of great hilarity, and knew that I was talking very quickly. Then I laughed at everything that others said, or that I said myself; every word seemed to me the purest wit and humour; I laughed at the servants, at my companions, at the figures on the plates, at the forms of the bottles, at the colour of the cheese I was eating. Suddenly I was aware that my wits were wandering, and I tried to fix my thoughts upon something serious. I thought of the boy who was to have been bastinadoed in the morning. Poor boy! I was moved with compassion. I should have liked to take him to Italy, educate him, give him a career. I loved him like a son. And the Caid, too, Abu-Ben-Gileli, poor old man! I loved the Caid like a father. And the soldiers of the escort!—all good fellows, ready to defend me, to risk their lives for me. I loved them like brothers. I loved the Algerians also, and why not? I thought; are they not of the same race?—and what a race! We are all brothers, we ought to love each other; and I threw my arms round the neck of the doctor, who was laughing. From this delight I suddenly fell into a deep and vague melancholy. I remembered the persons whom I had offended, the pain I had inflicted on those who loved me, and was oppressed by poignant remorse and regret; I seemed to hear voices in my ears speaking in tones of loving reproach; I repented, I asked pardon, I furtively wiped away big tears that were in my eyes. Then there rose in my mind a crowd of strange and contrasted images that vanished as quickly as they came; forgotten friends of my childhood, words of a dialect unused for twenty years, faces of women, my old regiment, William the Silent, Paris, my publisher Barbera, a beaver hat that I had when I was a boy, the Acropolis at Athens, the bill of an innkeeper at Seville, and a thousand other absurdities. I remember confusedly the amused looks of my companions at table. From time to time I closed my eyes, and opened them again, unconscious of the passage of time, and ignorant whether I had slept or not. My thoughts sparkled and went out like fireflies, intricate and inextricable. At one moment I saw Ussi, with his face lengthened like a reflection in a convex mirror; the Vice-Consul, with his visage a foot in breadth; all the others attenuated, swollen, contorted, like fantastic caricatures, making the most impossible grimaces; and I laughed, and wagged my head, and dreamed, and thought that they were all crazy, that we were in another world, that what I saw was not true, that I was ill, that I could not understand what had happened, that I did not know where I was. Then all was darkness and silence. When I came to myself I was in my tent, stretched on the bed, and the doctor, standing beside me with a candle in his hand, was saying, with a smile, " It is over; but let it be the last, as it was the first time."

CHAPTER X.

FROM ZEGUTA TO SAGAT.

WHILST I was running here and there in search of my mule—  which, I do not know how or why, was at last found among the baggage—the members of the Embassy departed. I still had time to come up with them, but in leaving the camp and going down a rocky path my mule stumbled, the saddle slipped, and literature, as represented in my person, was precipitated to the ground. It took half-an-hour to set matters straight again ; and meantime, adieu to the Embassy ! I had to make the journey alone, followed afar off by a limping servitor, who could hardly arrive in time, in case of an assault, to see me breathe my last breath. May the will of Allah be done ! The country is deserted, and the sky cloudy. From time to time I can see, on the summit of distant heights, a gay cavalcade, among which I recognise the Ambassador's white horse and Selim's red caftan, and then I do not feel so much alone; but the cavalcade vanishes, and solitude once more oppresses my heart. In an hour's time I rejoin the rear-guard of twelve horsemen, led by old Abu-Ben-Gileli, the Caid, who gives me a terrible glance that I feel all down my spine. I smile with humility and pass on. Coming out of the lovely valley on which our encampment looked, I enter another spacious valley, flanked by steep hills clothed with aloe and olive, forming two great green walls to the right and left of a broad straight road, closed at the end by a curtain of blue mountains. I meet a few Arabs, who stop and look amazed at seeing me without an escort. Will they attack me, or no? One goes to a tree, and, hastily tearing off a branch, runs towards me with it. It has come! I stop my mule and grasp my pistol. He laughs, and hands me the branch, explaining that it is to beat my lazy mule with. At that moment two soldiers of the escort come galloping to meet me: my hour is not yet come. The two soldiers place themselves one on either side, and drive forward my quadruped with blows from the butts of their muskets, saying, " *Embasceador! Embasceador!* " The Ambassador has sent them back to see what has become of me. They deserve a reward. I stop and offer them a small bottle of wine, which I take from my pocket. They say neither yes nor no, but look smiling at each other, and then sign to me that they have never drunk wine. " Try it," I say, with a gesture. One takes the bottle, pours a few drops in the palm of his hand, licks it up, and remains thoughtful for a moment. The other does the same. Then they laugh, look at each other, and make signs that it is good. " Drink, then." One empties half the bottle at a gulp; the other finishes it. Then they each place a hand on their stomach, and turn up their eyes to heaven. We resume our road. We meet Arabs —men, women, and children—who all look at me with surprise. One of them says something which is answered by the

soldiers with an emphatic negative.   He said, " Here is a
Christian who has been robbing the Ambassador."

We saw some white villages on the top of the rising ground
that bordered the valley.   *Cube,* palms, fruit-trees, flowering
oleanders, and rose-gardens were visible.   The country was
brilliantly green, and began to show here and there traces of
division into farms.   At last we entered a narrow, rocky gorge,
and, issuing thence, found ourselves at the camp.   We are
upon the banks of the Miches—an affluent of the Sebù—near
a little bridge built of masonry, and in a semicircle of rocky
hills.   The grey sky, like a leaden roof, sends down a pale
dull light.   The thermometer marks forty degrees Centigrade:
we are constrained to remain seven hours motionless in our
tents.   The air is heavy and burning.   No sound is heard
but the grasshopper's chirp and Ducalè's guitar.   A profound
ennui broods over the entire encampment.   But towards evening
there is a change.   A light shower refreshes the air; a shaft
of rays, darting like a stream of electric light through the
opening of the gorge, gilds one half the camp; couriers arrive
from Tangiers and Fez, and Arabs from the villages.   Two-
thirds of the caravan are in the river, and the dinner is enlivened by the apparition of a new personage, come from the
great city of the Schereefs : the Moor Schellah, another of
the protégés of the Legation, who has a suit pending with
the Sultan's Government—the most voluminous turban, the
most rotund visage, the most comfortable and unctuous of fat
Moors that we have seen between this and Tangiers.   The
next morning at dawn we resumed our march without other
escort than the forty soldiers commanded by Hamed Ben-
Kasen.   A revolt had broken out in the confines of Algiers,
and all the cavalry in Fez had been sent against the rebels.
" We shall see many heads hanging over the gates of Fez,"
said Ducalè.   After two hours' journey among the broom-clad
hills, we came out upon the vast table-land of Fez, encircled
by mountains and hills, golden with grain, sprinkled with large

duar, watered by the river of the Azure Fountain, which empties into the Miches, and by the Pearl river, affluent of the Sebù, which divides into two parts the sacred city of the empire. Flocks of cranes, wild geese, doves, pheasants, and heron flew over it; and the luxuriant vegetation, full of smiling peace and light, made it like one vast garden. We encamped on the bank of the Azure Fountain river. The day flew by with lightning speed, what with hunting, visiting the *duar,* Jews coming from Fez to relate the great preparations that were being made, and messengers from the Court bringing the Sultan's salutations. Arabs came, fording the river in families— first the camel, then the men, then the women with their children on their backs, then the boys and girls, then the dogs

Schellah, the Moor.

swimming. Caravans passed; crowds of curious lookers-on appeared. The sunset was exquisite, and the night more luminous than our eyes had ever beheld. In the morning at daybreak we were again on the march. We re-entered the hilly region, turned to descend into the plain, and

N

threaded a winding road between two banks that hid the horizon.

A sonorous voice cried out, " Behold Fez ! " Everybody stopped. Straight before us, at a few miles distance, at the foot of the mountains, lay a forest of towers, minarets, and palms, veiled by a light mist. A joyful shout of " Here we are ! " broke from every lip—in Italian, in Spanish, in French, Arabic, Genoese, Sicilian, and Neapolitan ; and to the first brief silence of astonishment succeeded a buzz of conversation. We encamped for the last time at the foot of Mount Tagat on the shore of the Pearl river, at about one hour and a half from Fez.

Here throughout the day there was a coming and going and a bustle that made it seem like the general head-quarters of an army in time of war. Messengers from the Sultan, from the Prime Minister, from the Grand Chamberlain, from the governor, officers, majordomos, merchants, relatives of the Moors of the caravan, all well-dressed people, neat, ceremonious, surrounded by the air of a court and a metropolis, speaking with grave voices and dignified gesture, and telling of the formidable army, the immense crowd, the delicious palace that awaited us. Our entrance into Fez was fixed for eight o'clock the next morning. At daydawn we were all afoot. There was great use of razors, brushes, combs, and currycombs, and an excitement of spirits that made up for all the tedium of the journey. The Ambassador put on his gilded cap, Hamed Ben-Kasen his dress sabre, Selim his red caftan, Civo a green handkerchief on his head (a sign of high solemnity) ; the servants came out in white mantles ; the soldiers' arms shone in the sun ; the Italians put on the best they had in their trunks. We were about a hundred in all, and it may be affirmed that Italy never had an embassy more oddly composed, more gorgeous in colour, more joyously impatient, or more eagerly expected than this one. The weather is splendid, the horses prance, robes float

out in the morning breeze, every face is animated, every
eye is fixed upon the Ambassador, who counts the minutes
on his watch. It is eight o'clock — a sign — every one is
in the saddle—and we advance with hearts beating high in
expectation.

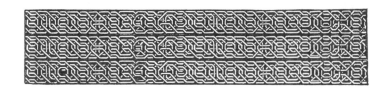

CHAPTER XI.

FEZ.

WE had not advanced half a mile towards the city when we were surrounded by a throng of Moors and Arabs, come from Fez and from the country round, on foot and on horseback, on mules and on donkeys, two and two, like the ancient Numidians, so eager to see us that the soldiers of our escort are obliged to make use of the butt-end of their muskets to keep them from pressing upon us. The ground being low, the city, whose castellated walls we had seen from the camp, remains for some time hidden. Then all at once it reappears, and between us and the walls we can see an immense white and crimson mass, like a myriad of lilies and roses trembling in the breeze. The city vanishes again, and again appears, but much nearer this time; and between us and it, the people, the army, the court, and a pomp and splendour and oddity that are beyond my powers of description.

A company of officers on horseback come galloping to meet us, and, dividing in the middle, pass to the rear and join themselves in our escort. Behind them comes a troop of horsemen, splendidly attired and mounted on superb horses, preceded by a Moor of tall stature, with a white turban and a rose-coloured caftan. He is the Grand Chamberlain, Hadji Mohammed Ben-Aissa, accompanied by his suite, who, having welcomed the Ambassador in the Sultan's name, joins the escort.

We advance between two rows of infantry soldiers, who with difficulty keep back the crowd. What soldiers they are ! There are old men and mature men, and boys of fifteen, twelve, and even nine years of age, dressed in scarlet, with bare legs and yellow slippers, ranged along in single file without regard to height, with their captains in front. Each one presents in his own fashion his rusty musket and his crooked bayonet. Some stand with one foot foremost, some with legs apart, some with their heads on their shoulders, some with their chins on their breasts. Some have put their red jackets on their heads to shelter them from the sun. Here and there is a tambourine, a trumpet, five or six banners, one beside the other — red, yellow,

The Grand Chamberlain, Hadji Mohammed Ben-Aissa.

green, orange—carried as crosses are carried in a procession. There seems to be no division into squadrons or companies. They look like paper soldiers stuck up in a row by boys. There are blacks, mulattoes, whites, and faces of an indefinable colour; men of gigantic stature beside boys who are scarcely old enough to hold a gun; bent old men with long white beards, leaning on their neighbours; savage faces, making the effect, in that uniform, of dressed-up monkeys. They all look at us with open eyes and mouth, and their line stretches farther than we can see.

A second troop of horsemen advances, on the left. It is the old Governor, Gilali Ben-Amù, followed by eighteen chiefs of inferior degree and by the flower of the aristocracy of Fez, all

Soldiers of the Sultan.

dressed in white from head to foot, like a company of priests— austere visages, black beards, silken caics, gilded housings. Saluting us, they circle round, and join our cortege.

We go forward, still between two lines of soldiers, behind whom presses a white and hooded crowd who devour us with their eyes. They are always the same soldiers, for the most part boys, wearing the fez, with red jackets and bare legs. They have blue, white, or green drawers. Some are in their shirt sleeves; some hold their muskets on their shoulder, some rest them on the ground; some press forward, some hang back.

The officers are dressed according to their fancy—zouaves, turcos, Greeks, Albanians, Turks—with arabesque embroidery of gold

The Governor of Fez, Gilali Ben-Amū.

and silver, with scimitars, swords, curved poignards, horse pistols. Some wear the boots of a groom, and some yellow boots without heels; some are all in crimson, some all in white;

some in green, and looking like masquerade devils. Here and there among them may be seen a European face, looking at us sadly and with sympathy. As many as ten banners are ranged in a row together. The trumpets sound as we pass. A woman's arm protrudes itself between the soldiers' heads, and threatens us with clenched fist. The walls of the city seem to recede before us, and the two lines of soldiers to extend interminably.

Another troop of cavaliers, more splendid than the first, comes to meet us. It is the aged Minister of War, Sid-Abd-Alla Ben-Hamed, black, mounted on a white horse with sky-blue trappings; and with him are the military governors of provinces, the commandant of the garrison, and a numerous staff of officers crowned with snowy turbans, and wearing caftans of every known colour.

It is now more than half-an-hour that we have been proceeding between the two lines of soldiers, and some one has counted more than four thousand. On one side is drawn out the cavalry; on the other a nameless and heterogeneous mass of men and boys, dressed in divers uniforms, or rather fragments of uniforms, some with arms and some without, cloaked and uncloaked, with uncovered heads, or heads bound with a shapeless rag, shirtless for the most part; faces from the desert, from the coast, from the mountains; shaven heads, and heads ornamented with long braids; giants and dwarfs—people gathered from Heaven knows where, to make a show and inspire terror. And behind them, on the rising ground that borders the way, an innumerable throng of veiled women, screaming and gesticulating, in wonder, anger, or pleasure, and holding up their children to see us.

We approach the walls at a point where there is a venerable gate crowned with battlements. A band bursts into music, and at the same moment all the drums and trumpets rend the air with a mighty crash. Then our ranks are broken up, and there is a general rush and confusion of magistrates, courtiers,

ENTRY INTO FEZ.

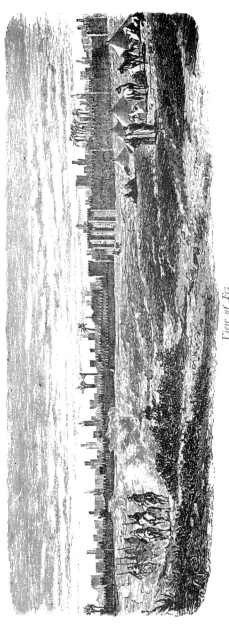

View of Fez

ministers, generals, officials and slaves; our escort is scattered, our servants dispersed, and we ourselves divided from each other. There is a torrent of turbans and horses rolling and twisting about us with irresistible impetus; a confusion of colours, a phantasmagoria of faces, a noise of harsh voices, a grandeur and savagery that at once delight and bewilder. Passing in at the gate, we expect to see the houses of the city, but are still between castellated walls and towers; to the left is a tomb, or *cuba*, with a green dome shaded by two palms; people about the cuba, upon the walls, everywhere. We pass another gate, and find ourselves at last in a street with houses on each side.

My memory here becomes confused, for I had as much as I

could do to save my neck, going as we were over great stones,
in the midst of a crowd of plunging horses : it would have been

Arrival at our House at Fez

all up with any one who had fallen. We passed, I remember,
through some deserted streets bordered by tall houses, suffocated

by dust, and deafened by the noise of the horses' hoofs; and in
about half-an-hour, after threading a labyrinth of steep and
narrow alleys where we were obliged to go in single file, we
reached a little door, where some scarlet soldiers presented
arms, and we entered our own house. It was a delicious sensation.

The house was a princely mansion in the purest Moorish
style, with a small garden shaded by parallel rows of orange and
lemon trees. From the garden you entered the interior court
by a low door, and thence into a corridor large enough only for
one person to pass. Around the court were twelve white
pilasters, joined by as many arches of a horseshoe form, which
supported an arched gallery furnished with a wooden balustrade.
The pavement of the court, gallery, and chambers was one
splendid mosaic of little squares of enamel of brilliant colours;
the arches were painted in arabesque; the balustrade carved in
delicate open work; the whole building designed with a grace and
harmony worthy of the architects of the Alhambra. In the
middle of the court there was a fountain; and another one, with
three jets of water, was in a carved and ornamented niche in the
wall. A large Moorish lantern depended from every arch.
One wing of the edifice extended along one side of the garden,
and had a graceful façade of three arches, painted in arabesque,
in front of which a third fountain sparkled. There were other
little courts, and corridors, and chambers, and the innumerable
recesses of an Oriental house. Some iron bedsteads, without sheets
or coverlets, a few clocks, one mirror in the court, two chairs and
a table for the Ambassador, and half-a-dozen basins and jugs,
completed the furniture of the house. In the principal rooms
the walls were hung with gold embroidered carpets, and some
white mattresses lay on the floors, and, except in the Ambassador's room, there was neither chair, nor table, nor wardrobe.
We had to send to the camp for some furniture. But, by way of
compensation, there was everywhere coolness, shade, the gurgle
of water, fragrance, and something deliciously soft and volup-

THE INNER COURT OF OUR HOUSE AT FEZ.

tuous in the lines of the building, in the air, in the light. The
whole edifice was encircled by a lofty wall, and surrounded by a
labyrinth of deserted alleys.

We had scarcely arrived in the court-yard when there began a
coming and going of Ministers and other high personages, each
one of whom had a few minutes' conversation with the Ambassador. The Minister of Finance was the one who attracted my
attention most. He was a Moor of about fifty years of age, of
a severe aspect, beardless, and dressed all in white, with an
immense turban. An interpreter told me that he was very
clever, and adduced as proof of the same that he one day had
brought to him one of those little arithmetical machines, and
both he and the machine had done the same sum in the same
time, and with the same results. It was worth while to see the
expression of sacred respect with which Selim, Ali, Civo, and the
rest regarded those personages, who, after the Sultan, represented in their eyes the highest grade of science, power, and
glory which could be attained on this earth.

These visits over, we took possession of our abode. The two
painters, the doctor, and myself occupied the rooms looking on
the garden ; the rest, those opening on the court. Interpreters,
cooks, sailors, servants, soldiers, all found their place, and in a
few hours the aspect of the house was changed.

The first to go out and visit the city were Ussi and Biseo,
the two artists ; and then the Commandant and the Captain.
I preferred to wait until the following morning. They went
out in couples, each encircled, like malefactors, by an infantry
guard, armed with muskets and sticks. After an hour they
returned, covered with dust, and all dripping from the heat ;
and their first words were, " Great city—great crowd—immense
mosques—naked saints—curses—sticks—wonderful things ! "
But Ussi had had the most interesting adventure. In one of
the most frequented streets, in spite of the soldiers, a girl
of fifteen or thereabouts had sprung upon his shoulders like
a fury, and had inflicted a vigorous pommeling, crying out,

"Accursed Christians! There is not a corner in Morocco where they do not push themselves!" Such was the first welcome given to Italian art within the walls of Fez.

Late in the night I made a tour through the house. On all the landing-places of the stairs, before the chamber doors, in the garden, were soldiers lying wrapped in their mantles, and sound asleep. Before the little door of the court-yard, the faithful Hamed Ben-Kasen, with his sabre by his side, snored in the open air. The dim light of the lanterns, touching the mosaic pavements here and there, made them look as if set with pearls, and gave an air of mysterious splendour to the place. The sky was thickly set with stars, and a light breeze moved the branches of the orange-trees in the garden. The murmur of the Pearl river could be distinctly heard ; the gurgle of the fountains, the ticking of the clocks, and now and then the shrill voices of the sentinels answering one another at the outer doors of the palace with their chanted prayer.

In the morning we went out, four or five of us together, accompanied by an interpreter, and escorted by ten foot-soldiers, one of whom wore buttons with the effigy of Queen Victoria— for many of these red coats are bought at Gibraltar from soldiers of the English army. Two of these placed themselves in front, two behind, and three on each side of us—the first armed with muskets, the others with sticks and knotted cords. They were such a rascally-looking set that when I think of them I bless the ship that brought me back to Europe.

The interpreter asked what we wished to see. "All Fez," was the answer.

We directed our steps first towards the centre of the city. Here I ought to exclaim, "*Chi mi darà la voce e le parole!*" * How shall I express the wonder, the pity, the sadness that overcame me at that grand and dismal spectacle ? The first impression is that of an immense city fallen into decrepitude and slowly decaying. Tall houses, which seemed formed of houses piled

* "Oh, for a voice and words!"

one upon the other, all falling to pieces, cracked from roof to
base, propped up on every side, with no opening save some loophole in the shape of a cross ; long stretches of street, flanked by
two high bare walls like the walls of a fortress ; streets running
up hill and down, encumbered with stones and the ruins of
fallen buildings, twisting and turning at every thirty paces ;
every now and then a long covered passage, dark as a cellar,
where you have to feel your way ; blind alleys, recesses, dens
full of bones, dead animals, and heaps of putrid matter : the
whole steeped in a dim and melancholy twilight. In some
places the ground is so broken, the dust so thick, the smell so
horrible, the flies are so numerous, that we have to stop to take
breath. In half-an-hour we have made so many turns that if
our road could be drawn it would form an arabesque as intricate
as any in the Alhambra. Here and there we hear the noise of a
mill, a murmur of water, the click of a weaver's loom, a chanting
of nasal voices, which we are told come from a school of children ;
but we see nothing and no one anywhere. We approach the
centre of the city ; people become more numerous ; the men
stop to let us pass, and stare astonished ; the women turn back,
or hide themselves ; the children scream and run ; the larger
boys growl and shake their fists at a distance, mindful of the
soldiers and their sticks. We see fountains richly ornamented
with mosaics, arabesque doors, arched courts, some few remains
of Arab architecture in decay. Every moment we find ourselves
in darkness, entering one of the many covered passages. We
come to one of the principal streets, about six feet wide, and full
of people, who crowd about us. The soldiers shout, and push,
and strike in vain, and at last make a sort of bulwark of their
bodies by forming a circle around us and clasping hands, face
outwards. There are a thousand eyes upon us ; we can scarcely
breathe in the press and heat, and move slowly on, stopping
every moment to give passage to a Moor on horseback, or a
veiled lady on a camel, or an ass with a load of bleeding sheep's
heads. To the right and left are crowded bazaars ; inn court-

yards encumbered with merchandise; doors of mosques, through which we catch glimpses of arcades in perspective, and figures

A Street in Fez.

prostrate in prayer. All along the street there is nothing to be seen but silent forms in white hoods, moving like spectres. The

o

air is impregnated with an acute and mingled odour of aloes,
spices, incense, and kif; we seem to be walking in an immense
drug-shop.   Groups of boys go by with scarred and scabby
heads; horrible old women, perfectly bald and with naked breasts,
making their way by dint of furious imprecations against us;

Conveying a Corpse to the Cemetery.

naked, or almost naked, madmen, crowned with flowers and
feathers, bearing a branch in their hands, laughing and singing
and cutting capers before the soldiers, who drive them away
with blows.   Turning into another street, we meet a saint, an
enormously fat old fellow, as naked as he was born, leaning upon
a lance bound with strips of red cloth.   He squints at us, and

SHOE SHOP, FEZ.

mutters something as we pass. Further on come four soldiers,
dragging along some poor unfortunate, all bleeding and torn,
who has been taken in the act of thieving ; and after them come
a troop of boys, calling out, " Cut off his hand ! cut off his
hand ! " Next come two men carrying an uncovered bier, upon
which is stretched a corpse, dry as a mummy, wrapped in a
white linen sack tied round the neck, waist, and knees. I ask
myself where I am, and whether I am awake or asleep, and whether
Fez and Paris are in the same planet ! We go into the bazaar.
The crowd is everywhere. The shops, as in Tangiers, are mere
dens opened in the wall. The money-changers are seated on the
ground, with heaps of black coin before them. We cross, jostled
by the crowd, the cloth-bazaar, that of slippers, that of earthenware, that of metal ornaments, which all together form a
labyrinth of alleys roofed with canes and branches of trees.
Passing through a vegetable market, thronged with women who
lift their arms and scream curses at us, we come out into the
centre of the city. There it is the same experience as before,
and we finally get out at a gate, and take a turn outside the
walls.

The city extends in the form of a monstrous figure of eight
between two hills, upon which still tower the ruins of two
ancient fortifications. Beyond the hills there is a chain of
mountains. The Pearl river divides the town in two—modern
Fez on the left bank, ancient Fez on the right—and a girdle of
old castellated walls and towers, dark and falling into ruin, binds
the whole together. From the heights the eye takes in the
whole city—a myriad of white, flat-roofed houses, among which
rise tall minarets ornamented with mosaics, gigantic palm-trees,
tufts of verdure, green domes, and castellated towers. The
grandeur of the ancient city can be divined from what is left,
though it is but a skeleton. Near the gates, and upon the hills,
for a long distance the country is covered with monuments and
ruins, tombs and houses of saints, arches of aqueducts, sepulchres,
zanie, and foundations that seem like the remains of a city

CLOTHES BAZAAR, FEZ.

destroyed by cannon and devoured by flames. Between the wall
and the highest of the two hills that flank the city it is all one
garden, a thick and intricate grove of mulberry-trees, olives,
palms, fruit-trees, and tall poplars, clothed with ivy and grape-
vines; little streams run through it, fountains gush and sparkle,
and canals intersect it between high green banks. The opposite
bank is crowned with aloes twice the height of a man. Along
the walls are great fissures and deep ditches, filled with vegetation; rude remains of bastions and broken towers—a grand
and severe disorder of ruin and greenery, recalling the more
picturesque parts of the walls of Constantinople. We passed by
the Gate of Ghisa, the Iron Gate, the Gate of the *Padre delle
Cuoia*, the New Gate, the Burned Gate, the Gate that Opens,
the Gate of Lions, the Gate of Sidi Busida, the Gate of the
Father of Utility, and re-entered new Fez by the Gate of the
Niche of Butter. Here are large gardens, vast open spaces,
large squares, surrounded by battlemented walls, beyond which
can be seen other squares and other walls, arched gateways and
towers, and beautiful prospects of hills and mountains. Some
of the doors are very lofty, and are covered with iron plates
studded with large nails. Approaching the Pearl river, we
come upon the decaying carcass of a horse, lying in the middle
of the street. Along the wall about a hundred Arabs are
washing and jumping upon the linen piled upon the shore. We
meet patrols of soldiers, personages of the court on horseback,
small caravans of camels, groups of women from the country
with their children tied on their backs, who cover their faces at
our approach; and at last we see some faces that smile upon us.
We enter the Mellà, the Hebrew quarter—truly a triumphal
entrance. They run to their windows and terraces, down into
the street, calling to one another. The men, with long hair
covered by a handkerchief tied under the chin like women, bow
with ceremonious smiles. The women, comely and plump,
dressed in red and green garments embroidered and braided with
gold, wish us *buenas dias,* and say a thousand charming things

with their brilliant dark eyes. Some of the children come and
kiss our hands. To escape from this ovation, and from the filth
of the streets, we take a cross street,
and, passing through the Jewish
cemetery, get back at last to the
palace of the Embassy, tired out and
with bewildered minds.

"O Fez!" says an Arabian
historian, "all the beauty of the
earth is concentrated in thee!"
He adds that Fez has always
been the seat of wisdom, science,
peace, and religion; the mother
and the queen of all the cities
of the Magreb; that its inhabitants have a finer and
deeper intelligence than that
of the other inhabitants of
Morocco; that all that is in
it and around it is blessed of
God, even to the waters of the
Pearl river, which cure the
stone, soften the skin, per-
fume the clothes, destroy
insects, render sweeter (if
drunk fasting) the pleasures
of the senses, and contain
precious stones of inestimable
value. Not less poetically
is related by the Arabian
writers the story of the
foundation of Fez. When

BARBERIS

Jew of Fez.

the Abassidi, towards the end of the eighth century, were
divided into two factions, one of the princes of the vanquished
faction—Edris-ebn-Abdallah—took refuge in the Magreb, a

short distance from the place where Fez now stands; and here
he lived in solitude, in prayer, and meditation, until, by reason
of his illustrious origin, as well as because of his holy life,
having acquired great fame among the Berbers of that region,
they elected him their chief.   Gradually, by his arms, and
by his high authority as a descendant of Ali and Fatima, he
extended his sovereignty over a large extent of country, con-
verting by force to Islamism idolators, Christians, and Hebrews;
and reached such a height of power that the Caliph of the
East—Haroun-el-Reschid—jealous of his fame, caused him to
be poisoned by a pretended physician, in order to destroy with
him his growing empire.   But the Berbers gave solemn sepul-
ture to Edris, and recognised as Caliph his posthumous son,
Edris-ebn-Edris, who ascended the throne at twelve years of
ge, consolidated and extended his father's work, and may be
said to have been the true founder of the empire of Morocco,
which remained until the end of the tenth century in the
hands of his dynasty.   It was this same Edris who laid the
foundations of Fez, on the 3rd of February of the year 808,
" in a valley placed between two high hills covered with rich
groves, and irrigated by a thousand streams, on the right bank
of the River of Pearls.

Tradition explains in several ways the origin of the name.
In digging for the foundations, they found in the earth a
great hatchet (called in Arabic *Fez*), which weighed sixty
pounds, and this gave its name to the city.

Edris himself, says another legend, worked at the foundations among his labourers, who, in gratitude, offered him a
hatchet made of gold and silver; and he chose to perpetuate,
in the name of the city, the memory of their homage.   According
to another account, the secretary of Edris had asked one day
of his lord what name he meant to give the city.   "The
name," answered the prince, "of the first person we shall
meet."   A man passed by, who, being questioned, said his
name was Farès; but he stammered, and pronounced it Fez.

Another account says that there was an ancient city called *Zef*, on the Pearl river, which existed eighteen hundred years, and was destroyed before Islam shone upon the world; and Edris imposed upon his metropolis the name of the old city reversed. However it may be, the new city grew rapidly, and already, at the beginning of the tenth century, rivalled Bagdad in splendour; held within its walls the mosque of El-Caruin and that of Edris, still existent, one the largest and the other the most venerated in Africa; and was called the Mecca of the West. Towards the middle of the eleventh century, Gregory IX. established there a bishopric. Under the dynasty of the Almoadi it had thirty suburbs, eight hundred mosques, ninety thousand houses, ten thousand shops, eighty-six gates, vast hospitals, magnificent baths, a great and rich library of precious manuscripts in Greek and Latin; also schools of philosophy, of physics, of astronomy, and languages, to which came all the learned and lettered men of Europe and the Levant. It was called the Athens of Africa, and was at one time the seat of a perpetual fair, into which flowed the products of three continents; and European commerce had there its bazaar and its inns; and there—between Moors, Arabs, Berbers, Jews, Negroes, Turks, Christians, and renegades—five hundred thousand people lived and prospered. And now, what a change! Almost all traces of gardens have vanished; the greater part of the mosques are in ruins; of the great library, only a few worm-eaten volumes remain; the schools are dead; commerce languishes; its edifices are falling into ruin; and the population is reduced to less than a fifth of the former number. Fez is no more than an enormous carcass of a metropolis abandoned in the midst of the vast cemetery called Morocco.

Our greatest desire, after our first walk about Fez, was to visit the two famous mosques of El-Caruin and Muley-Edris; but as Christians are not permitted to put a foot in them, we were obliged to content ourselves with what we could see from

Fragment of a Doorway at Fez.

the street: the mosaic doors, the arched courts, the long low aisles, divided by a forest of columns, and lighted by a dim, mysterious light. It must not be imagined, however, that those mosques are now what they were in the time of their fame; since, already in the fifteenth century, the celebrated historian Abd-er-Rhaman-ebn-Kaldun, describing that of El-Caruin (may God exalt it more and more, as he says), speaks of various

ornaments that were no longer in existence in his time. The
first foundations of this enormous mosque were laid on the
first Saturday of Ramadan, in the year 859 of Jesus Christ, at
the expense of a pious woman of Kairuan. It was at the
beginning a small mosque of four naves ; but, little by little,
Governors, Emirs, and Sultans embellished and enlarged it.
Upon the point of the minaret, built by the Imaum Ahmed ben
Aby-Beker, glittered a golden ball studded with pearls and
precious stones, on which was represented the sword of Edris-
ebn-Edris, the founder of Fez. On the interior walls were
suspended talismans which protected the mosque against rats,
scorpions, and serpents. The Mirab, or niche turned towards
Mecca, was so splendid that the Imaum had it painted white,
that it might no longer distract the faithful from their prayers.
There was a pulpit of ebony, inlaid with ivory and gems.
There were two hundred and seventy columns, forming sixteen
naves of twenty-one arches in each, fifteen great doors of entrance for the men, and two small ones for the women, and
seventeen hundred hanging lamps, which, in the season of
Ramadan, consumed three quintals and a half of oil. All which
particulars the historian Kaldun relates with exclamations of
wonder and delight, adding that the mosque could contain
twenty-two thousand and seven hundred persons, and that the
court alone had in its pavement fifty-two thousand bricks.
" Glory to Allah, Lord of the world, immensely merciful, and
king of the day of the last judgment ! "

Expecting that the Sultan would fix a day for the solemn
reception of the Embassy, we took several turns about the city,
in one of which I had an entirely new sensation. We were
approaching the Burnt Gate, *Bab-el-Maroc*, to re-enter the city,
when the Vice-Consul made an exclamation—" Two heads ! "
Lifting my eyes far enough along the wall to see two long
streams of blood, my courage failed me to see more ; but I
was told that the two heads were suspended by the hair over the
gate. One appeared to be that of a boy of not more than

fifteen, and the other a man of twenty-five or thirty; both Moors. We learned afterwards that they were heads of rebels from the confines of Algeria, which had been brought to Fez the day before; but the fresh blood made it probable that they had been cut off in the city, perhaps before that very gate. However that may be, we were informed on this same occasion that heads of rebels are always brought and presented to the Sultan; after which the imperial soldiers catch the first Jew whom they happen to encounter, and make him take out the brain, fill the skull with tow and salt, and hang it over one of the city gates. It is removed from one gate to another, and from one town to another, until it is destroyed. It does not appear, however, that this was done with the two heads of Bebel-Maroc, for a day or two after, asking an Arab servant what had become of them, he answered, with a gesture, " Buried," and then hastened to add, by way of consolation, " But there are plenty more coming."

Two days before the solemn reception, we were invited to breakfast by Sid-Moussa.

Sid-Moussa has no title: he is simply called Sid-Moussa. He was born a slave, and emancipated by the Sultan, who can to-morrow despoil him of all his property, cast him into prison, or hang his head over the gate of Fez, without being called to account for it. But he is the minister of ministers, the soul of the Government, the mind which embraces and moves all things all over the empire, and, after the Sultan, the most famous man in Morocco. Our curiosity may be imagined, therefore, on the morning when, surrounded as usual by an armed guard, accompanied by the Caid and interpreters, and followed by a tail of people, we went to his house in new Fez.

We were received at the door by a crowd of Arabs and blacks, and entered a garden enclosed by high walls, at the end of which, under a little portico, stood Sid-Moussa, dressed all in white, and surrounded by his officials.

The famous minister gave both hands with much heartiness

to the Ambassador, bowed smilingly to us, and preceded us into a small room on the ground-floor, where we sat down.

What a strange figure! A man of about sixty, a dark mulatto, of middle height, with an immense oblong head, two fiery eyes of a most astute expression, a great flat nose, a monstrous mouth, two rows of big teeth, and an immeasurable chin; yet in spite of these hideous features, an affable smile, an expression of benignity, and voice and manners of the utmost courtesy. But there are no people more deceptive in their aspect than the Moors. Not into the soul, but into the brain of that man would I have liked to peep! Certainly I should have found no great erudition. Perhaps no more than a few pages of the Koran, some periods of the imperial history, some vague geographical notions of the first States of Europe, some idea of astronomy, some rules of arithmetic. But instead, what profound knowledge of the human heart, what quickness of perception, what subtlety of craft, what intricate plottings and contrivings far from our own habits of mind, what curious secrets of government, and who knows what strange medley of memories of loves, and sufferings, and intrigues, and vicissitudes! The chamber, for a Moorish room, was sumptuously furnished, for it contained a small sofa, a table, a mirror, and a few chairs. The walls were hung with red and green carpets, the ceiling painted, the pavement in mosaic. Nothing extraordinary, however, for the house of a rich personage like Sid-Moussa.

After an exchange of the usual compliments, we were conducted into the dining-room, which was on the other side of the garden.

Sid-Moussa, according to custom, did not come with us. The dining-room was hung, like the other, with red and green carpets. In one corner was an armoire, with its two old bunches of artificial flowers under glass shades; and near it one of those little mirrors with a frame painted with flowers that are found in every village inn. On the table there were about twenty dishes containing big white sugar-plums in the form of

balls and carobs; the silver and china very elegant; numerous
bottles of water, and not a drop of wine. We seated ourselves,

Colonnade of a Mosque at Fez.

and were served at once. Twenty-eight dishes, without counting the sweets! Twenty-eight enormous dishes, every one of

which would have been enough for twenty people, of all forms, odours, and flavours; monstrous pieces of mutton on the spit, chickens (with pomatum), game (with cold cream), fish (with cosmetics), livers, puddings, vegetables, eggs, salads, all with the same dreadful combinations suggestive of the barber's shop; sweetmeats, every mouthful of which was enough to purge a man of any crime he had ever committed; and with all this, large glasses of water, into which we squeezed lemons that we had brought in our pockets; then a cup of tea sweetened to syrup; and finally an irruption of servants, who deluged the table, the walls, and ourselves with rose-water. Such was the breakfast of Sid-Moussa.

When we rose from table, there entered an official to announce to the Ambassador that Sid-Moussa was at prayers, and that as soon as he had finished he would have great pleasure in conferring with him. Immediately after there came in a tottering old man, supported between two Moors, who seized the Ambassador's hands and pressed them with great energy, exclaiming, with emotion, "Welcome! welcome! Welcome to the Ambassador of the King of Italy! Welcome among us! It is a great day for us!"

He was the grand Schereef Bacali, one of the most powerful personages of the court, and one of the richest proprietors of the empire, confidant of the Sultan, possessor of many wives, and a two years' invalid from dyspepsia. We were told that he relieved the ennui of his lord with witty words and comic action—a thing which would certainly never have been guessed from his ferocious face and impetuous gesture. After him appeared the two sons of Sid-Moussa, one of whom made his obeisance and vanished immediately; the other was an extremely handsome young man of twenty-five, private secretary to the Sultan: with the face of a woman, and two large brown eyes of indescribable softness; gay, graceful, and nervous, continually pulling with his hand at the folds of his ample orange-coloured caftan.

Bacalì and the Ambassador having gone out, we remained, with some officials seated on the floor, and the Sultan's secretary on a chair, in honour of us.

He immediately began a conversation through Mohammed Ducalè. Fixing his eyes on Ussi, he asked who he was.

"It is Signor Ussi," answered Ducalè; "a distinguished painter."

"Does he paint with the machine?" asked the young man. He meant the photographic instrument.

"No, Signore," replied the interpreter; "he paints with his hand."

He seemed to say to himself, "What a pity!" and remained a moment thoughtful. Then he said, "I asked, because, with the machine, the work is more precise."

The Commandant begged Ducalè to ask him whereabouts in Fez was the fountain called Ghalù, after a robber whom Edris, the founder of the city, had caused to be nailed to a tree near by. The young secretary was excessively astonished that the Commandant should know this particular story, and asked how he came to know it.

"I read it in Kaldun's history," answered the Commandant.

"In Kaldun's history!" exclaimed the other. "Have you read Kaldun? Then you understand Arabic? And where did you find Kaldun's history?"

The Commandant replied that the book was to be found in all our cities, that it was perfectly well known in Europe, and that it had been translated into English, French, and German.

"Really!" exclaimed the ingenuous young fellow. "You have all read it! and you know all these things! I never should have imagined it!"

Gradually the conversation became general, the officials also joining in it, and we heard some singular things. The English Ambassador had presented to the Sultan two telegraphic machines, and had taught some of the court people how to use them; and they were used, not publicly, because the sight of those mysterious wires in the city would cause disturbance,

The Sultan.

but in the interior of the palace; and words could not express the astonishment they excited. Not, however, to the point

P

that we might suppose, because, from what they had first heard,
they all, including the Sultan, had conceived a much more
wonderful idea of it; for they believed that the transmission
of the thought was not effected by means of letters and words,
but at once, instantaneously, so that a touch was sufficient to
express and transmit any speech. They recognised, however,
that the instrument was ingenious, and might be very useful
in our countries, where there were many people and much
traffic, and where everything had to be done in a hurry.
All of which signified in plain words, What should we do
with a telegraph?   And to what would the policy of our
Government be reduced if to the demands of the representatives of European States we were obliged to reply at once
and in few words? and renounce the great excuse of delays,
and the eternal pretext of lost letters, thanks to which we can
protract for two months questions that could be answered in
two days?   We learned also, or rather we were given to understand, that the Sultan is a man of a mild disposition and a
kind heart, who lives austerely, who loves one woman only,
who eats without a fork, like all his subjects, and seated on
the floor, but with the dishes placed upon a little gilded table
about a foot high; that before coming to the throne he
drilled with the soldiers, and was one of the most active
among them; that he likes to work, and often does himself
what ought to be done by his servants, even to packing his
own things when he goes away; and that the people love
him, but also fear him, because they know that, should a great
revolt break out, he would be the first to spring on horseback
and draw his sabre against the rebels.

But with what grace they told us all these things! with
what smiles and elegant gestures! What a pity not to be
able to understand their language, all colour and imagery,
and read and search at will in the ingenious ignorance of
their minds!

In about two hours' time the Ambassador came back with

Sid-Moussa, the grand Schereef, and the officials; and there was such an interchange of hand-pressings, and smiles, and bows, and salutations that we seemed to be engaged in some dance of ceremony ; and finally we departed, between two long rows of astonished servants. As we went out, we saw at a large grated window on the ground floor about ten faces of women—black, white, and mulatto—all be-jewelled and be-diademed; who, beholding us, instantly vanished with a great noise of flapping slippers and trailing skirts.

From the first day of our journey, the Sultan, Muley-el-Hassan, was, as may be imagined, the principal object of our curiosity. It was then a festival for us all when, at last, the Ambassador announced the reception for the following morning. I never in my life unfolded my dress-coat, or touched the spring of my *gibus,* with more profound complacency than on this occasion.

This great curiosity was produced, in part, by the history of his dynasty. There was the wish to look in the face of one of that terrible family of the Schereefs Fileli, to whom history assigns pre-eminence in fanaticism, ferocity, and crime, over all the dynasties that have ever reigned in Morocco. At the beginning of the seventeenth century, some inhabitants of Tafilet, a province of the empire on the confines of the desert, the Schereefs of which take the name of Fileli, brought from Mecca into their country a Schereef, named Ali, a native of Jambo, and a descendant of Mahomet, by Hassen, the second son of Ali and Fatima. The climate of the province of Tafilet, a little after his arrival, resumed a mildness that it had for some time lost. Dates grew in great abundance. The merit was attributed to Ali. Ali was elected king, under the name of Muley-Schereef. His descendants gradually, by their arms, extended the kingdom of their ancestor. They took possession of Morocco and Fez, drove out the dynasty of the Saadini Schereefs, and have reigned up to our day over the whole country comprised between the Muluia, the desert, and the

P 2

sea. Sidi-Mohammed, son of Muley-Schereef, reigned with
wise clemency; but after him the throne was steeped in blood.
El Reschid governed by terror, usurped the office of executioner, and lacerated with his own hands the breasts of women,
in order to force them to reveal the hiding-places of their
husbands' treasure. Muley-Ismail, the luxurious prince, the

A Barber's Shop in Fez.

lover of eight thousand women, and father of twelve hundred
sons, the founder of the famous corps of black guards, the
gallant Sultan who asked in marriage of Louis XIV. the
daughter of the Duchess de la Vallière, and stuck ten thousand
heads over the battlements of Morocco and Fez. Muley Ahmed el Dehebi, avaricious and a debauchee, stole the jewels of
his father's women, stupefied himself with wine, pulled out the
teeth of his own wives, and cut off the head of a slave who
had pressed the tobacco too much down into his pipe. Muley-
Abdallah, vanquished by the Berbers, cut the throats of the

inhabitants of Mechinez to satisfy his rage, aided the executioner in decapitating the officers of his brave but vanquished
army, and invented the horrible torture of cooking a man alive
inside a disembowelled bull, that the two might putrify together. The best of the race appears to have been Sidi-
Mohammed, his son, who surrounded himself with renegade
Christians, tried to live at peace, and brought Morocco nearer
to Europe. Then came Muley-Yezid, a cruel and violent
fanatic, who, in order to pay his soldiers, gave them leave to
sack and pillage the Hebrew quarters in all the cities of the
empire; Muley-Hescham, who, after a reign of a few days,
went into sanctuary to die; Muley-Soliman, who destroyed
piracy, and made a show of friendship to Europe, but, with
artful cunning, separated Morocco from all civilised States, and
caused to be brought to the foot of his throne the heads of
all renegade Jews from whom had escaped a word of regret
for their forced abjuration; Abd-er-Raman, the conqueror of
Isly, who built up conspirators alive into the walls of Fez;
and, finally, Sidi-Mohammed, the victor of Tetuan, who, in
order to inculcate respect and devotion in his people, sent the
heads of his enemies to the *duars* and cities, stuck upon his
soldiers' muskets. Nor are these the worst calamities that
afflicted the empire under the fatal dynasty of the Fileli.
There are wars with Spain, Portugal, Holland, England, France,
and the Turks of Algiers; ferocious insurrections of Berbers,
disastrous expeditions into the Sudan, revolts of fanatical tribes,
mutinies of the black guard, persecutions of the Christians;
furious wars of succession between father and son, uncle and
nephew, brother and brother; the empire by turns dismembered
and rejoined; Sultans five times discrowned and five times re-
instated; unnatural vengeance of princes of the same blood,
jealousies and horrid crimes, and monstrous suffering, and pre-
cipitate decline into antique barbarism; and at all times one
principle is triumphant: that, not being able to admit European civilisation unless upon the ruins of the entire political

and religious edifice of the Prophet, ignorance is the best bulwark of the empire, and barbarism an element necessary to its life.

With these recollections surrounding him, the Sultan became an object of special interest, and we were impatient to appear before him.

At eight o'clock in the morning, the Ambassador, the Vice-Consul, Signor Morteo, the Commandant, and the Captain, dressed in their best uniforms, were assembled in the court-yard, with a throng of soldiers, among whom the Caid appeared in great pomp. We—that is to say, the two artists, the doctor, and myself, all four in dress-coats, *gibus* hats, and white cravats—dared not issue from our rooms, in the fear that our strange costume, perhaps never before seen in Fez, might draw upon us the laughter of the public. " You go first."—" No, you."—" No, you,"—thus for a quarter of an hour, one trying to push the other out at the door. Finally, after a sage observation from the doctor that union made strength, we all came out together in a group, with our heads down and hats pulled over our eyes. Our appearance in the court-yard produced amazement among the soldiers and servants of the palace, some of whom hid themselves behind the pillars to laugh at their ease. But it was another thing in the city. We mounted our horses, and proceeded towards the gate of the *Nicchia del Burro*, with a company of the red division of infantry leading the way, followed by all the soldiers of the Legation, and flanked by officials, interpreters, masters of ceremony, and horsemen of the escort of Ben-Kasen-Buhammei. It was a fine spectacle, that mingling of tall hats and white turbans, diplomatic uniforms and red caftans, gold-mounted swords and barbaric sabres, yellow gloves and black hands, gilded pantaloons and bare legs; and the figure that we four made, in evening dress, mounted on mules, upon scarlet saddles as high as thrones, covered with dust and perspiration, may be left to the imagination. The streets were full of people. At our appearance, they all stopped and formed into two lines. They looked at the plumed hat of the Ambassador, the gold cord of the Captain, the medals of the

A Saint.

Commandant, and gave no sign of wonder; but when we four passed by, who were the last, there was an opening of eyes and an exhilaration of countenance that was truly trying. Mohammed-Ducalè rode near us, and we begged him to translate for us some of the observations which he caught in passing.

A Moor, standing with a number of others, said something to which the rest seemed to assent. Ducalè laughed, and told us that they took us for executioners. Some—perhaps because black is odious to the Moors—looked at us almost with anger and disdain; others shook their heads with a look of commiseration.

"Signori," said the doctor, "if we do not make ourselves respected it is our own fault. We have arms—let us use them. I will set the example."

Thus speaking, he took off his *gibus* hat, shut down the spring, and, passing before a group of smiling Moors, suddenly sprung it at them. The wonder and agitation of them at the sight cannot be expressed. Three or four sprang backwards, and threw a glance of profound suspicion upon the diabolical hat. The artists and I, encouraged by the example, imitated him; and thus, by dint of our *gibus*, we arrived, respected and feared, at the city walls.

Outside the gate of the *Nicchia del Burro* were ranged two rows of infantry soldiers—in great part boys—who presented arms in their usual fashion, one after the other, and, when we had passed, put their uniforms over their heads to shelter them from the sun. We crossed the Pearl river by a small bridge, and found ourselves in the place destined for the reception, where we all dismounted.

It was a vast square, closed on three sides by high battlemented walls with large towers. On the fourth side ran the River of Pearls. In the corner furthest from us opened a narrow road bordered by white walls, which led to the gardens and houses of the Sultan, completely concealed by bastions.

The square, when we arrived, presented an admirable *coup-d'œil*. In the middle a throng of generals, masters of ceremonies, magistrates, nobles, officials, and slaves, Arab and black, all dressed in white, were divided into two great ranks, opposite each other, and distant about thirty paces. Behind one of these ranks, towards the river, were disposed in files all the Sultan's horses—large and beautiful creatures, with trappings of velvet embroidered with gold, each one held by an armed groom. At the end of the files of horses stood a small gilded carriage, which the Queen of England had given to the Sultan, who always displays it at every reception. Behind the horses, and behind the other rank of court personages, were drawn up in interminable lines the imperial guard, dressed in white.

All around the square, at the foot of the wall and along the river bank, three thousand foot soldiers looked like four long lines of flaming red; and on the other bank of the river was an immense crowd of people all in white. In the middle of the place were arranged the cases containing the presents from the King of Italy—a portrait of the king himself, mirrors, pictures in mosaic, candelabra, and armchairs.

We placed ourselves near to the two ranks of personages, so as to form with them a square open towards that part of the place where the Sultan was to come. Behind us were the cases; behind the cases, all the soldiers of the Embassy. On one side, Mohammed Ducalè, the Commandant of the escort, Solomon Affalo, and the sailors in uniform.

A master of ceremonies, with a very crabbed expression of countenance, and armed with a knotty stick, placed us in two rows—in front, the Commandant, the Captain, and the Vice-Consul; behind, the doctor, the two painters, and myself. The Ambassador stood five or six paces in advance of us, with Signor Morteo, who was to interpret.

At one moment we seven advanced a few paces unconsciously. The master of ceremonies before mentioned made us all go back, and pointed out with his stick the exact place where we were to remain. This proceeding made a great impression on us, the more that we fancied we saw the gleam of an astute smile in his eye. At the same moment a great buzz and murmur arose from above. We looked up,

OUR FIRST MEETING WITH THE SULTAN.

and saw, at a certain height beyond the bastions, four or five windows, closed, with green curtains, behind which a quantity of heads seemed to be in movement. They were women's heads—the buzz came from them. The windows belonged to a kind of balcony, which communicated by a long corridor with the Sultan's harem; and the master of ceremonies had made us stand in that position by express order of the Sultan himself, who had promised his ladies that they should see the Christians. What a pity that we were not near enough to hear their observations upon our high hats and our swallow-tailed coats!

The sun was burning hot; a profound silence reigned in the vast square; every eye was turned towards the same point. We waited for about ten minutes. Suddenly a shiver seemed to run through the soldiers; there was a burst of music, the trumpets sounded ; the court personages bowed profoundly; the guards, grooms, and soldiers put one knee to the ground; and from every mouth came one prolonged and thundering shout—" God protect the Sultan ! "

He was on horseback, followed by a throng of courtiers on foot, one of whom held over his head an immense parasol. At a few paces from the Ambassador he stopped his horse, a portion of his suite closed the square, the rest grouped themselves about him.

The master of ceremonies with the knotty stick shouted in a loud voice—"The Ambassador from Italy ! "

The Ambassador, accompanied by his interpreter, advanced with uncovered head. The Sultan said in Arabic, " Welcome ! welcome ! welcome ! " Then he asked if he had had a good journey, and if he were content with the service of the escort, and with the reception of the governors. But of all this we heard nothing. We were fascinated. The Sultan, whom our imagination had represented to us under the aspect of a cruel and savage despot, was the handsomest and most charming young fellow that had ever excited the fancy of an *odalisque*. He is tall and slender, with large soft eyes, a fine aquiline nose, and his dark visage is of a perfect oval, encircled by a short, black beard: a noble face, full of sadness and gentleness. A mantle of snowy whiteness fell from his head to his feet; his turban was covered by a tall hood; his feet were bare, except for yellow slippers; his horse was large and white, with trappings of green and gold, and golden stirrups. All this whiteness and amplitude of his garments gave him a priestly air, which, with a certain majestic grace and affability, corresponded admirably with the expression of his face. The parasol (sign of command) which a courtier held a little inclined behind him—a great round parasol, three metres in height, lined with blue silk embroidered with gold, and covered on the outside with amaranth, topped by a great golden ball—added to the dignity of his appearance. His graceful action, his smiling and pensive expression, his low voice, sweet and monotonous as the murmur of a stream—his whole person and manners had something of ingenuous and feminine, and at the same time solemn, that inspired irresistible sympathy and profound respect. He looked about thirty-two or thirty-three years of age.

"I am rejoiced," he said, "that the King of Italy has sent an ambassador to draw more tightly the bands of our ancient friendship. The House of Savoy has never made war on Morocco. I love the House of Savoy, and have followed with pleasure and admiration the events which have succeeded each other under its auspices in Italy. In the time of ancient Rome, Italy was the most powerful country in the world. Then it was divided into seven states. My ancestors were friendly to all the seven states. And I, now that all are reunited into one, have concentrated upon it all the friendship that my ancestors had for the seven."

He spoke these words slowly, with pauses, as if he had studied them first, and was trying to remember them.

Among other things, the Ambassador told him that the King of Italy had sent him his portrait.

"It is a precious gift," he replied, "and I will have it placed in the room where I sleep, opposite a mirror, so that it shall be the first object on which my eyes fall when I wake; and so every morning I shall see the image of the King of Italy reflected, and will think of him." A little while afterwards he added, "I am content, and I hope that you will stay long in Fez, and that it will be a pleasant memory when you shall have returned to your beautiful country."

While he spoke he kept his eyes fixed almost constantly upon his horse's head. At times he seemed about to smile, but immediately bent his brows and resumed the gravity proper to the imperial countenance. He was curious, it was evident, to see what sort of beings were these seven ranged at ten paces from his horse; but not wishing to look directly at us, he turned his eyes little by little, and then with one rapid glance took in the whole seven together, and at that moment there was in his eye a certain indefinable expression of childish amusement that made a pleasant contrast with the majesty of his person. The numerous suite that were gathered behind and about him appeared to be petrified. All eyes were fixed upon him; not a breath could be heard, and nothing was seen but immoveable faces and attitudes of profound veneration. Two Moors with trembling hands drove away the flies from his feet; another from time to time passed his hand over the skirt of his white mantle, as if to purify it from contact with the air; a fourth, with an action of sacred respect, caressed the crupper of the horse; the one who held the parasol stood with downcast eyes, motionless as a statue, almost as if he were confused and bewildered by the solemnity of his office. All things about him expressed his enormous power, the immense distance that separated him from everybody, a measureless submission, a fanatic devotion, a savage, passionate affection that seemed to offer its blood for proof. He seemed not a monarch, but a god.

The Ambassador presented his credentials, and then introduced the Commandant, the Captain, and the Vice-Consul,
who advanced one after the other, and stood for a moment
bowing low. The Sultan looked with particular attention at
the Commandant's decorations.

"The physician"—then said the Ambassador, pointing us
out—"and three *scienzati*" (men of science).

My eyes encountered the eyes of the god, and all the
periods, already conceived, of this description, confounded themselves in my mind.

The Sultan asked with curiosity which was the physician.
"He to the right," answered the interpreter.

He looked attentively at the doctor. Then, accompanying
his words with a graceful wave of his right hand, he said,
"Peace be with you! Peace be with you! Peace be with you!"
and turned his horse.

The band burst out, the trumpets sounded, the courtiers
bent to the ground, guards, soldiers, and servants knelt on
one knee, and once more the loud and prolonged shout arose—
"God protect our Sultan!"

The Sultan gone, the two ranks of high personages met and
mingled, and there came towards us Sid-Moussa, with his sons,
his officers, the Minister of War, the Minister of Finance, the
Grand Schereef Bacalì, the Grand-Master of Ceremonies, all
the great ones of the court, smiling, talking, and waving
their hands in sign of festivity. A little later, Sid-Moussa
having invited the Ambassador to rest in a garden of the
Sultan's, we mounted, crossed the square to the mysterious
little road, and entered the august precincts of the imperial
residence.

Alleys bordered by high walls, small squares, courts, ruined
houses and houses in course of construction, arched doors,
corridors, little gardens, little mosques, a labyrinth to make
one lose one's way, and everywhere busy workmen, lines of
servants, armed sentinels, and some faces of slave women

behind the grated windows or at the openings in the doors : this was all. Not a single handsome edifice, nor anything,

beyond the guard, to indicate the residence of the sovereign. We entered a vast uncultivated garden, with shaded walks crossing each other at right angles, and shut in by high walls like the garden of a convent, and from thence, after a short rest, returned home, spreading by the way — the doctor, the painters, and myself —hilarity with our swallow-tails and terror with our *gibus*.

All that day we talked of nothing but the Sultan. We were all in love with him. Ussi tried a hundred times to sketch his face, and threw away his pencil in despair. We proclaimed him the handsomest and the most amiable of Mohammedan monarchs ; and in order that the proclamation might be truly a national one, we sought the suffrages of the cook and the two sailors.

The cook, from whom

A Street in Fez.

all the spectacles seen between Tangiers and Fez had never drawn anything but a smile of commiseration, showed himself generous to the Sultan :—

" He is a fine man—there is no doubt about that—a handsome man; but he ought to travel, *where he can get some instruction.*"

This naturally meant Turin. Luigi, the sailor, though a Neapolitan, was more laconic. Being asked what he had remarked in the Sultan, he thought a moment, and answered, smilingly, "I remarked that in this country even the kings do not wear stockings."

The most comical of all was Ranni. "How did the Sultan strike you?" asked the Commandant.

"It struck me," he answered, frankly and with perfect gravity, "that he was afraid."

"Afraid!" exclaimed the Commandant. "Of whom?"

"Of us. Did you not see how pale he grew, and he spoke as if he had lost his breath?"

"You are crazy! Do you think that he, in the midst of his army, and surrounded by his guard, could be afraid of us?"

"It seemed so to me," said Ranni, imperturbably.

The Commandant looked fixedly at him, and then took his head in both hands, like a profoundly discouraged man.

That same evening there came to the palace, conducted by Selim, two Moors, who having heard marvels of our *gibus* desired to see them. I went and got mine and opened it under their noses. Both of them looked into it with great curiosity, and appeared much astonished. They probably expected to find some complicated mechanism of wheels and springs, and seeing nothing were confirmed in the belief that exists among the Moorish vulgar that in all Christian objects there is something diabolical.

"Why, there is nothing!" they exclaimed, with one voice.

"But it is precisely in that," I answered, through Selim, "that the wonder of these supernatural hats appears; that they do what they do without any wheels or springs!"

Selim laughed, suspecting the trick, and I then tried to explain the mechanism of the thing to them; but they seemed to understand but little.

They asked also, as they took leave, whether Christians put such things in their hats "for amusement."

"And you," I said to Selim, "what is your opinion of these contrivances?"

"My opinion is," he answered, with haughty contempt, placing his finger on the offending hat, "that if I had to live a hundred years in your country, perhaps, little by little, I might adopt your manner of dressing—your shoes, your cravats, and even the hideous colours that please you; but that horrible black thing—ah! God is my witness, that I would rather die!"

At this point I begin my journal at Fez, which embraces all the time that transpired between our reception by the Sultan, and our departure for Mechinez:—

May 20th.

To-day the chief custodian of the palace gave me secretly the key of the terrace, warmly recommending us to observe prudence. It appears that he had received orders not to refuse the keys, but to give them only if urgently asked for; and this because the terraces at Fez, as in other cities of Morocco, belong to the women, and are considered almost as appendages of the harem. We went up to the terrace, which is very spacious, and completely surrounded by a wall higher than a man, having a few loopholes for windows. The palace being very high, and built on a height, hundreds of white terraces could be seen from thence, as well as the hills which surround the city, and the distant mountains; and below another small garden, from the midst of which rose a palm-tree so tall as to overtop the building by almost one-third of its own stature. Looking through those loophole windows, we seemed to see into another world. Upon the terraces far and near were many women, the greater part of them, judging by their dress, in easy circumstances—ladies, if that title can be given to Moorish women. A few were seated upon the parapets, some walking about, some jumping with the agility of squirrels from one terrace to the other, hiding, re-

Q

appearing, and throwing water in each other's faces, laughing merrily. There were old women and young, little girls of eight or ten, all dressed in the strangest garments, and of the most

A Pottery Dealer, Fez.

brilliant colours. Most of them had their hair falling over their shoulders, a red or green silk handkerchief tied round the head in a band, a sort of caftan of different colours, with wide sleeves, bound round the waist with a blue or crimson sash; a velvet jacket open at the breast; wide trowsers, yellow slippers, and

large silver rings above the ankle. The slaves and children had
nothing on but a chemise. One only of these ladies was near
enough for us to see her features. She was a woman of about
thirty, dressed in gala dress, and standing on a terrace a cat's
jump below our own. She was looking down into a garden,
leaning her head upon her hand. We looked at her with a glass.
Heavens, what a picture! Eyes darkened with antimony, cheeks
painted red, throat painted white, nails stained with henna : she
was a perfect painter's palette ; but handsome, despite her thirty
years, with a full face, and almond-shaped eyes, languid, and
veiled by long black lashes; the nose a little turned up ; a small
round mouth, as the Moorish poet says, like a ring ; and a
sylph-like figure, whose soft and curling lines were shown by
the thin texture of her dress. She seemed sad. Perhaps some
youthful bride of fourteen had lately entered the harem and stolen
her husband's caresses. From time to time she glanced at her
hand, her arm, a tress of hair that fell over her bosom, and sighed.
The sound of our voices suddenly roused her; she looked up,
saw that we were observing her, jumped over the parapet of the
terrace with the dexterity of an acrobat, and vanished. To see
better, we sent for a chair, and drew lots which should mount
it first. The lot falling to me, I placed the chair against the
wall, and succeeded in raising my head and shoulders above it.
It was like the apparition of a new star in the sky of Fez, if I
may be excused the audacity of the simile. I was seen at once
from the nearer houses, the occupants of which at once took to
flight, then turned to look, and announced the event to those on
the more distant terraces. In a few minutes the news had
spread from terrace to terrace over half the city ; curious eyes
appeared everywhere, and I found myself in a sort of pillory.
But the beauty of the spectacle held me to my post. There
were hundreds of women and children, on the parapets, on the
little towers, on the outer staircases, all turned towards me,
all in flaming colours, from those nearer ones whose features
I could discern, to those more distant, who were mere white,

Q 2

green, or vermilion points to my eye; some of the terraces were
so full that they seemed like baskets of flowers; and everywhere
there was a buzz, and hurry, and gesticulation, as if they were
all looking on at some celestial phenomenon. Not to put the
entire city in commotion, I *set*, or rather descended from my
chair, and for a moment no one went up. Then Biseo rose,
and he also was the mark for thousands of eyes, when, suddenly,
upon a distant terrace, all the women turned the other way,
and ran to look in the opposite direction, and, in a moment,
those on the other houses did the same. We could not at first
imagine what had happened, until the Vice-Consul made a happy
guess. " A great event," he said, " the Commandant and the
Captain are passing through the streets of Fez;" and in fact,
after a little time, we saw the red uniforms of the escort appear
upon the heights that overlook the city, and with the glass
could recognise the Commandant and Captain on horseback.
Another sudden turn about of the women on some of the
terraces gave notice of the passage of another Italian party;
and in about ten minutes we beheld upon the opposite hills the
white Egyptian head-dress of Ussi, and Morteo's English hat.
After this the universal attention was once more turned to us,
and we stayed a moment to enjoy it; but upon a neighbouring
terrace there appeared five or six brats of slave-girls, of about
thirteen or fourteen years of age, who looked at us and giggled
in such an insolent manner that we were constrained, in
Christian decorum, to deprive the metropolitan fair sex of our
shining presence.

Yesterday we dined with the Grand Vizier, Taib Ben-
Jamani, surnamed Boascherin, which signifies, according to
some, victor at the game of ball, and according to others,
father of twenty children;—Grand Vizier, however, by courtesy
only, his father having filled that office under the late Sultan.
The messenger bearing the invitation was received by the
Ambassador in our presence.

" The Grand Vizier, Taib Ben-Jamani Boascherin," said he,

ON THE TERRACES, FEZ.

with much gravity, "prays the Ambassador of Italy and his
suite to dine to-day at his house."

The Ambassador expressed his thanks.

"The Grand Vizier, Taib Ben-Jamani Boascherin," he continued, with the same gravity, "prays the Ambassador and his
suite to bring with them their knives and forks, and also their
servants to wait on them at table."

We went towards evening in dress-coats and white cravats,
mounted, and with an armed guard as before. I do not remember in what part of the city the house was situated, so many
were the turns and twists we made, the ups and downs, through
covered ways gloomy and sinister, holding up the mules from
slipping, and stooping our heads not to strike them against the
low damp vaults of those interminable galleries. We dismounted
in a dark passage, and entered a square court, paved in mosaic,
and surrounded by tall white pilasters, which upheld little arches
painted green and ornamented with arabesques in stucco—a
strange Moorish-Babylonian sort of architecture, both pleasing
and peculiar. In the middle of the court seven jets of water
shot up from as many vases of white marble, making a noise as
of a heavy rain. All around were little half-closed doors and
double windows. At the two shorter sides two great doors stood
open, giving access to two halls. On the threshold of one of
these doors was the Grand Vizier, standing; behind him two
old Moors, relations of his; to the right and left, two wings of
male and female slaves.

After the usual salutations, the Grand Vizier seated himself
upon a divan which ran along the wall, crossed his legs, hugged
to his stomach with both his hands a large round cushion—his
habitual and peculiar attitude—and never moved again for the
rest of the evening.

He was a man of about forty-five years of age, vigorous, and
with regular features, but with a certain false light shining in
his eyes. He wore a white turban and caftan. He spoke with
much vivacity, and laughed loud and long at his own words and

those of others, throwing back his head while he did so, and keeping his mouth open long after he had done laughing.

On the walls hung some small pictures with inscriptions from the Koran in gold letters; in the middle of the room there was a common wooden table and some rustic chairs; all about lay white matresses, on which we threw our hats.

Sidi Ben-Jamani began a vivacious conversation with the Ambassador, asking if he were married, and why he did not marry. He said that if he had been married he might have brought his wife to dinner; that the English Ambassador had brought his daughter, and that she had been much diverted by what she saw there; that all the ambassadors ought to marry, expressly to conduct their wives to Fez, and dine with him; together with other talk of the same kind, all of it interspersed with loud laughter.

Whilst the Grand Vizier was talking, the two painters and I, seated in the doorway, were looking out of the corners of our eyes at the slave women, who, little by little, and encouraged by our air of benign curiosity, had drawn near, unseen by the Grand Vizier, so that they could almost touch us; and there they stood, looking and being looked at, with a certain complacency. There were eight of them, fine girls of from fifteen to twenty years of age, some mulatto, some black, with large eyes and dilated nostrils; all dressed in white, with very broad embroidered girdles, arms and feet bare, bracelets on their wrists, great silver rings in their ears, thick silver anklets. It seemed as if they would not scruple very much to have their cheeks pinched by a Christian hand. Ussi pointed out to Biseo the beautiful foot of one of them; she noticed it, and began to examine her own foot with much curiosity. All the others did the same, comparing their own feet with hers. Ussi " fired off " his *gibus* hat; they drew back, then smiled, and came near again. The Grand Vizier's voice, ordering the table to be prepared, sent them flying.

The table was laid by our own soldiers. A servant of the

house placed upon it, in the middle, three thick waxen torches of different colours. The china-ware belonged to the Grand Vizier, and there were not two plates alike; but they were big and little, white and coloured, fine and common, plenty and to spare. The napkins also belonged to the house, and consisted of sundry

Women of the Grand Vizier of the Household.

square pieces of cotton cloth, of different sizes, unhemmed, and evidently just cut off in a hurry for the occasion.

It was night when we sat down. The Grand Vizier sat on his mattress, hugging his cushion, and talking and laughing with his two relatives.

I will not describe the dinner. I do not wish to recall painful memories. Enough to say that there were thirty dishes, or rather thirty unpleasant things, without counting the smaller annoyances of the sweets.

At the fifteenth dish, it becoming impossible to continue the struggle without the aid of wine, the Ambassador begged Morteo to ask the Grand Vizier if it would be displeasing to him to have some champagne sent for.

Morteo whispered to Selim, and Selim repeated the request in the ear of his Excellency. His Excellency made a long reply in a low voice, and we anxiously watched his face out of the corners of our eyes. But we found small hope there.

Selim rose with a mortified air, and repeated the answer into the ear of the intendant, who gave us the *coup de grâce* in the following words :—

"The Grand Vizier says that there would be no difficulty, that he would consent willingly, but that it would be an impropriety, and the glasses would be soiled, and perhaps the table; and that in any case the sight, the odour, and then the novelty of the thing "——

"I understand," answered the Ambassador; " we will say no more about it."

Our complexions all assumed a slight shade of green.

The dinner over, the Ambassador remained in conversation with the Grand Vizier, and the rest of us issued forth into the rain and darkness of the court. In the room at the other end of it, lighted by a torch, and seated on the ground, our Caid, his officers, and the Secretaries of our host were dining. At all the little windows in the walls, lighted from within, women's and children's heads could be seen, their dark outlines showing against the light. A half-open door showed a splendidly illuminated hall, where seated, lounging in a circle, and gorgeously arrayed, were the wives and concubines of the Grand Vizier ; dimly seen through the smoke of burning perfumes that rose from tripods at their feet. Slave women and servants came and went continually; there must have been at least fifty persons moving about, but there was no sound of voice, or step, or rustle of garment. It was like a phantasmagoria, at which we gazed for a long time, silent, and hidden in the darkness.

AN INTERVIEW WITH THE GRAND VIZIER.

As we were going away we saw, attached to a pillar in the court, a thick leathern thong with knots in it. The interpreter asked one of the men what it was for. "To beat us with," he answered.

We mounted and turned our faces homewards, accompanied by a troop of the Grand Vizier's servants carrying lanterns. It was very dark and raining heavily. The strange effect of that long cavalcade cannot be imagined, with the lanterns, the crowd of armed and hooded figures, the deafening noise of the horses' feet, the sound of savage exclamations, in that labyrinth of narrow streets and covered passages, in the midst of the silence of the sleeping city. It seemed like a funeral procession winding along under ground, or a party of soldiers advancing through subterranean ways to surprise a fortress. Suddenly the procession halted, there was a sepulchral silence, broken by a voice saying angrily in Arabic, "The road is closed!" A moment after there was a great noise of blows. The soldiers of the escort were trying to beat down with the butts of their muskets one of the thousand gates that during the night prevent circulation through the streets of Fez. The work took some time; it thundered and lightened, and the rain poured in torrents; the soldiers and servants ran about with lanterns, throwing their long shadows on the walls; the Caid, standing in his stirrups, threatened the invisible inhabitants of the surrounding houses; and we enjoyed the fine Rembrandt picture with infinite delight. Finally the door came down with a great noise, and we passed on. A little before we reached our house, under an arched passage, six foot soldiers presented arms with one hand, the other holding a lighted taper; and this was the last scene of the fantastic drama, entitled, A Dinner with the Grand Vizier. But, no; the last scene of all was when we, hardly in our own court-yard, precipitated ourselves upon sardines of Nantes, and bottles of Bordeaux, and Ussi, lifting his glass above our heads, exclaimed in solemn accents, "To Sidi Ben-Jamani, Grand Vizier of Morocco, our most gracious host, I, Stefano Ussi, with Christian forgiveness, consecrate this cup!"

The Sultan has received the Ambassador in private audience. The reception-hall is as big, as bare, and as white as a prison.

The Closed Gate.

There are no other ornaments but a great number of clocks of all forms and dimensions, of which some are on the floor, ranged along the walls, and some are huddled together on the table in the middle of the room. Clocks, it may be remembered, are very great objects of admiration and amusement among the Moors. The Sultan was seated cross-legged, in a little alcove, upon a wooden platform about a yard high. He wore, as at his public reception, a white mantle, with a hood over his head; his feet were bare, his yellow slippers in a corner, and a green cord crossed his breast, to which a poignard was probably suspended. In this way the Emperors of Morocco have always received ambassadors. Their throne, as Sultan Abd-er-Rhaman said, is the horse, and their pavilion the sky. The Ambassador, having first made known his wish to Sid-Moussa, found before the imperial platform a modest chair, upon which, at a sign from the Sultan, he seated himself; Signor Morteo, the interpreter, remained standing. His Majesty, Muley-el-Hassan, spoke for a long time, without ever raising his hands from beneath his mantle, without making a movement with his head, without altering by a single accent the habitual monotony of his soft deep voice. He spoke of the needs of his empire, of commerce, of industry, of treaties; going into minute particulars, with much order and method, and great simplicity of language. He asked many questions, listening to the answers with great attention, and concluded by saying, with a slight expression of sadness, "It is true; but we are constrained to proceed slowly"—strange and admirable words on the lips of an Emperor of Morocco. Seeing that he gave no sign, even in the intervals of silence, to break off the interview, the Ambassador thought it his duty to rise. "Stay yet a while," said the Sultan, with a certain expression of ingenuousness; "it gives me pleasure to converse with you." When the Ambassador took leave, bowing for the last time on the threshold of the door, he slightly bent his head, and remained motionless, like an idol in his deserted temple.

A company of Hebrew women have been here presenting I know not what petition to the Ambassador. No one could shelter his hands from the shower of their kisses. They were the wives, daughters, and relations of two rich merchants:

beautiful women, with brilliant black eyes, fair skins, scarlet lips, and very small hands. The two mothers, already old, had not a single white hair, and the fire of youth still burned in their eyes. Their dress was splendid and picturesque—a

Jewish Synagogue in Fez.

handkerchief of gorgeous colours bound about the forehead: a jacket of red cloth, trimmed with heavy gold braid; a sort of waistcoat all of gold embroidery; a short, narrow petticoat of green cloth, also bordered with gold; and a sash of red or blue silk around the waist. They looked like so many Asiatic princesses, and their splendour of attire contrasted oddly with their servile and obsequious manners. They all spoke Spanish. It was not until after some minutes that we observed that they had bare feet, and carried their yellow slippers under their arms.

" Why do you not wear your shoes?" I asked of one of the old women.

" What!" she said, in astonishment. " Do you not know that we Israelites must not wear shoes except in the Mellà, and that when we enter a Moorish city we must go barefoot?"

Reassured by the Ambassador, they all put on their slippers. Such is the fact. They are not absolutely obliged to go always with bare feet; but as they must take off their shoes in passing through certain streets, before certain mosques, near certain *cube*, it becomes the same thing in the end. And this is not the only vexation to which they are subjected, nor the most humiliating one. They cannot bear witness before a judge, and must prostrate themselves on the ground before any tribunal; they cannot possess lands or houses outside of their own quarter; they must not raise their hand against a Mussulman, even in self-defence, except in the case of being assaulted under their own roof; they can only wear dark colours;* they must carry their dead to the cemetery at a run; they must ask the Sultan's leave to marry; they must be within their own quarter at sunset; they must pay the Moorish guard who stands sentinel at the gates of the Mellà; and they must present rich gifts to the Sultan on the four great festivals of Islamism, and on every occasion of birth or matrimony in the imperial family. Their condition was still worse before the time of Sultan Abd-er-Rhaman, who at least prevented their blood from being shed. Even if they would, the Sultans could not much ameliorate their condition, without exposing this unfortunate people to an even worse fate than the horrible slavery they now endure, so fanatical and ferocious is the hatred of the Moors

* Apparently the women are exempt from this law.—*Trans.*

against them. Thus Sultan Soliman, having decreed that they
might wear their shoes, so many of them were killed in open
day in the streets of Fez that they themselves petitioned the
revocation of the decree. Nevertheless, they remain in the
country, and being willing to run the risks, they serve as
intermediaries between the commerce of Europe and that of

Jewish Children.

Africa; and the Govern-
ment, aware of their
importance to the pros-
perity of the State, op-
poses an almost insur-
mountable barrier to
emigration, prohibiting
the departure of any
Jewish woman from Mo-
rocco. They serve, they
tremble, and grovel in
the dust; but they
would not give, to ac-
quire the dignity of men
and the liberty of citi-
zens, the heaps of gold
which they keep hidden in
their gloomy habitations.
There are about eight

thousand of them living in Fez, divided into Synagogues,
and directed by Rabbis who enjoy high authority.

These poor women showed us a number of large bracelets
of chased silver, some rings set with jewels, and some gold
ear-rings, which they kept hidden in their bosoms. We asked
why they concealed them.

"*Nos espantamos de los Moros.*" "We are afraid of the
Moors," they said, in a low voice, looking timidly about them.
They were suspicious, too, of the soldiers of the Legation.

Among them there were several children, dressed with the

same splendour as the women. One of them stood close to her mother, seeming more timid than the rest. The Ambassador asked how old she was. "Twelve years old," the mother said.

" She will soon be married," remarked the Ambassador.

" *Che!* " exclaimed the mother ; " she is too old to marry."

We all thought she was joking. But she repeated, almost astonished at our incredulity, "I speak the truth ; look here at this one "—and she pointed to a smaller child. " She will be ten years old in six months, and she has already been married one year."

The child held down her head. We were still incredulous.

" What can I say ? " continued the woman. " If you will not believe my word, do me the honour to come to my house on Saturday, so that we may receive you worthily, and you will see the husband and the witnesses of the marriage."

" And how old is the husband ? " I asked.

" Ten years old, Signore."

Seeing that we still doubted, the other women all asserted the same, adding that it is quite rare for a girl to marry after twelve years of age ; that the greater part of them are married at ten, many at eight, and some even at seven, to boys of about their own age; and that, naturally, while they are so young, they live with their parents, who continue to treat them like children, feed, clothe, and correct them, without the least regard to their marital dignity; but they are always together, and the wife is submissive to the husband.

To us all this seemed news from another world than ours, and we listened with open mouths, divided between a desire to laugh, pity, and anger.

A breakfast at the house of the Minister of War.

We were received in a narrow court, enclosed by four high walls, and as dark as a well. On one side there was a door about three feet in height, on the other a great doorway without doors, and a bare room, with a mattress on the floor, and some

R

sheets of paper strung on a string, and hanging on one of
the walls: the daily correspondence, I imagine of his Excellency.

He is called Sid-Abd-Alla Ben Hamed, is the elder brother
of Sid-Moussa, is about sixty years old, black, small, lean,
infirm on his legs, trembling and decrepit. He speaks little,
shuts his eyes often, and smiles courteously, bowing his head,
which is almost concealed in an immense turban. Nevertheless,
his appearance and manners are agreeable.

After the exchange of a few words, we were invited into the
dining-hall. The Ambassador first, and then all the others
one by one, stooping almost to a right angle, passed the little
low door, and came out into another court, spacious, surrounded
by an elegant arcade, and covered with splendid and various
ornaments in mosaic. It is a palace which was presented to
Sid-Abd-Alla by the Sultan. He himself gives us this information, bowing his head and closing his eyes with an air of
religious veneration.

In one corner of the court there was a group of officials in
white turbans and robes; on the other side a troop of servants,
among whom towered a very handsome young giant, dressed
all in blue, with a long pistol at his belt. At all the little
doors and windows in the four walls, heads of women and
children of various shades of complexion appeared and disappeared, and on every side was heard the voice of infancy.

We sat down around a small table, in a little room encumbered by two enormous beds. The Minister placed himself
next to, but a little behind, the Ambassador, and sat there all
the time of the breakfast, vigorously rubbing his bare black
foot, which he had planted on his knee, so that the ministerial
toes appeared just above the edge of the table, at a few inches
from the Commandant's plate. The soldiers of the Legation
waited at table. Close to it stood the young blue giant, with
his hand on his pistol.

Sid-Abd-Alla was very polite to the Ambassador.

"I like you very much," he said, without preamble, through the interpreter.

Breakfast at the War Minister's.

The Ambassador replied that he experienced the same sentiment towards him.

R 2

" I had scarcely seen you," continued the Minister, " when my heart was all yours."

The Ambassador returned the compliment.

" The heart," concluded Sid-Abd-Alla, " cannot be resisted; and when it commands you to love a person, even without knowing the reason, you must obey."

The Ambassador gave him his hand, which he pressed to his breast.

Eighteen dishes were served. I speak not of them. Enough to say that I hope that my partaking of them will some day be counted in my favour. By way of variety the water was flavoured with musk, the table-cloth of many colours, and the chairs tottering on their legs. But these little calamities, instead of putting us into an ill-humour, only excited our comic vein, so that seldom were we so full of mischievous frolic as on that occasion. If Sid-Abd-Alla could only have heard us! But Sid-Abd-Alla was entirely absorbed in the Ambassador. Signor Morteo alarmed us for an instant, by whispering to us that the blue giant, who was from Tunis, might possibly understand a few words of Italian. But observing him attentively when certain jokes were made, and seeing him always impassible as a statue, we were re-assured, and went on without minding him. How many apt and unexpected similes did we find, and with what clamorously comic effect, but unfortunately not to be repeated, for those ragoûts and sauces!

The breakfast over, we all went out into the court, where the Minister presented to the Ambassador one of the highest officers of the army. He was the Commander-in-Chief of the artillery; a little old man, dry, and bent like the letter C, with an enormous hooked nose and two round eyes; the face of a bird of prey; overwhelmed, rather than covered, by an immeasurable yellow turban of a spherical form, and dressed in a sort of Zouave dress, all blue, with a white mantle on his shoulders. He wore at his side a long sabre, and had a silver

poignard in his belt.   The Ambassador inquired to what rank in
a European army his own corresponded.   He seemed embarrassed
by the question.   He hesitated a moment, and then answered,
stammering, "General;" then he thought again, and said,

The Officers' Breakfast.

"No; Colonel," and was confused.   He said he was a native
of Algeria.   I had a suspicion that he was a renegade.   Who
knows by what strange vicissitudes he has come to be Colonel
in Morocco ?

The other officers, meantime, were breakfasting in a room
opening on the court, all sitting in a circle on the floor, with the
dishes in the midst.   Seeing them eat, I understood how it was

that the Moors could do without knives and forks. The neatness
and dexterity, the precision with which they pulled chickens,
mutton, game, and fish to pieces cannot be described. With a
few rapid movements of the hands, without the least discom-
posure, each one took his exact portion. They seemed to have
nails as sharp as razors. They dipped their fingers in the sauces,
made balls of the *cùscùssù*, ate salad by the handful, and not a
morsel or crumb fell from the dish ; and when they rose, we saw
that their caftans were immaculate. Every now and then a
servant carried round a basin and a towel ; they gave themselves
a wash, and then all together plunged their paws into the next
dish. No one spoke, no one raised his eyes, no one seemed to
notice that we were looking on.

What officers they were, whether of the staff, or adjutants,
or chiefs of division, or what, it is impossible to know in
Morocco. The army is the most mysterious of all their myste-
ries. They say, for example, that in case of a Holy war, when
the Djehad law shall be proclaimed, which calls every man under
arms who is capable of bearing them, the Sultan can raise two
hundred thousand soldiers ; but if they do not know even
approximately the number of the population of the empire, on
what do they base their calculations ? And the standing army,
who knows how large it is ? And how can anything be known, not
only of the numbers, but of the regulations, if, except the chiefs,
no one knows anything, and these latter either will not answer,
or do not tell the truth, and cannot make themselves understood ?

Sid-Abd-Alla, the most courteous of hosts, made us write all
our names in his pocket-book, and took leave of us, pressing our
hands one by one to his heart.

At the door we were joined by the blue giant, who, looking
at us with a cunning grin, said, in good Italian, though with a
Moorish accent, " *Signori, stiano bene !*"

Our jesting talk at table flashed on our minds, and we were
all struck dumb. Finally, " Ah, dog ! " cried Ussi. But the
dog had already vanished.

Our every movement out of doors is a military expedition; we must warn the Caid, get together the escort, send for the interpreters, order horses and mules, and an hour at least is spent in preparation. Consequently we stay a great part of the day within. But the spectacle there largely rewards us for our imprisonment. There is a continual procession of red soldiers, black servants, messengers from the Court, city traders, sick Moors in search of the doctor, Jewish rabbins coming to do homage to the Ambassador, other Jews with bunches of flowers, couriers with letters from Tangiers, porters bringing the *muna*. In the court are some workers in mosaic, working for Visconti Venosta; on the terrace, masons; in the kitchens, a coming and going of cooks; in the gardens are merchants spreading out their stuffs, and Signor Vincent his uniforms; the doctor is swinging in a hammock slung between two trees; the artists are painting before the door of their chamber; soldiers and servants are jumping and shouting in the neighbouring alleys; all the fountains spout and trickle with a noise of heavy rain, and hundreds of birds are warbling among the orange and lemon trees. The day passes between ball playing and Kaldun's history; the evening with chess, and singing directed by the Commandant, first tenor of Fez. My nights would be better passed if it were not for the continual flitting to and fro, like so many phantoms, of Mohammed Ducalè's black servants, who are in a little room adjoining mine. The doctor also sleeps in my room, and between us we have a poor wretch of an Arab servant, who makes us die with laughter. They say that he belongs to a family who, if not rich, are in easy circumstances, and that he joined the caravan as a servant at Tangiers, in order to make a *pleasure trip*. He had hardly reached Fez, the half of his pleasure trip, when for some trifling fault he caught a beating. After that he did his service with furious zeal. He understands nothing, not even gestures; and always looks like one frightened to death; if we ask for the chess-board, he brings a spittoon; and yesterday, when the doctor wanted bread, he brought him a

crust that he had picked up in the garden. We may try our
best to reassure him ; he is afraid of us, tries to mollify us with
all sorts of strange unnecessary services, such as changing the
water in our basins three times before we rise in the morning.
Moreover, in order to do a pleasing thing, he waits every
morning erect in the middle of the room with a cup of coffee in
his hand for the doctor or me to awake, and the first one that
gives signs of life he precipitates himself upon, and thrusts the
cup under his nose with the fury of one who is administering an
antidote. Another delightful personage is the washerwoman—a
big woman with a veiled face, a green petticoat, and red trousers,
who comes to get our linen, destined, alas! to be trampled by
Moors. It is superfluous to say that they iron nothing ; in all
Fez there does not exist a smoothing iron, and we put on our
linen exactly as it comes from under the hoofs of the washer-
men. " Perhaps," said some one, " there might be an iron in
the Mellà ? " There might be, but the difficulty is to find it.
There *is* a carriage, but it belongs to the Sultan. It is said that
there is also a piano-forte ; it was seen to come into the city
some years ago, but it is not known who possesses it. It is
amusing also to send to buy something in the shops. " A
candle ?"—" There are none," is the answer ; " but we will
make some presently." " A yard of ribbon ? "—" It will be
ready by to-morrow evening." " Cigars ? "—" We have the
tobacco, and will have them ready in an hour." The Vice-
Consul spent several days looking for an old Arabic book, and
all the Moors he questioned looked at each other and said, " A
book ? Who has books in Fez ? There were some once ; if we
are not mistaken, so and so had them ; but he is dead, and we
do not know who are his heirs." " And Arabic journals, or
other journals, could we have them ? "—" One single journal,
printed in Arabic in Algiers, arrives regularly at Fez, but it is
addressed to the Sultan."

Yet, I have an idea that we are less than two hundred miles
from Gibraltar, where probably this evening they are giving *Lucia*

di Lammermoor, and that in eight days we could reach the *Loggia dei Lanzi* at Florence. But in spite of this conviction I feel a sentiment of immense remoteness. It is not miles but things and people that divide us most from our country. With what pleasure we tear off the bands of our journals, and break open our letters! Poor letters, that fly from the hands of the Carlists in Spain, pass through the midst of the brigands of the Sierra-Morena, overpass the peaks of the red mountain, swim, clasped in the hands of a Bedouin, the waters of the Kus, the Sebù, the Mechez, and the river of the Azure Fountain, and bring us a loving word in this land of reproaches and maledictions.

We pass many hours in watching the painters work. Ussi has made a fine sketch of the great reception, in which the figure of the Sultan is wonderfully well done; Biseo, an excellent painter of Oriental architecture, is copying the façade of the small house in the garden. It is worth while, for diversion, to hear the soldiers and shopkeepers of Fez who come to see that picture. They come on tiptoe behind the painter, and look over his shoulder making a telescope with their hand, and then they all begin to laugh, as if they had discovered something very odd. The great oddity is that in the drawing the second arch of the façade is smaller than the first, and the third smaller than the second. Devoid as they are of any idea of perspective, they believe that this inequality is an error, and they say that the walls are crooked, that the house totters, that the door is out of place, and they are much astonished, and go away saying the artist is a donkey. Ussi is more esteemed, since it is known that he has been at Cairo, and that he has painted the departure of the caravan for Mecca by the order of the Viceroy, who paid him fifteen thousand scudi. They say, however, that the Viceroy was mad to pay such a sum for a work on which the artist had expended perhaps about a hundred francs for colours. A merchant asked Morteo if Ussi could paint furniture also. But the best story is about Biseo, who goes every morning in New Fez to paint a mosque. He goes, of course, escorted by five or six

soldiers armed with sticks.   Before he has set up his easel, he is
surrounded by about three hundred people, and the soldiers are
obliged to yell furiously and make play with their sticks to keep
enough space open for him to see the mosque.   At every stroke

Shops in Fez.

of the brush, a blow with a stick; but they let themselves be
beaten, and do worse.   Every little while a saint appears with
threatening gestures, and the soldiers keep him off.   There are
also some progressive Moors, who come up with friendly aspect,
look, approve, and retire with signs of encouragement.   The

greater part of these progressists, however, admire a great deal more the structure of the easel and the portable seat than they do the picture. One day a savage-looking Moor shook his fist at the painter, and then, turning to the crowd, made a long speech with excited voice and gestures. An interpreter explained that he was exciting the people against Biseo, saying that that *dog* had been sent by the king of his country to copy the finest mosques in Fez, so that when the Christian army came to bombard the place, they could recognise and attack them first. Yesterday (I was present), a ragged old Moor, a good-natured old rascal, accosted him, appearing to have a great deal to say, and bringing out his words with much difficulty, he exclaimed with emotion, " France ! London ! Madrid ! Rome ! " We were much astonished, as may be supposed, and asked him if he knew how to speak French, Italian, or Spanish. He made signs that he could. " Speak, then," I said. He scratched his forehead, sighed, stamped his foot, and again exclaimed, " France ! London ! Madrid ! Rome ! " and pointed towards the horizon. He wanted to tell us that he had seen those countries, and perhaps that once he knew how to make himself understood in our tongues ; but he had forgotten them all. We put other questions to him, but could draw nothing from him but those four names. And he went away repeating, " Madrid ! Rome ! France ! London ! " as long as we could see him, and saluting us affectionately with his hand.

" We find all sorts of people here," said Biseo, provoked ; " even originals who wish us well and like us, but not a single dog that will let me paint him."

It is true that up to this moment the utmost efforts of the artists in that direction had failed. Even our faithful Selam refused.

" Are you afraid of the devil ? " demanded Ussi.

" No," he answered, with solemnity ; " I am afraid of God."

We have been up on the top of Mount Zalag—the Com-

mandant, Ussi, and I—guided by Captain de Boccard, a charming young fellow, equally admirable for the activity of his body,
the strength of his soul, and the acumen of his intelligence.
We were accompanied by an officer of the escort, three foot
soldiers, three cavalry soldiers, and three servants. At the
foot of the mountain, which is about an hour and a half from
the north-east of the city, we stopped to breakfast; after
which the Captain stuck an apple on a stick, put a *scudo* on the
apple, and made the soldiers and servants fire at it with his
revolver. The prize was tempting—they all fired with much
care; but as it was the first time they had ever had a revolver
in their hands, everybody missed, and the *scudo* was given
to the officer to be divided between them. It was laughable to
see the attitudes they took when taking aim. One threw
his head back, one bent forward, one put his chin quite over
the trigger, and one stood on guard as if fencing with a sabre.
Accustomed as they were to terrible attitudes, not one knew
how to adapt himself to the quiet, easy position which the
Captain tried to teach them. A soldier came to ask if we
would give something to a country-woman who had brought us
some milk. We said, Yes, on condition that the woman came
herself to get it. She came. She was a black, deformed
creature, about thirty years of age, covered with rags, and in
every way repulsive. She came towards us slowly, covering her
face with one hand; and when about five paces from us, turned
her back, and extended the other hand. The Commandant was
disgusted. "Be easy," he called out; "I am not in love.
I shall not lose my head; I can still control myself. Good
gracious, what frightful modesty!"

We put some money in her hand, she picked up her milk
jug, ran off towards her hut, and at the door smashed the profaned vessel against a stone.

We began the ascent on foot, accompanied by a part of
the escort. The mountain is about one thousand feet above
the level of the sea—steep, rocky, and without paths. In a

few minutes the Captain disappeared among the rocks; but for
the Commandant, Ussi, and I, it was one of the twelve labours
of Hercules. We had each an Arab at our side, who told

A Butcher's Shop in Fez.

us where to place our feet; and at some points we were obliged
to climb like cats, clinging to bushes and grass, slipping on
the rocks, stumbling, and seizing the arms of our guides as
drowning men seize a saving plank. Here and there we see
a goat, seemingly suspended above our heads, so steep is the

ascent; and the stones, scarcely touched, roll to the very
bottom of the mountain. With God's help, in an hour's
time we are on the top of the mountain, exhausted, but with
whole bones. What a lovely view! At the bottom, the
city, a little white spot in the form of an eight, surrounded
by black walls, cemeteries, gardens, *cube*, towers, and all the
verdant shell that holds them; on the left, a long shining
line, the Sebù; to the right, the great plain of Fez, streaked
with silver by the Pearl river and the River of the Azure
Fountain; to the south, the blue peaks of the great Atlas
chain; to the north, the mountains of the Rif; to the east,
the vast undulating plain where is the fortress of Teza, which
closes the pass between the basin of the Sebù and that of the
Mulaia; below us, great waves of ground yellow with grain
and barley, marked by innumerable paths, and long files of
gigantic aloes; a grandeur of lines, a magnificence of verdure,
a limpidity of sky, a silence and peace that steeped the soul in
paradise. Who would guess that in that terrestrial paradise
dwelt and dozed a decrepit people, chained on a heap of ruins.
The mountain that, seen from the city, appeared a cone, has an
elongated form, and is rocky on the top. The Captain mounted
to the highest point; we three, more careful of our lives,
scattered ourselves about among the rocks below, and went out
of sight of each other. I had made but a few steps, when at
the entrance of a little gorge I met an Arab. I stopped; he
stopped also, and looked much amazed at my appearance and
my being alone. He was a man of about fifty, of a truculent
aspect, and armed with a big stick. For a moment I suspected
that he might attack me and take my purse; but to my great
astonishment, instead of assailing me, he saluted me, smiled,
and taking hold of his own beard with one hand, pointed to
mine with the other, and said something, repeating it two or
three times. It sounded like a question, to which he desired an
answer. Moved by curiosity, I called for the officer of the
guard, who knew a little Spanish, and begged him to tell me

what the man wanted. Who would ever have guessed it? He wanted to pay me a compliment, and had asked me *ex abrupto* why I did not let my beard grow, when it would be more beautiful than his own!

The soldiers of the escort were following us all three at about twenty paces distance, and as we frequently called to each other in a loud voice, and it was the first time that they had heard our names, they found them strange, laughing and repeating them with their Moorish accent, in the oddest way: *"Isi! Amigi!"* At a certain point the officer said, abruptly, *"Scut!"* (Silence!) and they all were silent. The sun was high, the rocks were scorching; even the Captain, accustomed to the heats of Tunis, felt the need of shade; we gave a last look at the peaks of Atlas, scrambled down the mountain, and hastily

A Water Carrier.

getting into our crimson saddles, took the way back to **Fez**, where we had an agreeable surprise. The gate of El Ghisa, where we were to enter the city, was closed! "Let us go in by another," said the Commandant. "They are all closed,"

answered the officer of the guard; and, seeing us open our
eyes, he explained the mystery, saying that on all festivals
(this was Friday), from twelve o'clock to one, which is the hour
of prayer, all the city gates are closed, because it is a Mussulman belief that exactly at that hour, but no one knows in what
year, the Christians will take possession of their country by a
coup de main.

We had then to wait for the opening of the gates; and
when at last we got in, we were received with a flowery
compliment. An old woman shook her fist at us, and muttered
something which the officer refused to translate; but we in-
sisting, he finally consented, with a smile, and an assurance
that she was an old fool, and her words could do us no harm.
What she said was this: "The Jews to the hook (to be boiled),
the Christians to the spit!"

The doctor has performed the operation for cataract, *coram
populo,* in the garden of the palace. There was a crowd of
relations and friends, soldiers and servants, part disposed in a
circle around the patient, part ranged in a long file from the
spot where the operation was being done to the gate of the
street, where another crowd stood waiting. The patient was
an old Moor who had been quite blind for three years. At the
moment of taking his seat, he stopped as if frightened; then
sat down with a resolute air, and gave no further sign of
weakness. Whilst the doctor operated, the people stood as if
petrified. The children clung to their mothers' gowns, and the
latter embraced each other in attitudes of terror, as if they were
looking on at an execution. Not a breath could be heard.
We also, on account of the "diplomatic" importance of the
operation, were in great anxiety. All at once the patient gave
a cry of joy, and threw himself on his knees. He had seen the
first ray of light. All the people in the garden saluted the
doctor with a yell, to which another yell responded from those
in the street. The soldiers immediately made everybody,
except the patient, go out from the precincts of the palace, and

in a short time, the news of the marvellous operation was all over Fez. Fortunate doctor! He had his reward that very evening, when he was called upon to visit the harem of the Grand Schereef Bacalì, where the loveliest ladies showed themselves to him with uncovered faces, and in all the pomp of their splendid attire, and talked languidly of their pains and aches. . . . .

From time to time some renegade Spaniards come to see Señor Patxot. There are said to be about three hundred of these unfortunate men in the empire. Most of them are Spaniards, condemned for some common crimes, fugitives from the galleys of the coast; others, partly French deserters, are fugitives from Algeria; and the rest are rascals from all parts of Europe. In other times they rose to high positions in the Court and army, formed special military corps, and received large pay; but now their condition is much changed. When they arrive, they abjure the Christian religion, and embrace Islamism, without circumcision or other ceremony, merely pronouncing a formula. No one cares whether they fulfil their religious duties or not; the greater part of them never enter a mosque, and know no form of prayer. In order to bind them to the country, the Sultan exacts that they shall marry. He gives to whoever wants her one of his black women; the others can marry an Arab free woman or a Moor, and the Sultan pays the expenses of the wedding. They must all be enrolled in the army; but they can, at the same time, exercise a trade. They generally enter the artillery, and some belong to the bands of music, the head of which is a Spaniard. The soldiers receive five *sous* a day, and the officers twenty-five to thirty; if any one has a special talent, he can make as much as two francs a day. Lately, for instance, they were talking of a German renegade, endowed with a certain talent for mechanics, who had made for himself an enviable position. This man, for some reason unknown, had fled from Algeria in '73, and had gone to Tafilet, on the confines of the desert; there he stayed two years,

s

learned Arabic, and came to Fez, entered the army, and in a
few days, with some tools that he had, constructed a revolver.
The event made a noise; the revolver passed from hand to hand,
and reached the Minister of War; the Minister told the Sultan,
who sent for the soldier, encouraged him, gave him ten francs,
and raised his daily pay to forty *sous*.   But such good fortune
is rare.   Almost all of them live wretched lives, and their state
of mind is such, that although they are known to be stained
with serious crimes, they inspire pity rather than horror.   Yesterday two presented themselves, renegades since two years, with
wives, and children born at Fez.   One was thirty, the other
fifty years old, both Spaniards, fugitives from Ceuta.   The
younger one did not speak.   The elder said that he had been condemned to hard labour for life for having killed a man who was
beating his son to death.   He was pale, and spoke in a broken
voice, tearing his handkerchief with trembling hands.

   " If they would promise to keep me only ten years in the
galleys," he said, " I would go back.   I am fifty; I should
come out at sixty, and might still live a few years in my own
country.   But it is the thought of dying with the brand of
the galleys upon me that frightens me.   I would go back at
any rate, if I were sure of dying a free man in Spain.   This is
not living, this existence that we have here.   It is like being
in a desert.   It is frightful.   Every one despises us.   Our own
family is not our own, because our children are taught to hate
us.   And then, we never forget the religion in which we were
born, the church where our mothers used to take us to pray,
the counsels they gave us; and those memories—we are renegades, we are galley-slaves, it is true, but still we are men—
those memories tear our hearts !" and he wept as he spoke.

   The rain which has been pouring down for three days has
reduced Fez to an indescribable and incredible condition.   It
is no longer a city; it is a sewer.   The streets are gutters;
the crossings, lakes; the squares, seas; the people on foot sink
into the mud up to their knees; the houses are plastered with

it above the doors; men, horses, and mules look as if they had been rolling in mud; and as for the dogs, they were at

the outset plas-
tered in such a
way that they
have not a hair
visible. Few
people are to be
seen, and those
mostly on horse-
back; not an um-
brella, or even a
person hastening
to escape the rain.
Outside the quar-
ters of the bazaars
all is depressingly
dark and deser-
ted. Water is
running and rush-
ing everywhere,
carrying with it
every sort of pu-
tridity, and no
voice or other
human sound
breaks the mono-
tony of its deaf-
ening noise. It
looks like a city
abandoned by its
inhabitants after
an inundation.

A Street in Fez.

After an hour's turn, I came home in a most melancholy mood, and passed the time with my face pressed against the window-

s 2

bars, watching the dripping trees, and thinking of the poor
courier, who perhaps at that very moment was swimming a
flooded river at the risk of his life, carrying in his teeth the bag
that contained my letters from home.

It is said, and denied, that there has been within a few days
a capital execution before one of the gates of Fez. No head
has appeared upon the walls, however, and I prefer to think the
news is false. The description, which I once read, of an execution done at Tangiers, some years ago, deprived me of the
barbarous curiosity that I formerly had to be present at one
of these spectacles.

An Englishman, Mr. Drummond Hay, coming out one
morning at one of the gates of Tangiers, saw a company of
soldiers dragging along two prisoners with their arms bound
to their sides. One was a mountaineer from the Rif, formerly
gardener to a European resident at Tangiers; the other, a handsome young fellow, tall, and with an open and attractive
countenance.

The Englishman asked the officer in command what crime
these two unfortunate men had committed.

"The Sultan," was the answer—"may God prolong his
days!—has ordered their heads to be cut off because they have
been engaged in contraband trade, on the coast of the Rif, with
infidel Spaniards."

"It is a very severe punishment for such a fault," observed
the Englishman; "and if it is to serve as a warning and
example to the inhabitants of Tangiers, why are they not
allowed to be present at it?"

(The gates of the city had been closed, and Mr. Drummond
Hay had caused one to be opened for him by giving some money
to the guard.)

"Do not argue with me, Nazarene!" responded the officer;
" I have received an order and must obey."

The decapitation was to take place in the Hebrew slaughter-
house. A Moor of vulgar and hideous aspect, dressed like a

butcher, was there awaiting the condemned. He had in his hand a small knife, about six inches long. He was a stranger in the city, and had offered himself as executioner, because the Mohammedan butchers of Tangiers, who usually fill that office, had all taken refuge in a mosque.

An altercation now broke out between the soldiers and the executioner about the reward promised for the decapitation of the two poor creatures, who stood by and listened to the dispute over the blood-money. The executioner insisted, declaring that he had been promised twenty francs a head, and must have forty for the two. The officer at last agreed, but with a very ill grace. Then the butcher seized one of the condemned men, already half dead with terror, threw him on the ground, kneeled on his chest, and put the knife to his throat. The Englishman turned away his face. He heard the sounds of a violent struggle. The executioner cried out, "Give me another knife; mine does not cut!" Another knife was brought, and the head separated from the body.

The soldiers cried, in a faint voice, "God prolong the life of our lord and master!" But many of them were stupefied with terror.

Then came the other victim : the handsome and amiable-looking young man. Again they wrangled over his blood. The officer, denying his promise, declared he would give but twenty francs for both heads. The butcher was forced to yield. The condemned asked that his hands might be unbound. Being loosed, he took his cloak and gave it to the soldier who had unbound him, saying, "Accept this; we shall meet in a better world!" He threw his turban to another, who had been looking at him with compassion, and stepping to the place where lay the bloody corpse of his companion, he said, in a clear, firm voice, "There is no God but God, and Mahomet is His prophet!" Then taking off his belt he gave it to the executioner, saying, "Take it; but for the love of God cut my head off more quickly than you did my brother's." He stretched himself on the earth, in the blood, and the executioner kneeled upon his chest.

"A reprieve! Stop!" cried the Englishman. A horseman came galloping towards them. The executioner held his knife suspended.

"It is only the Governor's son," said a soldier. "He is coming to see the execution. Wait for him."

So it was, indeed. A few minutes after two bleeding heads were held up by the soldiers. Then the gates of the city were opened, and there came forth a crowd of boys, who pursued the executioner with stones for three miles, when he fell fainting to the ground, covered with wounds. The next day it was known that he had been shot by a relation of one of the victims, and buried where he fell. The authorities of Tangiers apparently did not trouble themselves about the matter, since the assassin came back into the city and remained unmolested.

After having been exposed three days, the heads were sent to the Sultan, in order that his Imperial Majesty might recognise the promptitude with which his orders had been fulfilled. The soldiers who were carrying them met on their way a courier, bearing a pardon, who had been detained by the sudden flooding of a river.

I frequently find merchants of Fez who have been in Italy. Forty or fifty of them go there every year, and many have Moorish or Arab agents in their cities. They go particularly to Upper Italy, where they buy raw silks, damasks, corals, velvets, thread, porcelain, pearls, Venice glass, Genoa playing-cards, and Leghorn muslin. In exchange they carry nothing but wax and wool, for trade in Morocco is much restricted; and it may be said that stuffs, arms, hides, and earthenware or pottery, are their only productions which attract a European's attention. The stuffs are made chiefly in Fez and Morocco. There are *caics* for women, lordly turbans, sashes, *foulards* of silk delicately woven with gold and silver, generally in stripes of soft and harmonious colours, very pretty at first sight, but unequal when examined, full of gum, and not wearing well. The red caps, on the contrary, which take the name from Fez, are very fine and durable, and the carpets made at Rabat, Casa Bianca, Morocco, Sciadma, and Sciania are admirable for solidity and richness of colour. From Tetuan come in great

A Deputation of Jews.

part the damascened muskets, inlaid with ivory and silver, carved, and set with precious stones, of light and elegant form; and Mechinez and Fez, and the province of Sus make the swords and daggers which are sometimes of such admirable workmanship.

Hides, the principal source of gain for the country, are well prepared in various provinces, and the scarlet leather of Fez, the yellow of Morocco, and the green of Tafilet, are still worthy of their ancient reputation. In Fez they boast particularly of their enamelled pottery, but it is rare to find the noble purity of form of the antique vase; and their chief merit is a brilliancy of colour, and a certain barbaric originality of design which attract the eye, but do not satisfy it. There are also in Fez a great number of jewellers and goldsmiths, who make some simple things in very good taste, but few, and of little variety, because the Amalechite rite proscribes the display of precious ornaments as contrary to Mahometan austerity. More notable than the jewellery is the furniture which comes from Tetuan: book-shelves, clothes-pegs, and little polygonal tea-tables, arched, arabesqued, and painted in many colours; copper vessels also, chased in complicated designs and ornamented with green, red, and blue enamel; and, above all, the mosaics of the pavements and walls, composed in exquisite taste by clever workmen, who form the designs with marvellous precision.

There is no doubt that these people are endowed with admirable faculties, and that their industries would increase immensely, as also their agriculture, which was once so flourishing, if commerce could make them live; but commerce is hampered with a thousand prohibitions, restrictions, monopolies, excessive tariffs, continual modifications, and the non-observance of treaties; and, although the European governments have obtained many privileges of late years, these are but small in comparison with what might be brought about, thanks to the wealth and geographical position of the country, under a civil government. The principal trade is that with England, after which come France and Spain, who give cereals, metals, sugar, tea, coffee, raw silk, woollen and cotton cloths, and take wool, hides, fruit, leeches, gum, wax, and a great part of the products of Central Africa. The trade which is carried on by Fez, Taza, and Udjda (and it is not of small importance, though less than that which the neighbourhood of the two countries should produce), comprehends, besides carpets, the cloths, belts, thick cords, and all the parts of the Arab and Moorish dress, bracelets and anklets of silver and gold, vases from Fez, mosaics, perfumes, incense, antimony for the eyes, *henna* for the nails, and all the other cosmetics used by the fair sex of Africa. Of more importance, more ancient, and

Cloth Bazaar.

more regular, is the commerce with the interior of Africa, for which place every year great caravans go forth, carrying stuffs from Fez, English cloths, Venetian glass, Italian corals, powder, arms, tobacco, sugar, small mirrors from Germany, feathers from Holland, little boxes from the Tyrol, hardware from

England and France, and salt, which they get on their way
in the Sahara; and their journey is like a travelling fair, where
their own merchandise is exchanged for black slaves, gold
dust, ostrich feathers, white gum from Senegal, gold ornaments
from Nigritia, which are afterwards sent to Europe and the
East; black stuffs which are worn on the heads of Moorish
women; *bezoar*, which preserves the Arabs from poison and
illness; and many drugs which have been abandoned in Europe,
but preserve their ancient value in Africa. Here is, for Europe,
the chief importance of Morocco : it is the principal gate of
Nigritia; where, being open, the commerce of Europe and that
of Central Africa will meet. Meanwhile, civilisation and
barbarism contend upon the threshold.

The Ambassador has frequent conferences with Sid Moussa.
His principal intent is to obtain from the Government of the
Schereefs certain concessions in trade by which Italy shall be
the gainer : more I may not say. These conferences last more
than two hours; but the conversation turns but briefly upon the
real question in discussion, because the Minister, following a
custom which seems traditional in the policy of the Government
of Morocco, never comes to the point until he has wandered over
a hundred extraneous subjects, and when he is dragged to it by
force. " Let us talk a little about something entertaining," he
says, in almost a beseeching tone. The weather, health, the
water of Fez, the properties of certain tissues, some historical
anecdotes, some proverbs, what may be the population of certain
states of Europe : all these are more agreeable subjects than the
one which is the purpose of the interview. " What do you say
of Fez ? " he asked one day ; and being answered that it was
beautiful, he added, " And it has another merit; it is clean ! "
Another day he wished to know what was the population of
Morocco. But at last the business must come ; and then there are
long phrases, hesitations, reticences, silences, a putting forth of
doubts when consent is already decided upon, a pretended denial
of condescension, a slipping through the fingers, a constant

SQUARE IN FEZ.

dropping of the subject just as the knot is about to be tightened, and then the eternal expedient " to-morrow."

The next day, recapitulation of things said the day before, new doubts, restrictions, recognition of equivocations, regrets for not having understood, and for not having been understood, and exhaustion of the interpreter charged with the duty of making things clear. And then it is necessary to wait for the return of the couriers from Tangiers and Tafilet, who have been sent to obtain information—information of little consequence, but which serves to put off the solution of the question for ten days longer. And, in fine, three great obstacles to everything : the fanaticism of the people, the obstinacy of the Ulemas and the necessity of proceeding cautiously, not exciting attention, with a slowness that looks like immobility. Under these conditions, Job himself might be expected to cry out; but then come the warm pressures of the hand, the sweet smiles, the demonstrations of an irresistible sympathy, and an affection that will only end in death. The most difficult affair is that of the big Moor Schellal, and they say that the fate of his whole life depends upon it ; consequently he is for ever at the palace, wrapped in his ample caic, anxious, thoughtful, sometimes with tears in his eyes, and he keeps them fixed upon the Ambassador with a supplicating look, like that of one condemned to death and begging for reprieve. Mohammed Ducalè, on the contrary, whose sails are swelled by favouring gales, is gay and sprightly, perfumes himself, smokes, changes his caftan every day, and strews on all sides his soft words, and jests, and smiles. Ah ! if it were not for Italian influence, how soon those smiles would be changed into tears of blood !

We are experiencing in these days the truth of what was told us at Tangiers with regard to the effects of the air of Fez. Are these effects produced by the air or by the water ? or by the rascally oil ? or by the infamous butter ? or by all these things together ? However it may be, it is a fact that we are all ill. Languor, loss of appetite, prostration of strength, and heaviness of head. And with all these ill-feelings there is a weariness, an irritability, a sort of horror, that in a few days have changed the face of the whole house. Every one longs for departure. We have reached that point, inevitable in all long journeys, at which curiosity is dulled, everything seems faded, memories of home rise up in crowds; all the longings, kept down at first, are alive and in tumult; and our own country is ever before our eyes. We have had enough of turbans, and black faces, and mosques; we are tired of being stared at by a thousand eyes; bored by this immense masquerade in white at which we have been looking for two months. What would we not give to see pass by, even at a distance, a European lady! to hear the sound of a bell! to see on a wall a printed play-bill! Oh, sweetest memories!

I have discovered among the soldiers of the guard one who has lost his right ear, and am told that it was legally cut off, in presence of witnesses, by another soldier whose ear the first one had mutilated some time before. Such is the *lex talionis* as it exists in Morocco. Not only has any relation of a person killed the right to kill the assassin on the same day of the week, at the same hour and place where the victim fell, using the same weapon, and striking in the same part of the body, but whoever has been deprived of a limb has the right to deprive his assailant of the same limb. A fact of this nature, accompanied by very singular circumstances, happened some years ago at Mogador, and was related to me by a member of the French Consulate, who knew one of the victims. An English merchant of Mogador was returning to the city on the evening of a market-day, at the moment when the gate by which he was entering was encumbered with a crowd of country people driving camels and asses. Although the Englishman called out as loud as he could, *"Bal-ak! bal-ak!"* (Make way!) an old woman was struck by his horse and knocked down, falling with her face upon a stone. Ill-fortune would have it that in the fall she broke the two last of her front teeth. She was stunned for an instant, and then rose convulsed with rage, and broke out into insults and ferocious maledictions, following the Englishman to his own door. She then went before the Caid, and demanded, that in virtue of the law of talion, he should order the English merchant's two front teeth to be broken. The Caid tried to pacify her, and advised her to pardon the injury; but she would listen to nothing, and

Ironing Cloth.

he sent her away with a promise that she should have justice, hoping that when her anger should be exhausted she would herself desist from her pursuit. But, three days having passed, the old woman came back more furious than ever, demanded justice, and insisted that a formal sentence should be pronounced against the Christian.

"Remember," said she to the Caid, "thou didst promise me!"

" *Che !* " responded the Caid. " Dost thou take me for a Christian, that I should be the slave of my word ? "

Every day for a month the old woman, athirst for vengeance, presented herself at the door of the citadel, and yelled, and cursed, and made such a noise, that the Caid, to be rid of her, was obliged to consent. He sent for the merchant, explained the case, the right which the law gave the woman, the duty imposed upon himself, and begged him to put an end to the matter by allowing two of his teeth to be removed, any two, although in strict justice they should be two incisors. The Englishman refused absolutely to part with incisors, or eye-teeth, or molars ; and the Caid was constrained to send the old woman packing, ordering the guard not to let her put her foot in the Casba again.

" Very well," said she ; " since there are none but degenerate Mussulmans here, since justice is refused to a Mussulman woman, mother of schereefs, against an infidel dog, I will go to the Sultan, and we shall see whether the prince of the faithful will deny the law of the Prophet."

True to her determination, she started on her journey alone, with an amulet in her bosom, a stick in her hand, and a bag around her neck, and made on foot the hundred leagues which separate Mogador from the sacred city of the empire. Arrived at Fez, she sought and obtained audience of the Sultan, laid her case before him, and demanded the right accorded by the Koran, the application of the law of retaliation. The Sultan exhorted her to forgive ; she insisted. All the serious difficulties which opposed themselves to the satisfaction of her petition were laid before her ; she remained inexorable. A sum of money was offered her, with which she could live in comfort for the rest of her days ; she refused it.

" What do I want with your money ? " said she ; " I am old, and accustomed to live in poverty ; what I want is the two teeth of the Christian ; I want them, I demand them in the name of the Koran ; and the Sultan, prince of the faithful, head

of Islamism, father of his subjects, cannot refuse justice to a
true believer."

Her obstinacy put the Sultan in a most embarrassing position;
the law was formal, and her right incontestable; and the ferment
of the populace, stirred up by the woman's fanatical declamations,

Moorish Grindstone.

rendered refusal perilous. The Sultan, who was Abd-er-Rhaman,
wrote to the English Consul, asking as a favour that he would
induce his countryman to allow two of his teeth to be broken.
The merchant answered the Consul that he would never consent.
Then the Sultan wrote again, saying that if he would consent, he
would grant him as a recompense any commercial privilege that
he chose to ask. This time, touched in his purse, the merchant

yielded. The old woman left Fez, blessing the name of the pious Abd-er-Rhaman, and went back to Mogador, where, in the presence of many people, the two teeth of the Nazarene were broken. When she saw them fall to the ground she gave a yell of triumph, and picked them up with a fierce joy. The merchant, thanks to the privileges that had been accorded him, made in the two following years so handsome a fortune that he went back to England toothless, but happy.

The more I study these people, the more I am inclined to believe that the judgment unanimously passed upon them by travellers is not far from the truth, and that they are a race of vipers and foxes—false, pusillanimous, cringing to the powerful, insolent to the weak, gnawed by avarice, devoured by egotism, and burning with the basest passions of which the human heart is capable. How could they be otherwise? The nature of the government and the state of society permit them no manly ambition. They traffic and bargain, but they have no knowledge of the labour that begets fatigue of body and serenity of mind; they are completely ignorant of any pleasure that is derived from the exercise of the intelligence; they take no care for the education of their sons; they have no high aims in life : therefore they give themselves up, with all their souls and for their whole lives, to the amassing of money; and the time that is left to them from this pursuit they divide between a sleepy indolence that enervates, and sensual pleasures that brutalise them. In this life of effeminacy they naturally become vain, small, malignant, tattling creatures; lacerating each other's reputation with spiteful rage; lying by habit with an incredible impudence; affecting charitable and pious sentiments, and sacrificing a friend for a scudo; despising knowledge, and accepting the most puerile superstitions; bathing every day, and keeping masses of filth in the recesses of their houses; and adding to all this a satanic pride, concealed, when convenient, under a manner both dignified and humble, which seems the index of an honourable mind. They deceived me in

T

this way at first; but now I am persuaded that the very least
of them believes, in the bottom of his heart, that he is infinitely
superior to us all. The nomadic Arab preserves at least the
austere simplicity of his antique customs, and the Berber, savage
as he is, has a warlike spirit, courage, and love of independence.
Only these Moors have within them a combination of barbarism,
depravity, and pride, and are the most powerful of the populations of the empire. From them come the merchants, the
ulemas, the *tholbas,* the caids, the pashas; they possess the
rich palaces, the great harems, beautiful women, and hidden
treasures. They are recognisable by their fat, their fair complexions, their cunning eyes, their big turbans, their majestic
walk, their arrogance, and their perfumes.

We have been to take tea at the house of the Moor Schellal.
We entered by a narrow corridor into a small, dark court, but
beautiful—beautiful and filthy as the filthiest house in the
ghetto of Alkazar. Except the mosaics of the pavement and
pilasters, everything was black, encrusted, sticky with dirt.
There were two little dark rooms on the ground-floor; round
the first floor ran a light gallery, and on the top was the
parapet of the terrace. The big Moor made us sit down before
the door of his sleeping-room, gave us tea and sweetmeats,
burned aloes, sprinkled us with rose-water, and presented his
children to us—two pretty boys, who came to us white with
terror, trembling like leaves under our caresses. On the
opposite side of the court there was a black slave-girl of about
fifteen, having on only a sort of chemise, which was open at the
side as far up as the hip, and confined round the waist with a
girdle, the slenderest, the most elegant, the most beautiful
female creature (I attest it on the head of Ussi) that I had seen
in all Morocco. She was leaning against a pilaster with her
arms crossed on her bosom, looking at us with an air of supreme
indifference. Presently there came out of a small door another
black woman, of about thirty years of age, tall in stature, of an
austere countenance and robust figure, straight as a palm-tree;

who, as it seemed, must have been a favourite with her master, for she advanced familiarly, whispered some words in his ear, pulled out a small bit of straw that was stuck in his beard, and pressed her hand upon his lips with an action at once listless

Negro Slave of Fez.

and caressing that made the Moor smile. Looking up, we saw the gallery on the first floor and the parapet of the terrace fringed with women's heads, which instantly disappeared. It was impossible for them all to belong to that house. The visit of the Christians had no doubt been announced in the neighbourhood, and friends from other terraces had come over

T 2

to Schellal's terrace. Just as we were gazing upwards, three
ghost-like forms passed by us, their heads entirely concealed,
and vanished through the small door. They were three friends,
who, not being able to come by the terraces, had been forced
to resign themselves to enter by the door; and a moment after
their heads appeared above the railing of the gallery. The
house, in short, had been converted into a theatre, and we were
the spectacle. The veiled spectators prattled, and with much
low laughter, popped up their heads, and withdrew them again
as if they had flown away. Each one of our movements produced a slight murmur; every time one of us raised his head
there was a great tumult in the first row of boxes. It was
evident that they were much entertained, that they were gathering material for a month's conversation, and that they could
scarcely contain themselves for delight at finding themselves
so unexpectedly in the enjoyment of so strange and rare a
spectacle! And we complacently obliged them for about an
hour—silent, however, and much bored, an effect produced, after
a time, by every Moorish house, however courteous its hospitality.

And then, after you have admired the beautiful mosaics, the
handsome slaves, and pretty children, you look about instinc-
tively for the person who is the incarnation of domestic life,
who represents the courtesy and honourability of the house,
who puts the seal on its hospitality, who gives its tone to the
conversation, who represents to your mind the altar of the
Lares,—you seek, in short, the pearl for this shell; and seeing
no one but women who have their master's embraces without
his affection, and children of unknown mothers, and the whole
house personified in one being only, its hospitality becomes a
mere empty ceremony; and in your host, instead of the
sympathetic features of an honoured friend, you see only the
aspect of a sensual and odious egotist.

There is no doubt that these people, if they do not hate
us absolutely, at least cannot endure us, and they are not

without some good reasons. Being among the descendants of the Moors of Spain, many of them still preserve the keys of cities in Andalusia, and titles to the possession of lands and houses in Seville and Granada, and their aversion to Spaniards is peculiarly acrid, their fathers having been despoiled and driven out by them. All the others nourish a general hatred to all Christians, not only because this hatred is instilled into them in their schools and mosques from their earliest infancy, with the purpose of rendering any commerce with civilised races odious to them, commerce which, scattering ignorance and superstition, would undermine the foundations of the empire; but because they all have in the bottom of their souls a vague suspicion of an expansive, growing, threatening force in the States of Europe, by which, sooner or later, they will be crushed. They hear the rising murmur of the French upon their eastern frontier; they see the Spaniards fortified on their Mediterranean coast; Tangiers is occupied by an advanced guard of Christians; the cities of the west are guarded by a line of European merchants, stretching along the Atlantic coast like a chain of sentinels; ambassadors come into the country from different directions, apparently to bring gifts to the Sultan, but in reality, as they believe, to look, and scrutinise, and pry, and corrupt, and prepare the ground; they hear, in short, a perpetual threat of invasion, and imagine this invasion accompanied by all the horrors of hatred and revenge, persuaded, as they are, that Christians nourish against Moors the same sentiments which the latter feel towards us. How can they change this aversion into sympathy when they see us, in our tight, immodest costume; dressed in gloomy colours; loaded with notebooks, telescopes, mysterious instruments which we direct at everything, noting all things, measuring all things, wishing to know all things; we, who are always laughing, and never pray; we, who are restless, chattering, drinking, smoking, full of pretensions and meanness, with only one wife, and never a slave in the whole country! And they form a dark idea of

Europe, as of an immense congeries of turbulent people, where
there reigns a feverish life, full of ardent ambitions, unbridled
vices, audacious enterprises, and tumult, a dizzy whirl, a confusion as of Babel, displeasing to God and man.

To-day great confusion in the palace, because of the first
and unique attempt at amorous conquest made by a Christian

Moorish Schoolmaster.

among the lower personages of the Embassy. This excellent
young man, upon whom, as it would seem, the diplomatic
austerity of our lives for the last forty days had begun to
weigh rather heavily, having seen, I know not whence, a
lovely Moor walking in a garden, thought (we all have our
weaknesses) that she would never be able to resist the attractions
of his fine person ; and without a thought of the danger,
insinuated himself through some hole in the wall into the
forbidden precincts. If, when arrived in the presence of his

nymph, he made a declaration of love, or whether he attempted
to suppress any preamble, whether the nymph lent a favourable
ear, or fled shrieking from the spot, no one knows; for in this
country all is mystery. It is known, however, that there
suddenly issued from behind the bushes four Moors armed
with daggers, two of whom sprang upon them on one side,
and two on the other; and that the unfortunate young man
would either never have issued from the garden, or would
have done so with some holes in his person, if the Caid
Hamed-Ben-Kasen Buhammei had not suddenly appeared upon
the scene, and with an imperious gesture arrested the four
assailants, and given the fugitive time to get back to the
palace with a whole skin. The news of the event flew about :
there was great excitement, and the culprit received a solemn
admonition in the presence of us all, while the Commandant,
always witty, added on his own account a little sermon which
produced a profound impression. " The wives of others," said
he, " and more especially the wives of Mussulmans, must be
let alone; and when one is with a European Embassy in
Morocco, one must make up one's mind not to be a man.
For, in Mahommetan countries, these woman questions speedily
become political questions. It would, indeed, be a fine re-
sponsibility, that of an honest young fellow, who, not having
been able to resist an inconsiderate impulse, should drag his
country into a war, the consequences of which could not
be foreseen." At this solemn discourse, the poor young man,
who already saw the Italian fleet with a hundred thousand
fighting men sailing towards Morocco because of him, showed
himself so overwhelmed with the sense of his guilt that no
further castigation was considered necessary.

I should much like to know what conception these people
have of their own military power, and their own valour in
war, with respect to the power and bravery of Europeans.
But I dare not question them directly on the subject, because
they are very ready to take offence, and I fear that my

COURT-YARD AND BATH IN THE PALACE.

questions might be mistaken for irony or brag. I have succeeded, however, touching lightly and with caution, in picking up something. As to the superiority of our military power they have no doubts; for, if any doubt remained in their minds thirty years since, when they had not yet met with any severe reverses from European armies, the wars with France and Spain, and principally the two famous battles of Isly and Tetuan, would have dissipated them for ever. But with regard to bravery, it seems to me that they still think themselves much superior to Europeans, whose victories they attribute to their artillery, to discipline, and to what with them takes the place of strategy and tactics, namely, craft; but not at all to their valour. It appears that they do not consider victories gained by these means as real victories, nobly obtained. The common people also add to these the alliance with evil spirits, without which neither artillery nor craft would avail to conquer the Mussulman armies. Certain it is that to the pure-blooded Arabs and to the Berbers, who are the warlike majority in Morocco, bravery cannot be denied, or even the recognition of it restricted to that common and indeterminate courage which in Europe is considered, with chivalric reciprocity, the property of all armies. For even taking into account the nature of the ground and the secret aid of England, the army of Morocco, scattered, badly commanded, badly armed, badly provisioned, could not have confronted, as it did, for nearly a year, with a tenacity unexpected in Europe, the Spanish troops, highly disciplined, and furnished with all the newest offensive weapons, unless they had possessed great bravery in compensation for the military power that they lacked. We may deny the name of true courage to that fanaticism which sends one man against ten, seeking a death that shall open for him the gates of Paradise; or to the savage fury which induces a soldier to dash his own brains out against a rock rather than fall into the enemy's hands; or to the wild rage of a wounded man,

who tears the bandages from his wounds and frees himself
at once from life and a prison; or to the contempt of pain,
the blind audacity, the brutal obstinacy, that seek death

Camel and Driver.

without any purpose to serve; but we must admit at least
that these are elements of courage, and it is incontestable that
this people gave many such tremendous examples to Spain.
After two months of warfare the Spanish army had taken but
two prisoners, an Arab from the province of Oran, and a lunatic
who had presented himself at the outposts; and at the san-

guinary battle of Castillejos five men only, and those five
wounded, fell into the hands of the victors. Their traditional
tactics are to advance *en masse* against the enemy, to extend

Caravan of Camels.

themselves rapidly, rush in, fire, and retreat precipitately to
reload. In great battles they dispose themselves in half-moon
shape, artillery and infantry in the centre, and cavalry at the
wings, which seeks to envelop the enemy and catch him
between two fires. The supreme head gives a general order,
but every inferior chief returns to the assault or retreats when

he thinks fit, and the army easily escapes from the control
of the head.   Indefatigable horsemen, dexterous marksmen,
unflinching at a defence, easily thrown into confusion in open
ground, they glide like serpents, climb like squirrels, run like
goats, pass rapidly from a bold assault to a precipitous flight,
and give an exaltation of courage that seems like furious
madness to a confusion and disorder without name.   There
are still in Morocco men who went mad with terror at the
battle of Isly; and it is known that when Marshal Bugeaud
began his cannonade, Sultan Abd-er-Rhaman cried out, " My
horse! my horse!" and leaping into the saddle fled precipitately, leaving in the camp his musicians, his necromancers, his hunting dogs, the sacred standard, the parasol,
and his tea, which the French soldiers found still boiling
hot.

I meet so many negroes in the streets of Fez that I
sometimes seem to find myself in the city of the Sudan,
and feel vaguely between me and Europe the immensity of
the desert of Sahara.   From the Sudan, in fact, the greater
part of them come—a little less than three thousand in a
year, many of whom are said to die in a short time from
home-sickness.   They are generally brought at the age of
eight or ten years.   The merchants, before exposing them for
sale, fatten them with balls of *cùscùssù*, try to cure them
of their home-sickness with music, and teach them a few
Arabic words; which last augments their price, which is
generally thirty francs for a boy, sixty for a girl, about four
hundred for a young woman of seventeen or eighteen who is
handsome, and knows how to speak, and has not yet had a
child, and fifty or sixty for an old man.   The Emperor takes
five per cent. on the imported material, and has a right to
the first choice.   The others are sold in the markets of Fez,
Mogador, and Morocco, and separately, at auction, in the
other cities.   They all, without difficulty, embrace the Mohammedan religion, preserving, however, many of their own

strange superstitions, and the queer festivals of their native country, consisting of grotesque balls, which last three days and three nights consecutively, accompanied by diabolical

Negro Slave Girl.

music. They serve generally in the houses, are treated with kindness, are for the most part freed in reward for their service, and the way is open for them to the highest offices of state. Here, as elsewhere, it is said that they are now

feverishly industrious, now torpidly lazy, sensual as monkeys,
astute as foxes, ferocious as tigers; but content with their
condition, and in general faithful and grateful to their
masters; which, it would seem, is not the case where slavery
is harder, as at Cuba, and where the liberty that they enjoy
is excessive, as in Europe. The Arab and Moorish women
refuse to accept them, and it is rare that a negro marries
another than one of his own colour; but the men, especially
the Moors, not only seek them eagerly as concubines, but
marry them as frequently as white women; from which cause
comes the great number of mulattoes of all shades who are
seen in the streets of Morocco. What strange chances! The
poor negro of ten years old, sold in the confines of the
Sahara for a sack of sugar and a piece of cloth, may—and
the case can be cited—discuss thirty years afterwards, as
Minister of Morocco, a treaty of commerce with the English
Ambassador; and still more possibly, the black girl baby,
born in a filthy den, and exchanged in the shade of an oasis
for a skin of brandy, may come to be covered with gems,
and fragrant with perfumes, and clasped in the arms of the
Sultan.

For some days, walking about Fez, there presents itself to
my mind with obstinate persistence, the image of a great
American city, to which people from all parts of the world
hasten, one of those cities which represent almost the type
of that to which all new cities are slowly conforming themselves, and whose life is, perhaps, an example of that which,
in another century, will be the life of all; a city whose
image cannot present itself to any European side by side
with that of Fez, without exciting a smile of pity, so enormous
is the difference which separates them in the road of human
progress; and yet the more I fix my thoughts upon that
city, the more I feel conscious of a doubt that saddens me.
I see those broad, straight, endless streets, with their long
perspectives of gigantic telegraph poles. "It is the hour for

closing the workshops and warehouses.   Torrents of workmen, workwomen, and children pass on foot, in omnibuses, in tramway cars, almost all following the same direction, towards a distant quarter of the town; and all have the same anxious, melancholy aspect, and seem worn out with fatigue.   Dense clouds of coal-smoke pour from the innumerable chimneys of the factories, descend into the streets, throw their black shadows over the splendid shop-windows, and the gilded lettering of the signs that cover the houses up to the roofs, and the crowd that, with bent heads and rapid step, swinging their arms, fly silently from the places where all day long they have laboured.   From time to time the sun parts the dismal veil which industry has spread over the capital of labour; but these sudden and fugitive beams, instead of making it more cheerful, only illuminate the sadness of the scene.   All the faces have the same expression.   Everybody is in haste to reach home in order to 'economise' his few hours of repose, after having drawn the largest possible advantage from the long hours of work.   Every

Negro Slave.

one seems to suspect a rival in his neighbour.   Every one bears the stamp of isolation.   The moral atmosphere in which these people live is not charity, it is rivalry.   A great number of families live in the hotels, a life which condemns the wife to solitude and idleness. All day long the husband attends to his business out of the house, coming in only at the hour for dinner, which he swallows with the avidity of a famished man. Then he returns to his galley. Boys, at the age of five or six years, are sent to school, they go and come alone, and pass the rest of their time as they please, in the enjoyment of perfect liberty. The paternal authority is almost *nil*. The sons receive no other education than that of the common school, arrive quickly at maturity, and from infancy are prepared for the fatigues and struggles of the over-excited, strained, and adventurous life which is before them. The existence of the man is merely one long and single *campaign*, an uninterrupted succession of combats, marches and counter-marches. The sweetness, the intimacy of the domestic hearth, have but a small part in his feverish and militant life. Is he happy? Judging by his sad, wearied, anxious countenance, often delicate and unhealthy, it is to be doubted. The excess of continued work breaks down his strength, forbids him the pleasures of the intellect, and prevents him from communing with his own soul. And the woman suffers even more. She sees her husband but once a day, for half-an-hour at most, and in the evening, when he returns tired out, and goes to bed; and she cannot lighten the burden which he carries, nor participate in his labours, cares, and pains, because she does not know them; for there is no time for an interchange of thought and feeling between the couple."

The city is Chicago, and the writer who describes it is the Baron de Hubner, a great admirer of America. Now my doubt is this: I do not know which of the two cities, Fez or Chicago, to compassionate most. I feel, however, that if I were a Moor of Fez, and a Christian should take me into one of these great civilised cities and ask me if I did not envy him, I should laugh in his face.

This morning Selim told me, in his own fashion, the famous history of the bandit Arusi—one of the many tales that go about from mouth to mouth from the sea to the desert; founded, however, on a real and recent fact, many witnesses to which are still living.

A short time after the war with France, Sultan Abd-er-Rhaman sent an army to punish the inhabitants of the Rif, who had burned a French vessel. Among the various Sheiks who were ordered to denounce the culprits was one named Sid-Mohammed Abd-el-Djebar, already advanced in years, who, being jealous of a certain Arusi, a bold and handsome youth, placed him, though innocent, in the hands of the General, who sent him to be incarcerated at Fez. But he only remained about a year in prison. After his release he went to Tangiers, remained there some time, and then suddenly disappeared, and for a while no one knew what had become of him. But shortly after his disappearance, there were rumours all over the province of Garb of a band of robbers and assassins which infested the country between Rabat and Laracce. Caravans were attacked, merchants robbed, Caids maltreated, the Sultan's soldiers poignarded; no one dared any more to cross that part of the country, and the few who had escaped alive from the hands of the bandits came back to the towns stupefied with terror.

Things remained in this state for a good while, and no one had been able to discover who was the chief of the band, when a merchant from the Rif, attacked one night by moonlight, recognised among the robbers the young Arusi, and brought the news to Tangiers, whence it spread rapidly about the province. Arusi was the chief. Many others recognised him. He appeared in the *duars* and villages, by day as well as by night, dressed as a soldier, as a Caid, as a Jew, as a Christian, as a woman, as an *ulema*, killing, robbing, vanishing, pursued from every quarter, but never taken, always unexpected in his approach, always under a

U

SCHOOL IN FEZ.

new disguise, capricious, fierce, and indefatigable; and he never went very far away from the neighbourhood of the citadel El Mamora—a fact which no one could understand. The reason was this: the Caid of the citadel El Mamora was no other than the old Sheik Sid-Mohammed Abd-el-Djebar, who had placed Arusi in the hands of the Sultan's General.

At that very time Sid-Mohammed had just given his daughter in marriage, a girl of marvellous beauty, named Rahmana, to the son of the Pasha of Salè, who was called Sid-Alì. The nuptial feasts were celebrated with great pomp, in the presence of all the rich young men of the province, who came on horseback, armed, and dressed in their best, to the citadel El Mamoro; and Sid-Alì was to conduct his bride to Salè, to his father's house. The cortége issued from the citadel at night. It had to pass through a narrow defile formed by two chains of wooded hills and downs. First went an escort of thirty horsemen; behind these, Rahmana, on a mule, between her husband and her brother; behind her, her father, the Caid, and a crowd of relations and friends.

They entered the defile. The night was serene, the bridegroom held Rahmana by the hand, the old Caid smoothed his beard; all were cheerful and unsuspecting.

Suddenly there burst upon the stillness of the night, a formidable voice, which cried—

"Arusi salutes thee, O Sheik Sid-Mohammed Abd-el-Djebar!"

At the same moment, from the top of the hill, thirty muskets flashed, and thirty shots rang out. Horses, soldiers, friends and relations, fell wounded or dead, or took to flight; and before the Caid and Sid-Alì, who were untouched, could recover from their bewilderment, a man, a fury, a demon, Arusi himself, had seized Rahmana, placed her before him on his horse, and fled with the speed of the wind towards the forest of Mamora.

U 2

The Caid and Sid-Alì, both resolute men, instead of
giving way to a vain despair, took a solemn oath never to
shave their heads until they had been fearfully avenged.
They demanded and obtained soldiers from the Sultan, and
began to give chase to Arusi, who had taken refuge with

Arusi carrying off Rahmana.

his band in the great forest of Mamora. It was a most
fatiguing warfare, carried on by *coups de main,* ambuscades,
nocturnal assaults, feints, and ferocious combats, and went
on for more than a year, driving, little by little, the band
of marauders into the centre of the forest. The circle grew
closer and closer. Many of Arusi's men were already dead
with hunger, many had fled, many had been killed fighting.
The Caid and Sid-Alì, as their vengeance seemed to draw

near, became more ferocious in its pursuit; they rested neither
night nor day, they breathed only for revenge. But of Arusi
and Rahmana they could learn nothing. Some said they were
dead, some that they had fled, some that the bandit had first
killed the woman and then himself. The Caid and Sid-Alì
began to despair, because the further they advanced into the
forest, and the thicker the trees, higher and more intricate became
the bushes, the vines, the brambles, and the junipers; so that
the horses and dogs could no longer force a passage through
them. At last one day, when the two were walking in the
forest almost discouraged, an Arab came towards them and
said that he had seen Arusi hidden in the reeds, on the river-
bank at the extremity of the wood. The Caid hastily called
his men together, and dividing them into two companies,
sent one to the right and the other to the left, towards
the river. After some time, the Caid was the first to see
rising from the midst of the reeds a phantom, a man of
tall stature and terrible aspect—Arusi. Everybody rushed
towards that point; they searched in vain, Arusi was not
there. "He has crossed the river!" shouted the Caid. They
threw themselves into the stream, and gained the opposite
bank. There they found some footprints, and followed them,
but after a little they failed. Suddenly the horsemen broke
into a gallop along the river brink. At the same moment
the attention of the Caid was drawn to three of his dogs,
who had stopped, searching, near a clump of reeds. Sid-
Alì was the first to run to the spot, and he found near the
reeds a large ditch, at the bottom of which were some holes.
Jumping into the ditch, he introduced his musket into one
of the holes, felt it pushed back, and fired; then calling the
Caid and the soldiers, they searched here and there, and
found a small round aperture in the steep bank just above
the water. Arusi must have entered by that opening.
"Dig!" shouted the Caid. The soldiers ran for picks and
shovels to a neighbouring village, and digging, presently

came upon a sort of arch in the earth, and under it a cave.

At the bottom of the cave was Arusi, erect, motionless, pale as death. They seized him : he made no resistance. They dragged him out : he had lost his left eye. He was bound, carried to a tent, laid on the ground, and as a first taste of vengeance, Sid-Alì cut off one by one all the toes of his feet and threw them in his face. This done, six soldiers were set to guard him, and Sid-Alì and the Caid withdrew to another tent, there to arrange what tortures they should inflict before cutting off his head. The discussion was prolonged ; for each one tried to propose some more painful torture, and nothing seemed horrible enough ; the evening came, and nothing was decided. The decision was put off until the next morning, and they separated.

An hour afterwards the Caid and Alì were asleep, each in his tent ; the night was very dark, there was not a breath of wind, not a leaf moving : nothing was heard but the murmur of the river, and the breathing of the sleeping men. Suddenly a formidable voice broke the silence of the night :—

"Arusi salutes thee, O Sheik Sid-Mohammed Abd-el-Djebar ! "

The old Caid sprang to his feet, and heard the rapid beat of a horse's feet departing. He called his soldiers, who came in haste, and shouted, " My horse ! my horse ! " They sought his horse, the most superb animal in the whole Garb : it was gone. They ran to the tent of Sidi-Alì : he was stretched to the ground, dead, with a poignard stuck in his left eye. The Caid burst into tears ; the soldiers went off on the track of the fugitive. They saw him for an instant, like a shadow ; then lost him ; again saw him ; but he sped like the lightning, and vanished not to be seen again. Nevertheless, they continued to follow all the night, until they reached a thick wood, where they halted to await the dawn. When daylight appeared, they saw far off the Caid's horse approaching, tired out and all bloody, filling the air with lamentable neighings. Thinking that Arusi must be in the wood, they loosed the dogs and advanced sword in hand. In a few minutes they discovered a dilapidated house half hidden among the trees. The dogs stopped there. The soldiers came to the door, and, levelling their muskets, let them fall with a cry of amazement. Within the four ruined walls lay the corpse of Arusi, and beside it a lovely woman, splendidly dressed, with her hair loose on her shoulders, was binding up his bleeding feet, sobbing, laughing, and murmuring words of despair and love. It was Rahmana. They took her to her father's house, where she remained three days without speaking one word, and then disappeared. She was found some time afterwards in the ruined house in the wood, scratching up the earth with her hands, and calling on Arusi. And there she stayed. "God," said the Arabs, "had called her reason back to Himself, and she was a saint." Whether she is still living or not, no one knows. She was certainly living twenty years ago, and was seen in her hermitage by M. Narcisse Cotte, attached to the Consulate of France at Tangiers, who told her story.

There is not now a corner of Fez that is unknown to us, and yet it seems as if we had only arrived yesterday, so varied is the aspect of the place, so much does every object revive in us the sense of our solitude, so little do we become habituated to the curiosity that we create. And this curiosity is in no wise lessened, although by this time we have been seen over and over again by every native of Fez. Timidity, on the other hand, is lessened, and antipathy, perhaps, a little; the children come nearer, and touch our garments, to feel what they are made of; the women look at us with forbidding glances, but they no longer turn back when they see us coming; curses are more rare, the soldiers do not use their sticks so much, and the blows that Ussi received were, it is to be hoped, the first and last blows with a fist that I shall have to report in Italy. And although, in our walks through the city, we are followed and preceded by a crowd, I think we could now go out alone without danger of death. Already

Slave of the War Minister.

the people, according to the soldiers' testimony, have given each of us a name, according to Moorish custom. The doctor is "the man with the spectacles;" the Vice-Consul is "the man with the flat nose;" the Captain is "the man with the black boots;" Ussi is "the man with the white handkerchief;" the Commandant, "the man with the short legs;" Biseo, "the man with the red hair;" Morteo, "the velvet man," because he is dressed in velvet; and myself, "the man with the broken shoe," because a pain in my foot obliged me to make a cut in my boot. They comment much upon our doings, it appears, and say that we are all ugly, not one excepted, not even the cook, who received this intelligence with a laugh of scorn, and clapped his hand on a pocket in his vest, where he had a letter from his sweetheart. And it seems to me that they find us, or pretend to find us, ridiculous, because, in the streets, they laugh with a certain ostentation every time that one of us slips, or hits his head against a branch of a tree, or loses his hat. Nevertheless, and despite the variety of the landscape, this population all of one colour, and without apparent distinction of rank, this silence broken only by an eternal rustle of slippers and mantles, these veiled women, these blind, mute houses, this mysterious life, all end by producing a dreadful tedium. We must be within doors at sunset, and may not go out again. With the daylight ceases all trade, every movement, every sign of life : Fez is no more than a vast necropolis, where, if perchance a human voice is heard, it is the howl of a madman, or the shriek of one who is being murdered ; and he who insists upon going about at any cost, must be accompanied by a patrol with loaded muskets, and a company of carpenters who, at every three hundred paces, must knock down a gate that stops the way. In the daytime the city supplies no news beyond some woman found in the street with a dagger in her heart, or the departure of a caravan, or the arrival of a governor or vice-governor of some province who has been thrown into prison, the bastinado administered to some dignitary, a festival in honour of some saint, or other things of the same character, brought to us in general by Mohammed Ducalè or Schellal, who are our two perambulating journals. And these events, with what I daily

see, and the singular life I lead, give me at night such
strangely intricate dreams of severed heads, and deserts, of
harems, prisons, Fez, Timbuctoo, and Turin, that when I wake
in the morning, it takes me some minutes to find out what
world I am in.

How many beautiful, grotesque, horrible, absurd, and strange
figures will live in my memory for ever! My head is full
of them, and when I am alone I make them pass before me
one by one, like the figures in a magic lantern, with inex-
pressible pleasure. There is Sid-Buker, the mysterious being
who comes three times every day, wrapped in a great mantle,
with head down, half-closed eyes, pale as death, stealthy as
a spectre, to confer secretly with the Ambassador, and vanishes
like a figure in a phantasmagoria, without any one observing
him. There is the favourite servant of Sid-Moussa, a handsome young mulatto, graceful as a girl, elegant as a prince,
fresh and smiling, who goes leaping up and down the stairs,
and salutes you with a sort of coquetry, bowing profoundly
and extending his hand as if he were throwing kisses. There
is a soldier of the guard, a Berber, born in the Atlas Mountains, a countenance that one cannot see without a shudder,
and who fixes upon me a cold, perfidious, immoveable glance,
as if he meant to kill me; and the more I try to avoid him
the more I meet him, and he seems to divine the dread with
which he inspires me, and to take a satanic pleasure in it.
There is a decrepit old woman whom I saw in the door of a
mosque, naked as she was born, except for a formless rag
about her hips, with her head as bald as the palm of my
hand, and a body so deformed that I made an exclamation of
horror, and was disturbed for some time by the sight of her.
There is the mischievous Moorish woman, who, entering her
house as we were passing by, threw off in furious haste the
caic that covered her, and, giving us a glimpse of her handsome, straight, and well-made figure, and a sparkling glance,
shut the door. There is the very old shopkeeper, with a face

at once ridiculous and frightful : so bent over that, when he
stands in the back of his dark niche, he seems almost to
touch his toes with his chin. He keeps only one eye open,
and that is hardly visible ; and every time I pass his shop,
and look in at him, that eye opens large and round, and shines
with a sort of mocking smile that gives me a kind of anxious
feeling. There is the beautiful little Moorish girl of ten
years old, with her hair loose about her shoulders, dressed in
a chemise bound round the waist with a green scarf, who, in
attempting to jump from one terrace to another lower one,
got caught by her chemise upon the corner of a brick, and
was held dangling; and she, knowing that she was seen from
the palace of the Embassy, and unable to get up or down,
raised the most despairing shrieks, and all the women in the
house came, shaking with laughter, to her assistance. There
is the gigantic mulatto, a madman, who, pursued by the fixed
idea that the Sultan's soldiers are seeking him to cut his hand
off, flies through the streets like some wild thing held in
chase, convulsively shaking his right arm as if it were already
mutilated, and giving the most frightful yells, which can be
heard from one end of the city to the other. There are many,
many more; but the one who rises oftenest before my memory
is a negro, of about fifty years of age, a servant of the
palace, a little more than a yard high, and a little less than
a yard wide—a contented spirit, who is always smiling and
twisting his mouth towards his right ear : the most grotesque,
the most absurdly ridiculous figure that ever appeared under
the vault of heaven ; and it is of no use for me to bite my
fingers, and tell myself that it is ignoble to laugh at human
deformity, and shame myself in many ways : the laugh breaks
out in spite of me—there must be in it some mysterious intention of Providence—it must break out. And—I really
cannot help it—the idea presents itself, what a capital pipe-
bowl he would make !

As the day of departure draws near, the merchants come in

crowds to the palace, and buying goes on with fury. The rooms, the court, and the gallery have taken the aspect of a bazaar. Everywhere long rows of vases, embroidered slippers, cushions, carpets, caics. Everything in Fez that is most gilded,

A Slave of the Sultan.

most arabesqued, most dear in price, is passed before our eyes. And it is worth while to see how they sell, these people, without a word, without a flitting smile, only making the sign of yes or no with the head, and going away, having sold or not having sold, with the same automaton faces that they brought. Above all, the painters' room is fine, converted into a great *bric-à-brac* shop, full of saddles, stirrups, guns, caftans, ragged scarfs, pottery, barbaric ornaments, old girdles of women, come from Heaven knows where, that have perhaps felt the pressure of the Sultan's arms, and next year will appear in some grand picture at Naples or New York. One kind of thing only is wanting, namely antique objects, records of the various peoples who have conquered and colonised Morocco ; and although it is known that such are often found underground and among the ruins, it is not possible to get them, because every object so found has to be carried to the authorities, and whoever finds one hides it ; and the authorities, ignorant of their value, destroy or sell as useless material the little that finds its way to them. In this way, a few years ago, a bronze horse and some small bronze statues, which were found in a well near the remains of an aqueduct, were broken up and sold for old copper to a Jew dealer in second-hand goods.

To-day I had a warm discussion with a merchant of Fez, with the intention of finding out what opinion the Moors held of European civilisation ; and for that reason I did not trouble myself to refute his arguments, except when it was necessary to give him line. He is a handsome man of forty, of an honest and severe countenance, who has visited, in his commerce, the principal cities of Western Europe, and who lived a good while at Tangiers, where he learned some Spanish. I had exchanged a few words with him some days ago, *à propos* of a small piece of stuff woven of silk and gold, which he pretended to be worth ten *marenghi*. But to-day, attacking him upon the subject of his travels, a conversation ensued which his companions listened to with astonishment, although they could not understand it. I asked him then what impression the great cities of Europe had made upon him ; not expecting, however, to hear any great expression of admiration, because I knew, as everybody knows, that of the four or five hundred merchants of Morocco who go every year to Europe the greater part return to their own country more stupidly

fanatical than at first, when they do not return more rascally
and vicious; and that if they were all amazed at the splendour
of our cities, and at the marvels of our industries, not one
of them would be touched in the soul, moved in the mind,
spurred on to imitate, to attempt; not one persuaded of the
complex inferiority of his own country; and certainly not

The Bread Market at Fez.

one, even if he experienced such sentiments, who would be
ready to express them, and still less to diffuse them, through
the fear of calling down upon himself the accusation of being
a renegade Mussulman and an enemy to his country.

"What have you to say," I asked, "of our great cities?"

He looked fixedly at me, and answered coldly, "Large
streets, fine shops, handsome palaces, fine offices—and all
clean."

With this he appeared to think that he had said all that
could be said in our honour.

" Did you see nothing else that was handsome and good ? " I asked.

He looked at me as if to inquire what I supposed he was likely to have found.

" Is it possible " (I insisted) " that a reasonable man like yourself, who has seen countries so wonderfully different and superior to his own, does not speak of them at least with astonishment, at least with the vivacity with which a boy from a *duar* would speak of a Pasha's palace ? What does astonish you then in the world ? What kind of people are you ? Who can comprehend you ? "

" *Perdóne Usted*," he answered, coldly ; " in my turn I do not understand you. When I have told you everything in which I think you superior to us, what do you wish more ? Do you wish me to say what I do not think ? I tell you that your streets are wider than ours, your shops finer, your palaces richer ; it seems to me that I have said all. I will say one thing more : that you know more than we do, because you have books and read."

I made a gesture of impatience.

" Do not be impatient, *caballero*," he went on quietly ; " you will acknowledge that the first duty of a man, the first thing which renders him estimable, and that in which it is of the utmost importance that a country should be superior to other countries, is honesty ; will you not ? Very well, in the matter of honesty I do not at all believe that you are superior to us. And that is one thing."

" Gently. Explain first what you mean by honesty."

" Honesty in trade, *caballero*. The Moors, for example, in trade sometimes deceive the Europeans, but you Europeans deceive us Moors much more often."

" The cases are rare," I answered, for the sake of saying something.

" Cases rare ! " he exclaimed, warmly. " Cases of every-day occurrence " (and here I would like to report exactly his

broken, concise, and childish language). "Proof! Proof! I
at Marseilles. I am at Marseilles. I buy cotton. I choose
the thread, thick like this. I say: this number, this stamp,
this quantity, send. I pay, I depart, arrive at Morocco,
receive cotton, open, look, same number, same stamp—thread
three times smaller! good for nothing! loss, thousands of
francs! I run to Consulate—nothing. *Otro,* another. Merchant of Fez orders blue cloth in Europe, so many pieces, so
wide, so long, agreed, paid. Receives cloth, opens, measures:
first pieces right; under, shorter; last, half a yard shorter!
not good for cloaks, merchant ruined. *Otro, otro.* Merchant
of Morocco orders in Europe thousand yards gold galloon for
officers, and sends money. Galloon comes, cut, sewed, worn—
copper! *Y otros, y otros, y otros!*" With this he lifted his
face to the sky, and then turning abruptly to me: "More
honest you?"

I repeated that these could only be exceptional cases. He
made no reply.

"More religious you?" he asked then, shortly. "No!"
and after a moment: "No! Enough to go once into one of
your mosques."

"You say," he went on, encouraged by my silence, "in
your country there are fewer *matamientos* (murders)?" Here
I should have been embarrassed to answer. What would he
have said if I had confessed that in Italy alone there are
committed three thousand homicides a year, and that there
are ninety thousand prisoners on trial and condemned?

"I do not believe it," he said, reading my answer in
my eyes. Not feeling myself secure upon this ground, I
attacked him with the usual arguments against polygamy.

He jumped as if I had burnt him.

"Always that!" he cried, turning red to his very ears.
"Always that! as if you had one woman only! and you
want to make us believe it! One wife is really yours, but
there are those of *los otros,* and those who are *de todos y de*

nadie, of everybody and nobody. Paris! London! Cafes full,
streets full, theatres full. *Verguenza!* and you reproach the
Moors!"

So saying, he pulled the beads of his rosary through his
trembling fingers, and turned from time to time with a faint

Moorish Turning Lathe.

smile to make me understand that his anger was not against
me, but against Europe.

Seeing that he took this question rather too much to
heart, I changed the subject, and asked him if he did not
recognise greater convenience in our manner of living. Here
he was very comic. He had his arguments all ready.

"It is true," he answered, with an ironical accent; "it
is true. Sun? Parasol. Rain? Umbrella. Dust? Gloves.

v

To walk? A stick. To look? An eye-glass. To take the
air? A carriage. To sit down? Elastic cushions. To eat?
Music. A scratch? The doctor. Death? A statue. *Eh !*
how many things you have need of ! What men, *por Dios !*
What children ! "

In short, he would not leave me anything. He even
laughed at our architecture.

" *Che ! che !* " said he, when I talked of the comfort of
our houses. " There are three hundred of you living in
one house, all a-top of one another, and then you go up,
and up, and up—and there is no air, and no light, and no
garden."

Then I spoke of laws, of government, of liberty, and
the like; and as he was a man of intelligence, I think I
succeeded, if not in making him understand all the differences
in these respects between his country and ours, at least, in
introducing some gleams of light into his mind. Seeing
that he could not meet me on this ground, he suddenly changed
the subject, and looking at me from head to foot, said, smiling,
" *Mal vestidos* " (Badly dressed).

I replied that dress was of small importance, and asked
him if he did not recognise our superiority in this, that
instead of sitting for hours idly, with our legs crossed on a
mattress, we employed our time in many useful and amusing
ways.

He gave me a more subtle answer than I had expected.
He said that it did not appear to him a good sign to have
need of so many ways of passing the time. Life alone,
then, was for us a punishment, that we could not rest an
hour doing nothing, without amusement, without wearing
ourselves out in the search for entertainment? Were we
afraid of ourselves ? Had we something in us which tormented
us ?

" But see," I said, " what a dull spectacle your city presents, what solitude, what silence, what misery. You have

been in Paris. Compare the streets of Paris with the streets of Fez."

Here he was sublime. He sprang to his feet laughing, and more in gesture than in words gave a jesting description of the spectacle which is presented by our city streets. "Come, go, run; carts here, wheelbarrows there; a deafening noise, drunken men staggering along, gentlemen buttoning up their coats to save their purses; at every step a guard, who looks as if at every step he saw a thief; old people and children who are in constant danger of being crushed by the carriages of the rich; impudent women, and even girls, horror! who give provoking glances, and even nudge the young men with their elbows; everybody with a cigar in his mouth; on every side people going into shops, to eat, to drink, to have their hair dressed, to look in mirrors, to put on gloves; and dandies planted before the doors of the cafés to whisper in the ears of other people's wives who are passing; and that ridiculous manner of saluting, and walking on the toes, and swinging, and jumping about; and then, good heavens, what womanish curiosity!" And touching this point, he grew warm, and told how one day, in an Italian city, having gone out in his Moorish dress, in a moment there had gathered a crowd, who ran before and behind him, shouting and laughing, and would scarcely let him walk, so that he had to go back to his hotel and change his dress. "And that is the way they act in your country!" he went on. "That they do so here is not surprising, for they never see a Christian; but in your country, where they know how we are dressed, because they have pictures of us, and send their painters here with machines to take our portraits: among you who know so much, do you think that such things ought to happen?"

After which he smiled courteously, as if to say, "All this is no reason why we should not be friends."

Then the conversation turned upon European manufactures, railways, telegraphs, and great works of public utility; and of these he allowed me to talk without interruption, assenting from time to time with a nod.

When I had finished, however, he sighed, and said, " After all, what are all these things worth if we must all die ? "

" Finally," I concluded, " you would not change your condition for ours ? "

He stood a moment thoughtful, and replied, " No, because you are no longer lived than we are, nor are you more healthy, nor better, nor more religious, nor more contented. Leave us, then, in peace. Do not insist that everybody should live as you do, and be happy according to your ideas. Let us all stay in the circle where Allah has placed us. For some good purpose Allah stretched the sea between Europe and Africa. Let us respect His decree."

" And do you believe," I demanded, " that you will always remain as you are ? that little by little we shall not make you change ? "

" I do not know," he answered. " You have the strength, you will do what you please. All that is to happen is already written. But whatever happens Allah will not abandon His faithful people."

With this he took my hand, pressed it to his heart, and went majestically away.

This morning at sunrise I went to see the review which the Sultan holds three times a week in the square where he received the Embassy.

As I went out at the gate of the Nicchia del Burro, I had a first taste of the manœuvres of the artillery. A troop of soldiers, old, middle-aged, and boys, all dressed in red, were running behind a small cannon drawn by one mule. It was one of the twelve guns presented by the Spanish Government to Sultan Sid-Mohammed after the war of 1860. Every now and then the mule slipped, or turned aside, or stopped, and the whole band began to yell and to strike at her, dancing and giggling, as if it was a carnival car they were conducting.

In a distance of about a hundred paces they stopped ten times.
Now the little bucket fell off, now the rammer, now something

Waiting for an Audience with the Sultan.

else; for everything was hung on the carriage. The mule
ziz-zagged along at her own caprice, or rather wherever the
cannon pushed her in coming down over the inequalities of the
ground; everybody gave orders which no one obeyed; the big
ones cuffed the small ones, the small ones cuffed the smaller

ones, and they all cuffed each other; and the cannon remained
pretty much in the same place. In was a scene to have thrown
General Lamarmora into a tertian fever.

On the left bank of the river there were about two thousand
foot soldiers, some lying on the ground, some standing about
in groups. In the square enclosed between the walls and the
river the artillery; four guns were firing at a mark. Behind
the guns stood some soldiers, and a tall figure in white—the
Sultan. From the place where I stood, however, I could
scarcely distinguish his outline. He seemed from time to time
to speak to the artillerymen, as if he were directing them. On
the opposite side of the square, near the bridge, there was a
crowd of Moors, Arabs, and blacks, men and women, people
from the city and country-people, gentlemen and peasants, all
assembled together, and waiting, I was told, to be called one
by one before the Sultan, from whom they wished favour or
justice; for the Sultan gives audience three times a week to
whosoever wishes to speak with him. Some of these poor
people had, perhaps, come from distant places to complain of
the exactions of the Governor, or to beg for pardon for their
relatives in prison. There were ragged women and tottering
old men; all the faces were weary and sad, and upon them
could be read both impatient desire and dread to appear before
the Prince of true Believers, the supreme judge, who in a few
minutes, with few words, would perhaps decide the fate of
their whole lives. I could not see that they had anything
at their feet or in their hands, and for this reason I believe
that the reigning Sultan has discontinued the custom, which
formerly existed, of accompanying every petition with a present,
which was never refused, however small, and consisted sometimes of a pair of fowls or a dozen of eggs. I walked about
among the soldiers. The boys were divided into companies
of thirty or forty each, and were amusing themselves by running
after one another and playing a sort of leap-frog. In some
of these groups, however, the diversion consisted in a sort of

pantomime, which, when I understood its meaning, made me
shudder. They were representing the amputation of the hands,
decapitation, and other kinds of punishment, which they had
doubtless often witnessed. One boy represented the caid,
another the victim, and a third the executioner; the victim,
when his hand was cut off, made believe to plunge the stump
into a vessel of pitch; another pretended to pick up the hand
and throw it to the dogs; and the spectators all laughed.

The gallows-bird faces of the greater part of these youthful
soldiers are not to be described. They were all shades of colour,
from ebony black to orange yellow; and not one of them,
even among the youngest, had preserved the ingenuous expression of childhood. All had something hard, impudent, cynical,
in their eyes, that inspired pity rather than anger. No great
perspicacity is necessary to understand that they could not be
otherwise. Of the men, the greater part of them were dozing,
stretched out on the ground; others were dancing negro
dances in the midst of a circle of spectators, and making all
sorts of jokes and grimaces; others, again, fencing with
sabres, in the same way as at Tangiers, springing about with
the action of rope-dancers. The officers, among them many
renegades, who were to be recognised by their faces, their
pipes, and a certain something of superior care in their dress,
walked about apart, and when I met them, turned their eyes
away. Beyond the bridge, in a place apart, about twenty
men, muffled in white mantles, were lying on the ground, one
beside the other, motionless as statues. I drew near, and
saw that they all wore heavy chains on wrist and ankle.
They were persons condemned for common offences, who were
dragged about by the army, and thus pilloried in the sight of
all. As I approached they all turned, and fixed upon me a
look that made me retreat at once.

I left the soldiers, and went to rest myself under the shade
of a palm tree, on a rising ground, whence I could command the
whole plain. I had been there but a few minutes, when I saw

an officer detach himself from a group, and come slowly towards me, looking carelessly about him, and humming a tune, as if to avoid notice. He was a short, stout man of about forty, wearing a sort of Zouave dress, with a fez, and without arms.

When I saw him near, I had a sensation of disgust. Never have I seen outside of the assize court a more perfidious coun-

Barber's Shop.

tenance. I would have sworn to his having at least ten murders on his conscience, accompanied by assaults on the person.

He stopped at a couple of paces from me, fixed two glassy eyes upon me, and said, coldly, " *Bon jour, monsieur.*"

I asked him if he were a Frenchman. " Yes," he replied. " I am from Algiers. I have been here seven years. I am a captain in the army of Morocco."

Not being able to compliment him on his position, I kept silence.

" *C'est comme ça,*" he continued, speaking quickly. " I came away from Algiers because I could not bear the sight of it any more. *J'étais obligé de vivre dans un cercle trop étroit*" (he meant, perhaps, the halter). " European life did not suit my tastes. I felt the need of change."

" And are you more contented now ? " I inquired.

" Most content," he answered, with affectation. " The country is lovely, Muley-el-Hassan is the best of sultans, the people are kind, I am a captain, I have a little shop, I exercise a small trade, I hunt, I fish, I make excursions into the mountains, I enjoy complete liberty. I would not go back to Europe, you see, for all the gold in the world."

" Do you not wish to see your own country again ? Have you forgotten even France ? "

" What is France to me ! " he replied. " For me France has no existence. Morocco is my country." And he shrugged his shoulders.

His cynicism revolted me ; I could scarcely believe it. I had the curiosity to probe him a little more deeply.

" Since you left Algeria," I asked, " have you had no news of events in Europe ? "

" *Pas un mot,*" he answered. " Here nobody knows any▪ thing, and I am very glad not to know anything."

" You do not know then that there has been a great war between France and Prussia ? "

He started. " *Qui a vaincu ?* " he asked, quickly, fixing his eyes upon me.

" Prussia," I replied.

He made a gesture of surprise. I told him in a few words of the disasters that had befallen France, the invasion, the taking of Paris, the loss of the two provinces. He listened with his head bent down and his eyebrows knit ; then he roused himself and said, with a kind of effort, " *C'est égal*—I have no country, it is no affair of mine," and bent his head again. I observed him steadily, and he saw it. " Adieu, monsieur," he said, abruptly, in an altered voice, and walked quickly away.

" All is not dead within him yet ! " I thought, and was glad.

Meantime the artillery had ceased its fire, the Sultan had retired under a white pavilion at the foot of a tower, and the

INTERIOR OF A MOSQUE AT FEZ.

soldiers began to defile before him, unarmed, and one by one, at
about twenty paces one from the other. As there was not
beside the Sultan or in front of the pavilion any officer to read
the names, as with us, in order to certify the existence of every
soldier on the rolls (and I am told there are no rolls in the army
of Morocco), I could not understand the purpose of the review,
unless it was for the Sultan's amusement; and I was tempted to
laugh. But, upon second thoughts, the primitive and poetic
idea in the sight of that African monarch, high-priest, and
absolute prince, young, gentle, and in all simplicity standing
three hours alone in the shadow of his tent, and three times in
every week seeing his soldiers pass before him one by one, and
listening to the prayers and lamentations of his unhappy subjects,
inspired me instead with a feeling of respect. And since it was
the last time that I should see him, I felt a sudden rush of
sympathy towards him as I turned away. "Farewell," I
thought, "handsome and noble prince!" and as his gracious
white figure disappeared for ever from my eyes, I felt a sensation
in my breast as if, in that moment, it had been stamped upon
my heart.

The ninth of June: the last day of the sojourn of the Italian
Embassy at Fez. All the Ambassador's demands have been
conceded, the affairs of Ducalè and Schellal arranged, visits of
leave-taking made, the last dinner of Sid-Moussa submitted to,
the usual presents from the Sultan received : a fine black horse,
with an enormous green velvet saddle embroidered with gold for
the Ambassador; gilded and damaskened sabres to the officials
of the Embassy; a mule to the second dragoman. The tents
and boxes were sent forward this morning, the rooms are empty,
the mules are ready, the escort awaits us at the gate of Nicchia
del Burro, my companions are walking up and down the court,
expecting the signal for departure, and I, seated for the last time
upon the edge of my imperial bed, note down in a book upon my
knee my last impressions of Fez. What are they? What is
left at last at the bottom of my soul by the spectacle of this

people, this city, this state of things? If my thought penetrates
at all under the pleasing impressions of wonder and gratified
curiosity, I find a mingling of diverse sentiments which leave
my mind uncertain.   There is a feeling of pity for the decay, the
debasement, the agony of a warlike and knightly race, who left
so luminous a track in the history of science and art, and now
have not even the consciousness of their past glory.   There is
admiration for what remains in them of the strong and beautiful,
for the virile and gracious majesty of their aspect, dress, de-
meanour, and ceremonies; for everything that their sad and
silent life retains of its antique dignity and simplicity.   There is
displeasure at the sight of so much barbarism at so short a
distance from civilisation, and that this civilisation should have
so disproportionate a force in rising and expanding, that in so
many centuries, and always growing on its own ground, it has
been unable to cross two hundred miles of sea.   There is anger
at the thought that, to the great interest of the barbarism of this
part of Africa, the civilised states prefer their own small local
and mercantile interests; and diminishing thus in the minds of
this people, by the spectacle of their mean jealousies, their own
authority, and that of the civilisation which they desire to spread,
render the undertaking always more difficult and slow.   Finally,
there is a sentiment of vivid pleasure, when I think that in this
country another little world has been formed in my brain, populous,
animated, full of new personages who will live for ever there,
whom I can evoke at will, and can converse with them, and live
again in Africa.   But with this glad feeling comes another which
is sad, the inevitable sentiment that throws a shadow over all
our serene hours and drops a drop of bitterness into all our
pleasures—that which the Moorish merchant expressed when he
demonstrated the vanity of the great efforts of civilised people
to study, to seek, to discover; and then this beautiful journey
seems to me only the rapid passage of a fine scene in the spectacle
of an hour, which is life; and my pencil drops from my hand,
and a dark discouragement takes possession of me.   Ah! the

voice of Selam calls me ? We must go, then. To return to the
tent, to the warlike manœuvres, the wide plains, the great light,
the joyous and wholesome life of the encampment. Farewell,
Fez ! Farewell, sadness ! My little African world is again
illuminated with rose colour.

CHAPTER XII.

MECHINEZ.

AFTER twenty-four days of city life the caravan impressed me as a new spectacle. And yet nothing was changed except that beside Mohammed Ducalè rode the Moor, Schellal, who, although his business had been amicably settled, thought it more prudent to return to Tangiers under the wing of the Ambassador than to remain in Fez under that of his Government. An acute observer might also have observed upon our faces, if he were a pessimist, a certain annoyance; if an optimist, a calm serenity, which was derived from a profound consciousness in all that we had left behind in the imperial capital no pining beauty, no offended husband, no distracted family. On all our faces also shone the thought of return—that is, on as much as could be seen of them under the umbrellas, veils, handkerchiefs, with which most of us had concealed our heads for shelter against the ardent sun and suffocating dust. Alas! here was the great

change. The sun of May was changed into the sun of June,
the thermometer marked forty-two degrees (centigrade) at the
moment of departure, and before us lay two hundred miles of
African soil.

To return to Tangiers we had to go to Mechinez, from
thence to Laracce, then along the shore of the sea to Arzilla,
and from Arzilla to Ain-Dalia, where we had first encamped.

We took three days to go to Mechinez, distant from Fez
about fifty kilometres.

The country did not present any marked differences to that
which we had traversed in going to Fez : always the same fields
of grain and barley, in some of which they were beginning to
reap ; the same black *duars*, the same vast spaces covered with
dwarf palms and lentiscus, those grand undulations of the land,
rocky hills, dry beds of torrents, solitary palms, white tombs of
saints, splendidly peaceful and infinitely sad. But because of
the neighbourhood of the two great cities, we met more people
than on the way between Tangiers and Fez : caravans of camels,
droves of cattle; merchants bringing troops of beautiful horses
to the markets of Fez ; saints preaching in the desert ; couriers
on foot and on horseback ; groups of Arabs armed with reaping
hooks ; and some rich Moorish families going to Fez with their
servants and chattels. One of these—the family of a wealthy
merchant known to Ducalè—formed a long caravan.   First
came two servants armed with muskets; and behind them the
head of the family, a handsome man of a stern countenance,
with a black beard and a white turban, riding a richly
caparisoned mule ; with one hand he held the reins, and sustained a child of two or three years old, seated before him in the
saddle; with the other he clasped the hand of a woman completely veiled—perhaps his favourite wife—who rode behind
him astride of the mule's crupper, and who held him round the
waist as if she meant to suffocate him, perhaps in fear of us.
Other women, all with veiled faces, came riding on other mules
behind the master; armed relations, boys, black servants;

women with babies in their arms ; Arab servants with muskets
on their shoulders; mules and asses laden with mattresses,
pillows, coverings, plates, and other matters; and finally,
more servants on foot, bearing cages full of canary-birds and
parrots.

The women, as they passed us, wrapped their veils more
closely about them, the merchant did not look at us, the
relations gave us a timid glance, and two of the children began
to cry.

From these spectacles we were diverted on the third day
by a sad event. Poor Doctor Miguerez, attacked at our second
resting-place by the atrocious pain of sciatica, had to be transported to Mechinez in a litter, hastily made of a hammock and
two curtain-poles, and suspended between two mules; and this
depressed us all. The caravan was divided into two parts. I
cannot express how painful it became to see, as we often did,
that litter appear behind us on the top of a hill and slowly
descend into the valley, surrounded by soldiers on horseback,
muleteers, servants and friends, all grave and silent as a funeral
cortége, now and then stopping to bend over the sick man, and
then going on, signing to us from afar that our poor friend was
growing worse. It was a painful spectacle, but a fine one also,
giving to the caravan the air of the afflicted escort of a wounded
Sultan.

On the first day we encamped still in the plain of Fez ; on
the second, on the right bank of the Mduma river, at about five
hours from Mechinez. Here we had a very pleasant adventure.
Towards evening we all went down to the bank of the river,
about half a mile from the camp, near a large *duar*, from which
all the inhabitants came out to meet us. There was a bridge
there of masonry : one single arch, of Arab construction, and
old, but still entire and solid ; and beside it the remains of
another bridge, partly embedded in the high rocky bank, and
partly fallen into the bed of the river. On the opposite shore,
at about fifty paces from the bridge, there was a dilapidated

wall, some traces of foundations, and a few big hewn stones
that seemed to have once belonged to an important building.

A Merchant of Mechinez.

The country all about was deserted. The ruins, we were told,
were those of an Arabian city, called Mduma, built upon the
remains of another city anterior to the Mussulman invasion.
We set to work to search among the stones for any traces of

w

Roman construction; but we found or recognised none, to the manifest satisfaction of the Arabs, who doubtless believed that we were seeking, on the faith of some of our diabolical books, some hidden treasures of the *Rumli* (Romans), from whom, according to them, all Christians are direct descendants.

Captain de Boccard, however, re-crossing the bridge to return to the camp, saw down in the river, on the top of an enormous fragment of almost pyramidal form, some small square stones, which looked to him as if they had characters engraved upon them; and the fact that they were there, as if placed there on purpose to be seen from the bridge, made the supposition of value. The Captain manifested his intention of going to see what they were. Everybody advised him not to. The river banks were very steep, the bottom encumbered with pointed rocks, scattered at some distance from each other, the current strong and rapid, the fragment of ruin on which the stones lay was very high, and either impossible or very dangerous of access. But Captain de Boccard is one of those persons who are impossible to move when once their purpose is fixed: they will do it, or die. We had not yet done dissuading him when he was already down the bank, just as he was, with his horseman's boots and spurs. A hundred Arabs were looking on, some fringed along the river banks, some leaning over the parapet of the bridge. As soon as they understood what the Captain was going to do, the enterprise appeared to them so desperate that they began to laugh. When they saw him stop on the edge of the water and look about as if seeking a passage, they imagined that his courage had failed, and all burst out into insolently sonorous laughter. "Not one of us," one cried, in a loud voice, "has ever succeeded in climbing up there: we shall see whether a Nazarene can do it."

And certainly no other of us Italians could have done it. But he who attempted it was, as it happened, the most active personage in the Embassy. The laughter of the Arabs gave him the final impulse. He gave a spring, disappeared into the midst of the bushes, reappeared upon a rock, vanished again, and so from rock to rock, springing like a cat, clinging and climbing, and slipping, over and over again risking a fall into the river, or the breaking of his bones, came to the foot of the piece of ruin, and without taking breath, clinging to every root and every projection, he reached the top, and stood

Mechinez.

erect upon it like a statue. We all drew a long breath, the Arabs were amazed, and Italian honour was safe. The Captain, like a noble victor, deigned not even a glance at his crestfallen adversaries; and, as soon as he had satisfied himself that the supposed engraved stones were nothing but fragments of mortar that had fallen from the bridge, came down by the other side, and with a few jumps gained the shore, where he was received with the honours of a triumph.

The transit from Mduma to Mechinez was a succession of optical illusions of so singular a character, that, if it had not been for the suffocating heat, we should have been immensely

w 2

amused by them. At about two hours from the encampment,
we saw, vaguely gleaming afar off in a vast naked plain, the
white minarets of Mechinez, and rejoiced that we were so near
our journey's end. But what had seemed to us a plain was
in reality an interminable succession of parallel valleys, separated
by large waves of land all of equal height, which presented
the aspect of one continued surface; so that, as we went forward, the city was perpetually hidden and again revealed, as
if it were peeping at us; and, besides that, the valleys being
broken, rocky, and traversed only by winding and difficult
paths, our road yet to be accomplished was at least double in
distance to what it appeared to be; and it seemed as if the
city withdrew as we advanced; at every valley our hearts
opened to hope, and at every hill we despaired again, and
voices weak and high were heard, and lamentable sighs, and
angry propositions to renounce any future voyage to Africa,
for whatever purpose or under whatever conditions; when
suddenly, as we came out of a grove of wild olives, the city
rose before us, and all our lamentations were lost in exclamations
of wonder.

Mechinez, spread upon a long hill, surrounded by gardens,
bound by three ranges of battlemented walls, crowned with
minarets and palms, gay and majestic, like a suburb of Constantinople, presented herself to our eyes, with her thousand
terraces drawn white against the azure of the sky. Not a
cloud of smoke issued from all that multitude of houses;
there was not a living soul to be seen, either on the terraces
or before the walls; nor was there a sound to be heard: it
seemed a deserted city, or a scene in a theatre.

The dinner tent was pitched in a bare field, at two hundred paces from one of the fifteen gates of the city, and
in a few minutes we sat down to satisfy, as some elegant
prose writer remarks, "our natural talent for food and
drink."

We were scarcely seated when there issued from the city

GATEWAY AT MECHINEZ.

gate, and advanced towards the encampment, a company of
horsemen, superbly dressed, and preceded by foot soldiers.

It was the Governor of Mechinez, with his relatives and
officials. At about twenty paces off they dismounted from
their horses, which were covered with trappings in all the
colours of the rainbow, and rushed towards us, shouting all
together in one voice, " Welcome! welcome! welcome!"

The Governor was a young man of a mild countenance,
with black eyes and blacker beard; all the others—men of
forty or ,fifty—were tall, bearded, dressed in white, and as
neat and perfumed as if they had come out of a box. They
all pressed our hands, passing round the table with a tripping
step, and smiling graciously, and then took their places behind the Governor. One of them, seeing a bit of bread on
the ground, picked it up and put it on the table, saying
something which probably meant, " Excuse me; the Koran
forbids the wasting of bread: I am doing my duty as a good
Mussulman." The Governor offered us the hospitality of his
house, which was accepted. Only the two artists and I remained in the camp, and waited until it should be cool before
going into the city.

Selam kept us company, and related to us the wonders of
Mechinez.

"At Mechinez are the most beautiful women in Morocco,
the finest gardens in Africa, and the most beautiful imperial
palace in the world." Thus he began; and, in fact, Mechinez
does enjoy such fame in the empire. To be a native of
Mechinez is, for a woman, to be beautiful, and for a man,
to be jealous. The Imperial Palace, founded by Muley-Ismael,
who, in 1703, had in it four thousand women and eight hundred and sixty-seven children, had an extent of two miles of
circuit, and was ornamented with marble columns, brought
partly from the ruins of the city of Pharaoh, near Mechinez,
and partly from Leghorn and Marseilles. There was a great
hall, or alkazar, where the most precious European tissues

were sold ; a vast market, joined to the city by a road ornamented with a hundred fountains ; a park of immense olive-
trees ; seven large mosques ; a formidable garrison with artillery,
that held the Berbers of the mountains in check ; an imperial
treasure of five hundred millions of francs ; and a population
of fifty thousand inhabitants, who were considered as the most
cultured and the most hospitable in the empire.

Selam described in a low voice and with mysterious gestures
the place where the treasure was kept, the amount of which
no one knows ; but it must have been much decreased in the
last wars, if even it is still worthy of the name of treasure.
" Within the palace," he said, " there is another palace all of
stone, which receives the light from above, and is surrounded
by three ranges of walls. It is entered by an iron door, and
within there is another, and yet another iron door. After
these three doors there is a dark, low passage, where lights
are necessary, and the pavement, walls, and roof are all of
black marble, and the air smells like that of a sepulchre. At
the end of the corridor there is a great hall, and in the middle
of it an opening which leads to a deep subterranean place, where
three hundred negroes, four times a year, shovel in the gold
and silver money which the Sultan sends. The Sultan looks on
while this is done. The negroes are shut up for life in the
palace, and never come out until they are carried out dead.
And around the great hall there are ten earthen jars which
contain the heads of ten slaves who once tried to steal. Muley
Soliman cut off all their heads as soon as the money was in its
place. And no man ever came out of that palace alive except
our lord the Sultan."

He related these horrors without the least sign of dis-
approval, even with an admiring accent, as if they were
superhuman and fatal events, which a man must not judge,
nor feel any other sentiment concerning them save one of
mysterious respect.

" There was once a king of Mechinez," he resumed, with

unalterable gravity, standing erect before our tent, with his hand on the hilt of his sabre, "who wished to make a road from Mechinez to Morocco, bordered by two high walls, so that even the blind could go from one place to the other without a guide. And this perverse and cruel king had a ring by whose power he could call all the demons to his service. And he called them, and made them work at the road. There were thousands and thousands of them, and every one of them carried stones that a hundred men could not have moved an inch, and those who would not work the king had built up alive in the wall, and their bones can still be seen." (They can still be seen, indeed, but they are the bones of Christian slaves, which are also found in the walls of Salè and Rabat.)

"And the wall was built for the length of a day's journey, and everybody rejoiced, thinking that it would soon be finished. But that king was displeasing to Allah, and Allah did not choose that the wall should be finished. One day, when he was riding along, a poor country-woman stopped him, and said, 'Where, O audacious king, is this road to end?' 'In hell,' answered the king, in a rage. 'Go down there, then!' cried the woman. At these words the king fell from his horse dead, the walls crumbled away, the demons scattered the stones over the country, and the road remains to this day unfinished for ever."

"And do you believe that all this is true, Selam?" I asked.

"Certainly," he answered, astonished at my doubt.

"Do you believe in demons?"

"Of course I believe in them! I should like to see the time when we would not believe in them!"

"But have you ever seen one?"

"Never! And for that reason I believe that there are no more of them on earth, and when I hear any one say, 'Take care how you pass at night through such or such a place, because there are demons there,' I go at once, and go in first myself, because I know that the demons are men, and with a good horse between my knees, and a good musket in my hand, I am afraid of nobody."

"And why, in your opinion, are there no more demons now, if there were some once?"

"Why, because the world was not always the same as it is now. I might as well ask you why men were once taller, and the days longer than they are now, and why beasts could talk." And he went off, shaking his head with a compassionate air.

On that day, as the Ambassador was dining in the city, Selam and the others did nothing but gallop between the town and the tents, to the great amusement of the artists and myself, because the contrast between the majesty of their aspect and the humility of their office had never struck us before. There, for instance, was Hamed, mounted on a superb black horse, coming out at a gallop from the battlemented gate of Mechinez, and darting off at full speed across the country. His tall turban gleamed in the sun with the whiteness of snow; his large blue mantle floated on the wind like a royal garment; his poignard glittered; the whole of his martial and gracious figure presented the dignity of a prince and the boldness of a warrior. What romantic fancies are excited in the mind by the vision of that handsome Mussulman cavalier flying like a phantom under the walls of a mediæval city! Whither goes he? To carry off the loveliest daughter of the Pasha of Faraone? to defy the valorous Caid of Uazzan, betrothed to the lady of his love? to pour out his griefs into the bosom of the aged saint who has prayed for eighty years on the top of Mount Zerhun, in the sacred *zania* of Muley-Edris?

Nothing of the sort; he is coming back to camp to get a plate of fried potatoes for the Ambassador.

Towards sunset the two painters and myself, mounted on mules, and escorted by four foot-soldiers of the Governor of

THE PALACE OF THE GOVERNOR OF MECHINEZ.

Mechinez, set out for the city, our guard having put away their muskets, and being armed only with sticks and knotted cords. Before starting, however, we arranged with them, through interpreter Hamed, that whenever we should all clap our hands thrice, in whatever quarter of the city we might be, they were to conduct us at once back to the encampment.

Passing two outside gates, divided by a steep ascent, we found ourselves in the centre of the city. The first impression was one of agreeable surprise. Mechinez, which we had fancied as more melancholy than Fez, was, on the contrary, a gay city, full of verdure, traversed by many winding streets, but broad, and bordered by low houses and garden walls that allowed the tops of the beautiful hills around to be seen. On every side there rose above the houses a minaret, a palm, a battlemented wall; at every step a fountain or an arabesqued door appeared; there were oaks and leafy fig-trees in the streets and squares, and everywhere air, and light, and the odour of the fields, and a certain gentle peacefulness, as of a princely city, fallen, but not dead. After many turns, we came out in a vast square, opposite the monumental palace of the Governor, resplendent with many-coloured mosaics of great beauty; and, at that moment, the level rays of the setting sun striking full upon it, it glittered like the pearl-encrusted palaces of the Oriental legends. A few soldiers were going through the powder-play (*guioco della polvere*), about fifty servants and guards were sitting on the ground before the door; the piazza was deserted. It was a fine spectacle. That illuminated façade, those horsemen, the towers, the solitude, and the sunset formed altogether a picture so completely Moorish, breathed so vivid an air of other times, presented in one frame so many stories, so much poetry, so many dreams, that we stood rapt before it. From thence the soldiers led us to see a great exterior gate of noble design, covered from top to bottom with delicate and many-coloured mosaics, which glowed in the sun like jewels set in ivory;

and the painters sketched it in all haste before we returned
to the city. Until now, the people we met by the way had
shown themselves only curious, and it seemed to us that
they even regarded us with more benevolent eyes than the
population of Fez. But suddenly, without a shadow of reason,
their humour changed. Some old women began to show us

Street Singer at Mechinez.

the whites of their eyes, then some boys threw stones at our
mules' legs, and then a troop of ragamuffins began to run
beside us and behind us, making a most infernal noise. The
soldiers, meantime, were in no humour for compliments. Two
placed themselves in front and two behind us, and they began
a real combat with the rabble, striking the nearest with their
sticks, throwing stones at those far away, and chasing the
most insolent. But it was all labour thrown away. Not
daring to retort with stones, the rabble began to throw

rotten oranges, bits of lemon-peel, dry sticks, and the shower
became so heavy, that it seemed to us more prudent to advise
the soldiers to desist from further provocation. But the soldiers
were provoked, and either did not or would not hear us, and
continued the battle with increasing fury. Indignant at
their brutality, we warned them with imperative gestures to
desist. But the wretches thought we were reproving them
for too much mildness, and went on worse than ever. By
way of addition, two boys of ten and twelve years old now
joined us—possibly relations of the soldiers—and armed with
sticks; they too began to distribute the most desperate blows
to men, women, asses, mules, near and far, until even the
soldiers themselves counselled moderation. And at every blow
they turned and looked at us, as if to ask us to take note
of their zeal in our defence ; and as we were in fits of laughter,
they were encouraged and went on worse than ever. Now
what will happen ? we said to each other. A scandal ! A
revolution ! Already the beaten ones grumbled, and some
raised their hands against the boys ; we must get out of the
city as soon as may be. But Biseo still hesitated, when a
stone struck my mule on the head, and a carrot alighted on
the back of Ussi's neck. Then we decided to clap our hands
as agreed upon. But even this innocent signal provoked a
tumult. The soldiers, to show that they understood, responded
by clapping their own hands ; the people in the square, thinking
that they were being made game of, clapped theirs, and the
oranges and lemons continued to rain upon us, together with
curses loud and deep; and when at last we reached the gate,
and rode down towards the camp, they still yelled after us
from the walls, " Accursed be thy father ! May thy race be
exterminated ! May God roast thy great-grandfather ! "

Thus did Mechinez receive us, and fortunate for us it was
that she is the " most hospitable city in the empire."

On the following morning there was brought to the camp
a litter for the doctor, made in twenty-four hours by the

best carpenters in Mechinez, who would certainly have taken
twenty-four days in its construction if the Governor had not
used certain arguments to which there was great risk in being
deaf. It was a heavy and badly made machine, which looked
more like a cage for the transportation of wild beasts than
a litter for a sick man ; much better made, however, than
anything we could contrive ; and the workmen who completed
it under our eyes were so proud of it, and so sure of our
admiration, that they trembled with emotion at their work,
and at every word from us sent flashes from their eyes.
When Morteo put the money in their hands they thanked
him gravely, and went away with a triumphant smile, which
meant—" Ignorant proud ones, we have let you see what we
can do ! "

Towards evening we left Mechinez, and travelled for two
hours over the loveliest country that was ever seen in his dreams
by an enamoured painter. I see, I feel still the divine grace of
those verdant hills, sprinkled with rose-trees, myrtles, oleanders,
flowering aloes ; the splendour of that city gilded by the sun,
hiding from our sight minaret by minaret, palm-tree by palm-
tree, terrace by terrace, and the air impregnated with inebriating
perfume, and the waters reflecting the thousand colours of the
escort, and the infinite melancholy of that rosy sky. I still see
and feel all this, and know not how to describe it.

CHAPTER XIII.

ON THE SEBÙ.

IT was noon of the fifth day after our departure from Fez, when, after a five hours' ride through a succession of deserted valleys, we passed once more through the gorge of Beb-el-Tinca, and saw again before us the vast plain of the Sebù, inundated by a white, ardent, implacable light, of which the memory alone makes my face glow. All, except the Ambassador and the Captain, who participated in the fabled virtue of the salamander, that lives in fire without being burned, covered their heads like brethren of the Misericordia, wrapped themselves in their mantles and cloaks, and without a word, with heads down, and eyes half closed, descended into the terrible plain, confiding in the clemency of God. Once the voice of the Commandant was heard announcing that a horse was dead *already*. One of the baggage-horses had fallen dead. No one made any comment. "Horses"—added the Commandant, spitefully—"always die *first*." These words also were received in mortal silence. In about half-an-hour another faint voice was heard, asking Ussi to whom he had *bequeathed* his picture of Bianca Cappello. Throughout the journey these were the only words heard. The heat oppressed all. Even the soldiers were silent. The Caid, Hamed Ben-Kasen, in spite of the great turban that shaded his visage, was dripping with sweat. Poor general! That very

morning he had shown me an attention that I shall remember
all my life. Noticing that I lagged behind, he came up, and
banged my mule with such heartfelt zeal, that in a few moments
I was carried at a gallop in front of all the others, bouncing in
my saddle like an india-rubber automaton, and reached the camp
five minutes in advance of them all, with my inside upside down,
and my heart full of gratitude.

That day no one came out of his tent until the dinner hour,
and the dinner was silent, as if all were still oppressed by the
heat of the day. One event alone aroused some excitement in
the camp. We were at dessert, when we heard a sound of
lamentation proceeding from the escort's quarters, and at the
same time the noise of regular blows, as of some one being
whipped. Thinking it to be some joke of the servants and
soldiers, we took, at first, no notice of it. But suddenly the
cries became excruciating, and we heard distinctly, in an accent
of supplicating invocation, the name of the founder of Fez—
"Muley-Edris! Muley-Edris! Muley-Edris!"

We all rose at once from the table, and, running to the
quarter whence the noise proceeded, arrived in time to see a sad
spectacle. Two soldiers held suspended between them, one by
the shoulders, the other by the feet, an Arab servant; a third
was furiously flogging him with a whip; a fourth held up a
lantern; the rest stood round in a circle, and the Caid looked on
with folded arms.

The Ambassador ordered the instant release of the victim,
who went off sobbing and crying, and asked the Caid what this
meant. "Oh, nothing, nothing," he answered; "only a little
correction." He then added that the man was punished because
he had persisted in throwing little balls of *cùscùssù* at his companions, a grave offence, in a Mussulman a sacrilege, because he
is commanded to respect every kind of aliment produced by the
earth as a gift of God. As he spoke, the poor Caid, a kind man
at heart, did not succeed in concealing, however he might wish
to do so, the pain and pity that he felt at being forced to inflict

the castigation; and this sufficed to restore him to his place in
my heart.

In the night we were awakened by a burning hot wind from
the east, which drove us panting from our tents, in search of air
that we could breathe; and at dawn we resumed our journey
under a sky that announced a hotter day than the preceding one.
The heavens were covered with clouds, on one side all on fire
with the rising sun, and broken here and there by dazzling
beams of light; on the opposite side all was black, striped by
oblique streaks of rain. From this troubled sky there fell a
strange light, which seemed to have passed through a yellow
veil, and tinted the stubble fields with an angry sulphurous
colour that offended the eye. Far off the wind raised and
whirled about with furious rapidity immense clouds of dust.
The country was solitary, the air heavy, the horizon hidden by a
veil of leaden-coloured vapour. Without ever having seen the
Sahara, I imagined that it might sometimes present that same
aspect, and was about to say so, when Ussi, who has been in
Egypt, stopping suddenly, exclaimed in wonder, "This is the
desert!"

After four hours' journey we arrived upon the bank
of the Sebũ, where we were met by twenty horsemen of
the Beni-Hassen, led by a handsome boy of twelve, the
son of the Governor, Sid-Abdallah. They came to meet
us at a gallop, with the usual shouts and discharges of
musketry.

The camp was pitched in all haste near the river, in a bare
piece of ground, full of deep gullies; and having breakfasted
quickly, we withdrew to our tents.

This was the hottest day of the journey.

I will try to give a distant idea of our torments. Let the
gentle reader prepare his or her heart to feel profound compassion. I wipe my dripping brows, and begin.

At ten o'clock in the morning, when my two companions and
I withdrew to our tent, the thermometer marked forty-two

x

degrees centigrade in the shade (about 106° Fahrenheit). For
about an hour the conversation continued animated. After that
we began to find a certain difficulty in terminating our periods,
and were reduced to simple propositions. Then, as it caused too
much fatigue to put subject, verb, and attribute together, we
stopped talking, and tried to sleep. It was useless. The hot
beds, the flies, thirst, and restlessness, would not let us close an

In the Desert.

eye. After much fretting and fuming, we resigned ourselves to
stay awake, and tried to cheat the weary time in some occupation. But it could not be done. Cigars, pipes, books, maps,
all dropped from our nerveless hands. I tried to write : at the
third line the page was bathed in the perspiration that streamed
from my forehead like water from a squeezed sponge. I felt
my whole body traversed by innumerable springs, which inter-
sected, followed, joined each other, forming confluents and
streams, running down my arms and hands, and watering the
ink in the point of my pen. In a few minutes, handkerchiefs,

towels, veils, everything that could serve the purpose, were as wet as if they had been dipped in a bucket. We had a barrel full of water: we tried to drink, it was boiling. We poured it out: it had hardly touched the earth when no trace of it could be seen. At noon the thermometer marked forty-four and a half degrees. The tent was an oven. Everything we touched scorched us. I put my hand on my head, and it felt like a stove. The beds heated us so that we could not lie down. I tried to put my foot outside the tent, and the ground was scorching. No one spoke any more. Only now and then was heard a languid exclamation: "It is death." "I cannot bear this." "I shall go mad." Ussi put his head out of the tent for an instant, his eyes starting out of his head, murmured in a suffocated voice, "I shall die," and disappeared. Diana, the poor dog, lying down near the Commandant's bed, panted as if she were at her last gasp. Outside of the tent no human voice was heard, no human being was visible, the camp seemed deserted. The horses neighed in a lamentable manner. The doctor's litter, standing near our tent, cracked as if it were splitting in pieces. Suddenly we heard the voice of Selam running by, and calling out, "One of the dogs is dead."

"One!" answered the faint voice of the Commandant, facetious to the last.

At one o'clock the thermometer marked forty-six and a half degrees. Then even complaints ceased. The Commandant, the Vice-Consul and I lay stretched on the ground motionless, like dead bodies. In the whole camp the Ambassador and the Captain were perhaps the only Christians who still gave signs of life. I do not remember how long this condition lasted. I was steeped in a sort of stupor, dreaming with my eyes open, and a thousand confused images of cool spots and frozen objects chased each other through my brain: I was springing from a rock into a lake, I was putting the back of my neck against the spout of a pump, I was building a house of ice, I was devouring all the ices in Naples, and the more I sprinkled myself with water and

x 2

drank cool drinks, the hotter, the thirstier, the wilder I
became. At last the Captain exclaimed in a sepulchral voice:
"Forty-seven!" * It was the last voice I remember to have
heard.

Towards evening the son of the Governor of the Beni-Hassen,
the boy whom we had seen in the morning, came to visit the
Governor in the name of his father, who was ill. He entered
the camp on horseback, accompanied by an officer and two
soldiers, who took him in their arms when he dismounted, and
advanced with solemn step towards the Ambassador, trailing his
long blue mantle like a robe, with his left hand upon the hilt
of a sabre longer than himself, and his right extended in
salutation.

In the morning, seen on horseback, he had seemed a handsome boy; and he had indeed beautiful pensive eyes, and a small
pallid oval face; but on foot we saw that he was ricketty and
deformed. From this no doubt came his melancholy looks. In
all the time he remained with us, no smile moved his lip, his
face never brightened for a moment. He looked at us all with
a profound attention, and answered the Ambassador's questions
with short sentences, spoken in low tones. Once only a gleam
of pleasure came into his eyes; it was when the Ambassador
told him that he had admired, in the morning, his bold and
graceful riding; but it was only a gleam.

Although all our eyes were upon him, and this was probably
the first time that he had appeared in an official capacity before
a European embassy, he showed no shadow of embarrassment.
He slowly drunk his tea, ate some sweatmeats, whispered in the
ear of his officer, settled two or three times his little turban on
his head, looked attentively at our boots, and showed that he
was a little bored; then, in taking leave, he pressed the Ambassador's hand to his breast, and returned to his horse
with the same royal gravity with which he had approached
the tent.

* About 114½° Fahrenheit.

Lifted into the saddle by his attendants, he said once more, " Peace be with you ! " and galloped off, followed by his small and hooded staff.

That same evening several sick people came to consult the doctor, who, with the dragoman Solomon and a company of soldiers, had started a little earlier for Tangiers, by the way of Alkazar. Among the rest came a poor half-naked boy, lean, and with his eyes in such a state that he could see with diffi- culty, while he seemed exhausted with fatigue. " What do you want ? " asked Morteo. " I seek the Christian physician," he answered in a trembling voice. When he heard that he was gone, he stood a moment as if stunned, and then cried out in despair : " Am I to lose my sight then ! I have come eight miles to be cured by the Christian physician ! I must see him ! " and he broke out into sobs and tears. Morteo put some money into his hand, which he received with indifference, and pointing out the way which the doctor had taken, told him that if he walked quickly he might perhaps overtake him. The boy stood a moment uncertain, looking with eyes full of tears, and then slowly limped away.

The sun went down that evening under an immense pavilion of gold and flame colour, and striking across the plains his last blood-coloured beams, set behind the straight line of the horizon like a monstrous glowing disk that was sinking into the bowels of the earth.

And the night was almost cold !

In the morning, at sunrise, we were on the left bank of the Sebù, at the same point where we had crossed coming from Tangiers; and we had hardly reached it before we saw appear upon the opposite bank, with his officers and soldiers, the Governor Sid-Bekr-el-Abbassi, with the same white vesture, and the same black horse caparisoned in sky blue, with which he had the first time appeared.

But the passage of the river presented this time an unfore- seen difficulty.

Of the two boats on which we were to cross, one was in pieces; the other broken in more than one place, and half sunk in the mud of the shore. The little *duar* inhabited by the boatmen's families was deserted; the river was dangerous to ford, and no other boat to be had except at a distance of a day's journey. How were we to cross, and what was to be done? A soldier swam across and carried the notice to the Governor, who

Crossing the Sebú.

sent another soldier by the same road to explain. The boatmen had been notified the night before to hold themselves in readiness for the passage of the Ambassador and his suite, who would arrive in the morning; but finding the boats in an unserviceable condition, and not being capable, or not choosing to endure the fatigue of mending them, they had fled during the night, heaven knows where, with their families and animals, to avoid punishment by the Governor. There was nothing to be done but to try and mend the least broken of the two boats, and this we did. The soldiers went off to get men from the neighbouring *duars*, and the work was begun under the direction of Luigi, one of the two sailors, who on that, to him memorable, occasion

gloriously sustained the honour of the Italian marine. It was
good to see how the Arabs and Moors laboured. Ten of them
together, yelling and flying about, did not do in half an hour
the work that Luigi and Ranni, in military silence, did in five
minutes. Everybody gave orders, everybody criticised, everybody got angry, everybody cut the air with imperious gestures,
until they all seemed like so many admirals, and not one of
them accomplished anything. Meantime the Governor and the
Caid conversed in loud voices across the river; the soldiers
careered about at a gallop seeking the fugitives along the banks;
the sumpter beasts forded the river in a long file with water up
to their necks; the workmen chanted the praises of the Prophet,
and on the opposite shore arose a great blue tent under which
the slaves of Sid-Bekr-el-Abbassi were busy in preparing an
exquisite collation of figs, sweetmeats, and tea, which we
watched through our glasses, humming the while a chorus from
a semi-serious opera, composed during our sojourn at Fez, and
called "*Gl' Italiani nel Marocco.*"

With the aid of the Prophet, the boat was ready within two
hours; Ranni took us on his shoulders, and deposited us one
by one on the prow, and we reached the other side, with our feet
up to the ankles in water, that came in on every side, but without having been forced to swim for it; a good fortune, of which
we were not sure at our departure.

The Governor, Sid-Bekr-el-Abbassi, who had heard of the
praises which the Ambassador had bestowed upon him to the
Sultan, was more amiable and fascinating to us than ever.
After a little rest, we went on to Karia-el-Abbassi, which we
reached about noon, and were received and passed the hot hours
in the same white chamber in which thirty-five days before we
had seen the pretty little daughter of our host peep at us from
behind the paternal turban.

Here Sid-Bekr-el-Abbassi presented to the Ambassador,
among other people, a Moor of about fifty years of age, of a
noble aspect and agreeable manners, whom none of us, I think,

have since forgotten, because of the strange things we were told about his family. He was the brother of one Sid-Bomedi, formerly Governor of the province of Ducalla, who languished for eight years in the dungeons of Fez. A tyrant and a prodigal, after having bled his people, he contracted ruinous loans with European merchants, accumulated debt upon debt, brought the wrath of God within and without his house, was arrested and taken to Fez by order of the Sultan, who, believing him to be the possessor of hidden treasures, had his house pulled down and search made among the ruins and under the foundations, and banished from the province, under pain of death, all his family, in the fear that they, knowing the hiding-place, would get possession of the money. But, nothing being found —perhaps because there was nothing—and the Sultan still persisting in his belief in a treasure which the prisoner knew and refused to reveal, the latter had never more beheld the light of the sun, and was, perhaps, condemned to die in prison. And the case of Sid-Bomedi is not rare among the Governors of Morocco, who, being all more or less enriched at the expense of their people, furnish the government that wishes to get possession of their wealth the advantage of doing so under colour of punishing a guilty man.

The Governor, or the Pasha upon whom the Governor has set his eye, is called in a friendly manner to Fez, or to Morocco, or perhaps arrested suddenly in the night by a company of the imperial soldiers, who take him by forced marches to the capital, tied on the crupper of a mule, with his head hanging down and his face turned to the sun. As soon as he arrives he is loaded with chains and thrown into a dungeon. If he reveals the hiding-place of his wealth, he is sent back with honour to his province, where in a little while, by worse exactions than before, he can make up again that which has been taken from him. If he will not reveal it, he is left to rot in his prison, and bastinadoed every day until the blood comes, until, reduced to extremity, he decides to speak rather than perish in chains. If he reveals

only in part, he is bastinadoed just the same, until he has made
a clean breast of it. Some of the more astute ones, foreseeing
the catastrophe in time, turn it aside by going in person to the
Court with a long caravan of camels and mules laden with

Sid-Bekr-el-Abbassi and Suite.

precious gifts; but in order to make these gifts they are
obliged to spend a large part of their wealth; and it follows
that their safety is scarcely less fatal to the provinces governed
by them than if they were to return from their prison despoiled
of all their treasure. Some also die in prison, and under the
stick make no revelations, in order to leave all they have to their
families, who know where it is concealed; and others die be-

cause they have nothing to reveal. But these are rare, because
in Morocco it is the custom to hide money, and it is known that
the Moors are masters in the art.   They talk of treasures built
up under the sill of the house door, in the pilasters of the court,.
in the stairs, in the windows; of houses demolished stone by
stone to the foundations, without the discovery of a treasure
that was really there; of slaves killed and secretly buried, after
having helped their masters to conceal it; and the vulgar mix.
with these horrible and painful truths their pretty legends of
spirits and prodigies.

The Governor el-Abbassi accompanied us towards evening
as far as the camp, which was about two hours distant from
his house, in a field full of flowers and tortoises, between the
river Dà, which divides itself just there into an infinity of
canals, and a beautiful hill crowned by the green cupola of a
saint's tomb.   At a gunshot from our tents was a large *duar,*
surrounded with aloes and the Indian fig. All the inhabitants
rushed out at sight of us.   Then we saw how much the
Governor was beloved by his people. Old men, young men,.
youths and children, all ran to him to have his hands placed
upon their heads, and then went away content, turning back
to look at him with an expression of affection and gratitude.
The presence, however, of the beloved Governor did not serve
to protect us from the usual bitter glances and the usual reproaches.   The women, half hidden behind the hedges, with one
hand pushed forward a child to go and be blessed by the Governor,
and with the other sent his brother to tell us that we were
dogs. We saw babies about two feet high, quite naked, and
hardly able to stand, come tottering towards us, and, showing
a fist about as large as a nut, cry, " Accursed be thy father!"
and because they were afraid to come alone, they made groups
of seven or eight, so compact that they might all have been
carried on a tray; and advancing with a threatening air to
within ten paces of us, stammered out their small insolence.
How they amused us!   One group among others advanced

against Biseo to wish that some relation or other of his might be roasted. Biseo raised his pencil; the two first falling back upon the others, they in their turn upon those behind, half the army presently lay with their legs in the air. Even the Governor burst out laughing.

CHAPTER XIV.

ARZILLA.

AFTER the spectacle of great cities in decadence, a moribund people and a lovely but melancholy landscape; after such sleep, such old age, and such ruin, here is the work of the eternal hand, and here is immortal youth; here is the air that revives the blood, the beauty that refreshes the heart, the immensity in which the soul expands! Here is the ocean! With what a thrill of delight we salute it! The unexpected apparition of a friend or a brother could not have been dearer to our hearts than the sight of that distant shining curve that gleamed before us like an immense sickle, mowing down Islamism, slavery, barbarism, and bearing our thoughts direct and free to Italy.

"*Bahr-el-Kibir!*" exclaimed some soldiers. (The great sea.) Others said, "*Bahr-ed-Dholma!*" (The sea of darkness.) All involuntarily hastened their steps; conversation, which had begun to languish, was re-animated; the servants set up sacred songs; the whole caravan, in a few minutes, assumed an air of cheer and festivity.

On the evening of June 19th we encamped at three hours' distance from Laracce, and the following morning entered the city, received at the gate by the son of the Governor; by twenty soldiers, without muskets or breeches, drawn up along the road; by almost a hundred ragged boys, and by a band

composed of a tambourine and a trumpet, who came afterwards to ask for money—giving us an excruciating concert
in the court of the Italian Consular-Agent.

Upon that coast, sprinkled with dead cities—such as Salè,
Azamor, Safi, Santa Cruz—Laracce still preserves a little
commercial life, which is sufficient to cause her to be considered as one of the principal ports of Morocco. Founded
by a Berber tribe in the fifteenth century, fortified at the end
of the same century by Muley-ben-Nassar, abandoned to Spain
in 1610, retaken by Muley Ismael in 1689, still flourishing at
the beginning of this century, with a population of about four
thousand, between Moors and Hebrews, it rises upon the
incline of a hill to the left of the mouth of the Kus, the
Lixus of the ancients, which forms for it an ample and
secure port, closed, however, by a sand-bank against the
entrance of large vessels. In the port lie rotting the carcasses
of two small gun-boats, the last miserable remnant of the fleet
that once carried the victorious army into Spain and alarmed
European commerce. Behind the hill there is a large grove
of gigantic trees. The town has nothing notable in it except
a market-place, surrounded by a portico sustained by small
stone columns; but seen from the port, all white upon the
dark green background of its hills, surrounded by a circle of
high battlemented walls of a dark calcareous tint, reflected
in the azure waters of the river, under that limpid sky, it
presents a dignified aspect, and despite the vividness of its
colours, almost a melancholy one, as if one felt compassion
at the sight of the picturesque city silent and alone upon that
barbarous coast, by that deserted port, in the face of that
immense sea.

The camp was pitched that evening on the right bank of
the Kus, and raised early the following morning. We were
to go to Arzilla, four hours distant from Laracce. The baggage
was sent on in the morning; the Embassy left towards evening.
I left with the baggage convoy, in order to see the caravan

under a new aspect; and I was glad I did, for it was a journey
full of adventure.

The laden mules, accompanied by muleteers and servants,
went in groups, at a great distance one from the other. I

The Ambassador's Groom.

went on alone, and rode for nearly an hour over the hills,
where I saw only one mule, driven by an Arab servant, and
carrying two sacks of straw, of which one supported the head
and the other the feet of a groom of the Ambassador's, who
had been seized by a violent fever, and who groaned enough
to move the very stones with pity. The poor fellow lay thus
across the mule, with his head hanging down, his body bent,
the sun in his eyes, and in this way had he come all the way
from Karia-el-Abbassi, and was to go to Tangiers! And in

this way are all the sick transported in Morocco who have no money to hire a litter and two mules, and fortunate is he who can have a bag of straw!

On the shore I was joined by the cook, Ranni, and Luigi, who did not leave me again until we reached Arzilla.

We trotted for an hour over the sands, turning out here and there from the direct road to avoid a marsh.

At this time the cook, who for the first time in all the journey was able to speak freely, opened his heart to me.

Poor fellow! all the adventures we had had, all the great things we had seen, had not freed him from a painful thought which had destroyed his peace from the first week of his sojourn at Tangiers. And this thought was an unsuccessful jelly made by him one day when we were dining with the French Minister—a jelly which had given the first blow to his reputation in the mind of the Ambassador, and whose ill-success was due, not to him, but to the bad Marsala wine. Fez, the Court, Mechinez, the Sebù, the ocean, he had seen and still saw them all through this medium of jelly. Or rather, he had seen and saw nothing, because, although his body was in Morocco, his spirit was in Turin. I asked him to tell me his impressions, and they were these, as nearly as I can set tnem down. He could not comprehend who the beast could have been who had stamped that country. He related his fatigues, his quarrels with his two Arab scullions, the difficulties of preparing food in the desert, and his immense desire to see Turin again; but he always fell back upon that deplorable jelly at the French Minister's. "I do not know how to cook? Do me the favour when you are at Turin," he said, touching my arm to withdraw me from my contemplation of the ocean, "go and ask Count so-and-so, Countess such a one, &c., whom I served for years and years! Go to General Ricotti, Minister of War, who has been five years Minister, and can do just what he pleases; go and ask him whether or no I can make a jelly! Do go; give me that

satisfaction; it will not take a moment when you are back
in our country!" And he insisted so, that in order to contemplate the ocean in peace, I was obliged to promise.

Meanwhile we came up at every hundred paces or so with
two or three laden mules, soldiers on horseback, and servants
on foot; fragments of the caravan that stretched along an
hour's journey before us. Among the soldiers there were some
from Laracce, ragged fellows, with a handkerchief bound round
their heads, and a rusty musket in their hands; and among
the servants, boys of twelve or fourteen years old, whom I
had not seen before, and who had escaped, I was told, from
Mechinez and Karia-el-Abbassi, and joined the caravan, with
nothing on them but a shirt, to seek their fortune at Tangiers,
living meantime on the charity of the soldiers.

In some of these groups there would be one telling a
story; others singing; and all seemed cheerful.

We stopped half-way to breakfast in the shadow of a
rock. And here I saw a scene that revealed to me the nature
of the people better than a volume of psychological disserta-
tion.

Near us there was a soldier seated on the sand, beyond
him another, further on a servant, and about fifty paces from
this last another servant, seated near a spring, with a jug
between his knees. Wishing to drink, I called to the first
soldier, " *Elma !* " (Water), and pointed to the spring. The
soldier answered with a courteous gesture of acquiescence, and
imperiously ordered the second soldier to go and get some
water. The latter made a gesture of obedience, and with
threats and reproaches, asked the nearest servant why he had
not brought the water. The servant in question sprang to his
feet, made three hasty steps towards the one seated near the
spring, and called to him to bring water instantly. The last,
observing that I was not paying attention, did not move.
Five minutes passed, and the water did not come. I turned
to the first soldier, and the same scene was enacted over

again. Finally, if I wanted water, I had to shout to the man who had the jug, who, after a few moments for reflection, decided to get it, and brought it with about the speed of a tortoise.

We resumed our journey. A fresh breeze blew, and a cloud covered the sun, so that the ride was delicious; but as the tide continued to rise, and restricted us more and more to the sandy path, upon which we proceeded in single file, we soon found ourselves imprisoned between the sea and the rocky heights which rose almost perpendicularly above our heads, and obliged to go on among the stones, where the waves were already breaking. Several times the mule came to a stand in terror, and I found myself surrounded by water and wrapped in a cloud of spray. But our hour, as the cook said, was not yet come; and after about a mile, we reached a hill up which we climbed in haste, looking back " *a rimirar lo passo.*"

With us there was an old soldier of Laracce, a little touched in the head, who laughed constantly, but who knew the road. He made us skirt the hill, and led us through a thick grove of dwarf oaks, cork-trees, broom, and shrubs of various kinds; by a hundred twists and turns; through thorns, and mud, and water, and darkness; in recesses where no human creature appeared ever to have penetrated; and always laughing, brought us, tired and torn, to the shore again, where we found a strip of sand uninvaded by the waters.

Here, the caravan not having yet arrived, the beach was deserted, and we rode for some time seeing nothing but sea and sky, and the foot of the steep little hills, which forming so many little harbours, hid the horizon behind us. We were going on in silence, one behind the other, over the soft, carpet-like sand, every one of us occupied with his thoughts miles away from Morocco, when suddenly there sprang from behind a rock a spectre, a horrible old man, half naked, with a crown of yellow flowers on his head—a saint—who began to inveigh against us, howling like a madman, and making

Y

with both hands the gesture of scratching our faces and tearing
our beards. We stopped to look at him. He became more
ferocious. Ranni, without further ceremony, advanced to give
him the stick; but I stopped him and threw some money to
the saint. The rascal stopped, picked up the coin, looked at
it all over, put it in his bosom, and began to yell worse than
before. "Ah! this time," said Ranni, "he shall have a good
beating," and raised his stick. But the soldier, becoming

On the Sea Coast.

serious in a moment, stopped him, and saying a few words
to the saint in accents of profound respect, induced him to
be silent. The horrible old wretch gave us one fulminating
glance, and hid himself once more among the rocks, where,
it appears, he lives, feeding on roots, with the sole purpose
of cursing the Nazarene ships that pass on the horizon.

We climbed the hills again, and rode for a long time
through winding paths among rocks and bushes. At some
points, where the path ran along the edge of the steep
precipice, we could see far down the sea beating upon the
rocks, and a long stretch of beach, with the caravan straggling
along, and the immense horizon of the blue ocean dotted with
distant sails. The mountains where our road lay formed with

their checkered tops a vast undulating plain, where there was no trace of cultivation, nor tomb, nor cabin, nor human creature, and no sound but the distant murmur of the sea. "What a country!" exclaimed the cook, looking about him with an anxious glance. "I hope we may not meet with any unpleasant adventure." As for me, I asked myself whether there was no danger of lions. Going up and going down, losing sight of each other, and meeting again among the bushes, we travelled for two hours through these mountain solitudes, and began to fear that we had missed the way, when from a height we suddenly discovered the towers of Arzilla, and the whole coast as far as Cape Spartel, whose blue outline was drawn sharply against the limpid clearness of the sky.

It was a delight for all the little caravan, but of brief duration.

As we descended towards the sea we saw far off a group of horses and men lying down, who, as soon as they discovered us, sprang to their feet, and to their saddles, and came towards us, spreading themselves out in the form of a half moon, as if they intended to prevent our advance towards the town.

"Here we are at last," thought I; "this time we shall not escape; it is a band," and I made a sign for the rest to halt.

"Let the Moor be sent forward!" called out the cook. The Moorish soldier ran on in advance.

"Give them a shot!" screamed the trembling cook.

"One moment," said I; "before we kill them, let us see whether they mean to kill us."

I looked attentively at them; they advanced at a trot; there were ten of them, some in dark colours, some in white; I could see no muskets; at their head was an old man with a white beard; I felt reassured.

"Let us form a square!" cried the cook.

"There is no need," I said. The old man with the white beard had uncovered his head, and came towards us cap in hand.

He was an Israelite. At ten paces off he stopped with his followers, who were composed of four other Israelites and five Arab servants, and made signs that he wished to speak with me.

"*Hable Usted,*" I replied (" Speak ! ").

" I am so and so," he said in Spanish, with a sweet voice, and bending in an attitude of respect, " Consular agent for Italy and all the other European states in the city of Arzilla. Have I the honour to be in the presence of his Excellency the Italian Ambassador, returning from Fez, on his way to Tangiers ? "

I was amazed. Then I assumed a grave and courteous air, and glanced round at my followers who were beaming with delight ; and after having tasted for an instant the honour of an official reception, I undeceived the old Hebrew, with a sigh, and told him who I was. He seemed for a moment displeased, but did not change his manner. He offered me his house to rest in, and when I declined his hospitality, he would at any rate accompany me to the spot destined for the encampment.

We all went on together, skirting the city, towards the seashore. Ah ! if Ussi and Biseo could only have seen me ! How picturesque I must have been, sitting on a mule, with a white scarf round my head, followed by my staff, composed of a cook in his shirt sleeves, two sailors armed with sticks, and a ragged Moor ! O Italian art, what hast thou not lost !

Arzilla, the Zilia of the Carthagenians, the *Julia Traducta* of the Romans, passed from the hands of the latter into those of the Goths, was sacked by the English towards the middle of the tenth century, remained for thirty years a heap of stones, was rebuilt by Abd-er-Rhaman-ben-Ali, Caliph of Cordova, taken by the Portuguese, and retaken by Morocco, and is now nothing but a little town of about one thousand inhabitants between Moors and Hebrews, surrounded on the sea and land sides by high battlemented walls, which are falling into ruin ; white and quiet as a cloister, and imprinted, like all the small Mahometan towns, with that smiling melancholy which recalls the last look on the face of the dying who are glad to die.

In the evening, at sunset, the Ambassador arrived, and came to the encampment across the city; and I have still before my eyes the spectacle of that beautiful cavalcade, full of colour and life, issuing out of a battlemented gate, advancing in picturesque disorder along the shore, and throwing across the sands in the rosy sunset light its long black shadows; and here, in fact, it may be said that our journey came to an end, since the following morning we encamped at Ain-Dalia, and

Departure from Arzilla.

two days afterwards we re-entered Tangiers, where the caravan broke up in that same little market-place where it had formed two months before.

The Commandant, the Captain, the two painters, and I left together for Gibraltar. The Ambassador, the Vice-Consul, all the people of the Legation accompanied us to the shore, and the farewells were very affectionate. All were moved, even the good General Hamed-ben-Kasen, who, pressing my hand against his mighty chest, repeated three times the only European word he knew—"*A Dios!*"—with a voice that came from his heart. We had scarcely put our foot upon the deck of the ship when,

oh ! how distant in space and time seemed all that phantasmagoria of pashas, and negroes, and tents, and mosques, and
battlemented towers.　It was not a country, it was an entire
world that in a moment vanished from our eyes, and a world
that we should never see again.　A little of Africa accompanied
us on board, however, in the two Selims, Ali, Hamed, Abd-er-
Rhaman, Civo, Morteo's servants, and other kind young fellows
whom Mussulman superstition had not prevented from wishing
well to the Nazarenes and serving them with fidelity.　And they
also took leave of us with warm demonstrations of affection
and regret, Civo more than the others, who, causing his long
white shirt to float for the last time before my eyes, threw
his arms about my neck, and planted two kisses in my
ear.　And when the steamer moved they saluted us still
from a boat, waving their red fezes, and shouting as long
as we could see them, "Allah be with you !　Come back
to Morocco !　Farewell, Nazarenes !　Farewell, Italians !　*A
Dios !　A Dios !*"

Farewell.

INDEX.